BLACK & WHITE & NOIR

BLACK & WHITE & NOIR

AMERICA'S PULP MODERNISM

Paula Rabinowitz

COLUMBIA UNIVERSITY PRESS   NEW YORK

COLUMBIA UNIVERSITY PRESS
Publishers Since 1893
New York   Chichester, West Sussex

Copyright © 2002 Columbia University Press

Library of Congress Cataloging-in-Publication Data
Rabinowitz, Paula.
Black & white & noir : America's pulp modernism /
Paula Rabinowitz.
p. cm.
Includes bibliographical references and index.
ISBN 0–231–11480–X (cloth)
ISBN 0–231–11481–8 (paper)
1. Film noir–United States–History and criticism.
2. Popular culture–United States–History–20th century.
I. Title: Black and white and noir. II. Title.

PN1995.9.F54 R33   2002
791.43'655–dc21   2002019270

⊗

Columbia University Press books are printed
on permanent and durable acid-free paper.

Printed in the United States of America
Designed by Audrey Smith

c 10 9 8 7 6 5 4 3 2 1
p 10 9 8 7 6 5 4 3 2 1

For Charlotte Nekola
sisters under the screen

CONTENTS

After her beautiful face has been permanently disfigured, scarred by a pot of hot coffee hurled at her primary asset by Vince Stone (Lee Marvin), her gangster lover in *The Big Heat*, Debby Marsh (Gloria Grahame) takes a trip to visit Bertha Duncan (Jeanette Nolan), the more respectable but still utterly corrupt widow of a police officer. Debby finds Bertha dressed in mink, a coat far more luxurious than one might afford on a policeman's pension, all ready to party. She knows that Bertha too is hooked up with the syndicate that controls the city and their lives, and Debby pleads with her to come clean and expose Mike Lagana's racket. Debby's terse observation thrills: "We're sisters under our minks," she tells Bertha. Fritz Lang's bleak depiction of the widespread sleaze oozing from the rackets to the police department also reveals a central theme of a temporarily submerged feminism—marriage, like prostitution, is just another form of the rackets. A man can offer no real protection for a woman, so she needs to get whatever goods she can by any means. Cloaked in her dark mink, Debby kills Bertha, ultimately sacrificing herself to save Dave Bannion (Glenn Ford), whose loyal but sexy wife was blown up by the mob in retaliation for his investigation into Duncan's suicide, and thus all the women end up sisters six feet under the earth. Their thick furs provide no protection from the coldness of death; yet, as Gilles Deleuze shows in his brilliant gloss on Leopold von Sacher-Masoch's *Venus in Furs*, the texture of mink covering the icy white body of the desired woman resexualizes death itself: "icy—sentimental—cruel," he calls her (51). It's a grim and perverse picture, and, like the many film noirs it mirrors, it fascinates me.

Since 1972, when I was living two blocks away from the Orson Welles Cinema on Massachusetts Avenue in Cambridge and wandered one afternoon into a screening of *Double Indemnity*, returning every day for the entire month-long revival of film noirs, I have spent long hours in cafes or on the telephone with my girlfriends recounting the plots of these movies. Back then, I quit my noir job at a Central Square florist shop, which fronted for a bookie joint, in order to soak up these films that seemed oddly familiar yet chillingly strange. I could not get over Fred McMurray—that sweet, funny, single dad of Chip and his brothers from *My Three Sons*—wisecracking double entendres much less murdering two people. And Barbara Stanwyck—that soft, sloppy, over-the-top mom in *Stella Dallas*—turned out to be, as she says, "a hard, rotten case." I had never seen anything like these films, I thought; yet they seemed utterly recognizable. I knew them all—the characters, settings, plots, dialogue, and lighting—from somewhere, sometime, outside the plush red velvet seats of the movie theater. In fact, I had been watching these B-movies all my life on the afternoon television shows, *Million Dollar Movies* or *Dialing for Dollars* or the midnight reruns crowding late 1950s and early 1960s television sets. So had my friends; they were our education into a bizarre grown-up adulthood far from that of our parents' staid lives, a black-and-white world glimpsed in snapshots from their pasts in the ghettoes of New York: the men dashing, dressed in uniforms returned from war; the women, hair marcelled, posing on the stoops before setting out to jobs in the city.

I came up with the title of this book five years ago, while lying on my couch in my dream apartment overlooking Trastevere. I was on a Fulbright scholarship in Rome, the culmination of a quarter-century fantasy of mine, rereading all the great American novels—*Moby-Dick*, *The Scarlet Letter*, *Daisy Miller*, because these were what was available in the used English-language bookstore down the block— I had loved as an undergraduate, but which I had not looked at in decades. On late-night television, RAI Uno played old black-and-white American movies dubbed into Italian, and the nearby cinema club was named Detour. So I spent many hours trying to figure out why, old and weird as the history of Rome was, it could not be a noir city, despite the murders of Beatrice Cenci, Giordano Bruno, and the martyrs of Fosse Ardeatino. I realized I had been writing around these questions—why America is so perverse in its racism and its Puritanism—for years. It was time to write about my secret obsession. But when I came to finish the book in the foggy, time-frozen noir-like town of Corvallis, Oregon, a place whose downtown still sports a bright orange Rexall Drugstore sign and whose outskirts are ringed by paper mills stinking of pulp, I found I still avoided investigating film noir as such. This book, instead, interrogates noir sensibility, the "effetto noir" as an exhibition mounted in the summer of 2000 in the Italian Alps called it, but it barely talks about the movies I love so much. In part this is because there are already many excellent books on the subject—the bibliography on this style, genre, form, code, whatever you want to call it, is long and rich— but it is also that I find I resist writing about them. Talking is one thing, writing another. So this is a book in which a deep debt to noir is paid through avoidance; it's a typical noir strategy, I'm afraid. Still, I hope I say something new about film noir; I know film noir has much to offer photography, literature, politics, and history. Call it political theory masking as pulp, or, more accurately, pulp masking as political history; at any rate, this book interrogates the essential trashiness of modern American culture, America's pulp modernism.

Many people and institutions have helped me research and write this book, sustaining me financially and intellectually. Support has come from the University of Minnesota: its Graduate School Grants-in-Aid of Research, which funded my terrific graduate assistants, Carol Mason, Rebecca Hill, and Laura Schere; International Travel Grants; Scholar of the College Award, and help with juggling leaves. I thank Shirley Nelson Garner, former chair of the Department of English Language and Literature, who unstintingly endorsed my many requests for time and money. I was lucky to have been named senior fellow at the Oregon State University Center for the Humanities during 2000–2001 so that I could complete the manuscript. In addition to a generous stipend, Peter Copek, Wendy Madar, and Jerry Sabin gave me a lovely corner office, solitude, and expert computer assistance. Tragically, Peter Copek died unexpectedly just weeks after I completed this manuscript. I have had the opportunity to present much of this work before rigorous audiences in the United States and in Europe. I thank Daniele Fiorentino at Rome's Centro Studi Americani for inviting me to participate in the Third and Fourth Seminars on American Studies there; portions of the book were developed for a symposium at the Centro on American women writers and a conference on the American city, both organized by Cristina Giorcelli, my colleague at Roma Tre where I taught as Fulbright Professor of American Studies. I delivered lectures from some of the material at the Universities of Siena and Arezzo. Many thanks to Rick McCormick of the University of Minnesota's German Forum for inviting me to his conference on "Thirty Years After: The Legacy of 1968 in German and American Culture," at which I delivered much of chapter 8. Thanks also to Giuliana Colaizzi, Marta Selva, and the women at Drac Magic in Barcelona for inviting me to deliver an address to the Sixth International Exhibition of Women's Films. Other places where I delivered parts of this book include the Rethinking Marxism conference at University of Massachusetts-Amherst, the Weisman Art Museum at the University of Minnesota, the Center for the Humanities at Oregon State University, and SUNY Albany. In addition, I have been lucky to have taught a number of intensive undergraduate seminars on political pulp and film noir to some of Minnesota's smartest, hippest students; they immediately recognized, in the words of one, that "Melville [both Herman and Jean-Pierre] is way weirder than Anne Rice."

I received enormous help from reference librarians at the Wilson Library at the University of Minnesota, the Library of Congress in Washington, D.C., the New York Public Library, and the Centro Studi Americani in Rome; David Klaassen archivist at the Social Welfare History Archive at the University of Minnesota aided my search for arcane information on Caroline Slade. Jean Bubley, executor of Esther Bubley's estate, along with her archivist, Tracy Schmid, gave me free rein to examine Esther's private papers, contact sheets, and unpublished photographs. I met her through the help of Bonnie Yochelson. Maureen Heher at Yale University's Beinecke Rare Book and Manuscript Library in addition to helping me while I was working there, valiantly retrieved my corrupted files after I'd left. Sharon Frost (NYPL), Nancy Goldman (PFA), Maja Keech and Barbara Oliver (LOC), Mary Corliss (MOMA), David Ferber, Dorothy Wiley, and Gunvor Nelson helped with images. Everyone at London's BFI was helpful, digging up ancient prints of *Yield to the Night* and many other British noirs from their collection for me to watch. I could not have written this book without the existence of repertory theaters willing to recycle old movies for the abject; Bob Cowgill and the Oak Street Cinema run a weekly film noir series for those of us in Minneapolis. I owe him a huge debt for letting me see dozens of black-and-white movies during the past five years. My editors at Columbia University Press, Ann Miller and Jennifer Crewe, and assistant editors, Jennifer Barager and Godwin Chu, saw the book through from idea to print.

Many of the chapters in this book began as essays invited by others for special issues of journals or anthologies. Each of the editors cut me enough slack so that my contribution could serve two purposes—that of their volumes and that of mine. A version of chapter 2 appears in a *Modern Fiction Studies* special issue on working-class literature, edited by Stephen Ross; a condensed version of chapter 3 appeared in *Città Reali ed Immaginaire*, edited by Cristina Giorcelli, Camilla Catarulla, and Anna Scacchi. Chapter 4 began as an essay in *Brave New Words: Strategies of Language and Communication in the United States of the 1930s*, edited by Biancamaria Bosco Tedeschini-Lalli and Maurizio Vaudagna. Versions of chapter 5 have appeared in a special issue on documentary of *Media International Australia* and in Janet Walker and Diane Waldman's superb collection *Feminism and Documentary*, published by University of Minnesota Press. Parts of chapter 6 appeared in *Legacy*'s special issue on class and gender, edited by Jeanne Pfaelzer, and in an issue of *Social Text* that was devoted to welfare. A shorter version of chapter 7 appears in volume four (accessories) of *Abito e Identità*, edited by Cristina Giorcelli. Chapter 8 appears in a slightly different form in a special issue on 1960s cultural politics of *Science and Society*, edited by Alan Wald and Paul Mishler; a section of chapter 9 was collected in Amitava Kumar's *Poetics/Politics*, published by St. Martin's Press. I thank all of these friends and colleagues for encouraging my work to develop in so many directions.

Most of my intellectual debts go to my many friends and relatives who have spent hours listening to me go on and on about movies and everything else. My son Raphael Rabinowitz is always willing to see any film noir; moreover, he remembers every plot twist and each character's name. My other son, Jacob Bernstein, and their father, David Bernstein, however, refuse to join me in my decadent pleasures; nevertheless, they too are willing to talk endlessly about the noirish elements of America's past. Countless conversations and movie dates over the years with Lake of the Isles walking partners Maria J. Fitzgerald and Cecily Marcus were essential to distilling my ideas. Past and present Minnesota colleagues Rita Copeland, Maria Damon, John Wright, Jani Scandura, John Mowitt, Mary Roth, Rita Raley, and Tom Pepper talk to me about history, theory, and politics in astounding ways. Coffee and phone calls with Patty Zimmermann, Ruth Bradley, Kathleen Fraser, Connie Samaras, Sara Antonelli, Alice Echols, Sandro Portelli, Cheryl Johnson, Bruce Robbins, Nelson Lichtenstein, Bradley Butterfield, Alan Wald, Sheri Stein, and my mother, Shirley Rabinowitz, kept me going through long winters and short summers. Finally, this book is dedicated to my sister under the screen, Charlotte Nekola, the blonde always available on the other end of the line.

BLACK & WHITE & NOIR

INTRODUCTION: ON PULP MODERNISM

The only town for certain where a Philadelphia first-baseman can answer an attractive brunette's invitation to step into her room: "I have a surprise for you"—and meet a shotgun blast under the heart. "The urge kept nagging at me and the tension built up. I thought killing someone would relieve it."

—*Nelson Algren on Richard Wright's Chicago*

But is not every square inch of our cities the scene of a crime? Every passer-by a culprit?

—*Walter Benjamin on Eugene Atget's Paris*

EMPTYING THE STREETS

Driving through Los Angeles with her friend N[athalie Sorokine Moffat] in February 1947, feminist philosopher and tourist par excellence Simone de Beauvoir notes: "We cross one suburb after another—nothing but suburbs. The city slips away like a phantom city. The streets thrown down any which way on the sides of hills, in the hollows of valleys, have been laid out at random as needed."[1] Her view echoes Theodor Adorno's baleful commentary from 1944 on the "shortcoming of the American landscape . . . that it bears no traces of the human hand. This applies not only to the lack of arable land, the uncultivated woods often no higher than scrub, but above all to the roads. These are always inserted directly in the landscape, and the more impressively smooth and broad they are, the more unrelated and violent their gleaming track appears against its wild, overgrown surroundings." The roads through are "uncomforted and comfortless;" glimpsed by "the hurrying eye . . . from the car . . .

the vanishing landscape leaves no more traces behind than it bears upon itself."[2] This nightmare vision, however, thrills de Beauvoir. Highly attuned, as she is, to the cinematic quality of her tour, almost all of America comes to resemble a film noir. "American cities are too big. At night their dimensions proliferate," she comments as she describes how difficult it was to walk to a movie house to see *The Killers*. "We set out on foot. . . . Suddenly, we were on a dark road lined with tracks, unmoving trains, and hangars, crossed now and then by other deserted streets. We were in the heart of town yet in a desert. It began to rain violently, and in the wind and rain, we felt as forlorn as on a treeless plain—no shelter, no cars in sight" (139). Eventually, they find some workmen and a pay phone to call a cab and make it to the theater in time for the movie.

De Beauvoir, who spent only four months in the United States, cannot see the country outside of the movies she constantly uses as reference points—California deserts equal Von Stroheim's *Greed* (157), Las Vegas nightclubs bring out "Edward G. Robinson [a movie actor known for gangster roles]" (159), the Sierra Nevada mountains make her "think of the snow in *The Gold Rush* (145). San Francisco is "the perfect place for Humphrey Bogart to murder his wife and claim it was an accident" (131). For de Beauvoir, America was dreamed through its movies. Particularly through its crime films, America circulated its fantasy of dangerous modernity, of pulpy concerns with sex and violence, that both repelled this sophisticated European and entranced her: "Movies show a conventional, papier-mache America in which only the landscapes and the material details have some reality" (173). Mary McCarthy would skewer de Beauvoir, "Mlle. Gulliver," she called her, for her fatuous conflation of image and reality; but then she was on a moral rampage against this trait she found in all Stalinists.[3] De Beauvoir's prose fuses her actual views of America with its cinematic construction that she had feasted on in the immediate postwar years in Paris, where she and Richard Wright, to whom she dedicated *America Day by Day*, often watched newly arrived American movies together. The United States itself, noir America, was a land of weirdly empty cities, of neon motel signs looming out of its deserts, of movie palaces tucked into lonely corners. It was crisscrossed with highways stopping abruptly to detour through washed-out small towns where a steak and whiskey might be had.

Her travel journal is filled with the names of the black-and-white pictures she has seen: *Gilda, The Best Years of Our Lives, Lost Weekend, Lady in the Lake*. These films provide metaphor and perspective; they offer a landscape. They not only invest the sights she sees with significance, they invent it. Upon arriving in New York, she takes the ferryboat to the Statue of Liberty because "I just want to see a view of Battery as I've so often seen it in the movies." This view and her visit to the hairdresser make her feel "less uprooted." America is fabricated in and through its fabrications. In the immediate postwar moment, those constructions were brilliantly differentiated between deep shadows and key lighting; the precise definition between sun and shadow, the insistent vertical lines of New York seem "fragile. . . . What a field day a bomber would have!" she concludes. The "house of cards" that is postwar America becomes apparent only through the obscure, darkly-lit films flowing from this sun-filled nation. After Pearl Harbor, no bombers would have a field day on this terrain. But de Beauvoir's instincts are correct, the potential for destruction is ever present. She knew this from the movies she saw and the highways she traveled. The explosions to come, however, the fire next time, would erupt from the bedrock below these glittering cities, the dark shadows "where no sun penetrates" that she discerned while walking Broadway (9).[4]

Cities—living cities, according to Jane Jacobs—are places where people walk the streets. Random people, many people, night and day, collide amid the traffic of commerce, industry, leisure, and play. But the cities of postwar North American popular imagination—cities perhaps reflecting the devastation of bombings abroad, or presentiments of urban renewal and planning at home, appeared dead and lifeless: empty streets filled menacingly not with bodies but with deep shadows, silent pools of light and the sound of one lone man's steps on the pavement, where anyone might just find that dame with a surprise, because, as Nelson Algren said of Chicago, "every 3 A.M. corner looks hired" and "every day is D-day under the El."[5] In this noir world, a man walks to the outskirts of town, collar turned up against the rain, and hopes for a ride; a man wanders into the bleak city night alone—the glow of a cigarette dangling from his lips the only light to guide his way; a man curls against the side of a building, his white shirt stained black as a pool of blood leaks from him;

3

a man runs desperately through the fog, nobody follows, yet still he runs. These scenes from 1940s B-movies—*Detour, Out of the Past, Double Indemnity, Night and the City*—are among the hundreds made, sometimes in two or three weeks for as little as $30,000, between 1942 and 1958. We know them: a lone man, a regular Joe, an average guy, perhaps slightly crooked or a bit too interested in the beautiful blonde whom he happens upon by chance—if there is such thing in this determined world—gets in over his head; the past catches up with him; the frame is too big; and he ends up, where? Dead, if he's lucky; walking those lonely streets, waiting, if he's not. The French called them *films noirs*, and they are emblematic of a cultural process, the pulp modernism of America.[6]

When the War ended, Hollywood turned the documentary techniques of the 1930s and early 1940s on its own backyard, filming the many 1930s hard-boiled detective novels of James M. Cain, Dashiell Hammett, and Raymond Chandler set in California. In the words of a *Life* magazine report, "homicide, always popular, became an obsession with the movies in 1946, and thrillers that racked up less than four or five murders before the final fade-out seemed almost sissified. Movie killers were no longer drawn exclusively from the ranks of gangsters, however. Hollywood's sudden discovery of psychology late in 1945 meant that any character in a film might turn out to be an undiscovered murderer."[7] French movie critics celebrated these dark thrillers, finding art in the chiaroscuro lighting, poetry in the clipped dialogue, philosophy in the doomed insatiable desire, and a smoldering sexuality in the curves of snake women played by such all-American ethnic working girls as Barbara Stanwyck and Rita Hayworth.[8] Un-American, yet thoroughly American. Like the HUAC hearings convening simultaneously, these films tracked urban anxiety, contracting the city into a region of inner terror as they spread its claustrophobia across the vast landscape of the nation.

The heroes of these films are often returning vets, out of place in the newly scrubbed world of home appliances and of women's shoulder-padded assertiveness. After the violence of war, they encounter a new world not of their making and strangely dangerous beyond imagination. The America they left behind, crumbling under the weight of the Depression—a country still located on Main Street—is gone forever. They had no address there anyway, so good riddance, but their place was at least secured—"If you're white, you're all right," croaks Algren in his anti-ode to Chicago. Now, nothing is certain; yet with used car lots full of Chevys and neon spilling from bar and hotel windows, a man can slip into an unknown and invisible life: change his name, head west, walk in some else's shoes. The anonymity of the living, teeming city gives way to another, scarier form: the uniformity of the Garden City; tidy bungalows rimming the Los Angeles hills house an inner violence. These regular guys can't go home. As early as the 1930s, urban planners had been dreaming of the city's disappearance. Rexford G. Tugwell, director of the Farm Security Administration responsible for the New Deal's Green Belt suburbs, put it bluntly: "My idea is to go just outside centers of populations, pick up cheap land, build a whole community and entice people into it. Then go back into the cities and tear down whole slums and make parks of them."[9] These slums, since the great migration of the 1910s and 1920s, had become home to millions of African Americans, as well as impoverished Eastern and Southern European, Mexican and, to some extent, Asian immigrants who had entered the United States before the 1924 Immigration Act restrictions. The face of the city had quite literally darkened; but it took postwar defense subsidies for highways and housing to fulfill Tugwell's dream.

The rise of 1950s car culture was smoothly integrated into home furnishings and women's fashion. The efforts of manufacturers to lure female consumers with car interiors decorated like living rooms culminated in a 1957 Chrysler model, La Femme, whose pink exterior and rose embroidered interior came complete with matching lipstick and nail polish (the exterior paint job) and raincoat and umbrella (the upholstery). The image of 1950s endless effortless mobility—both social, as working-class white ethnics slid into middle-class suburbia (parking the ubiquitous 1956 Chevy in the garage), and geographic, as families headed out on the same road as the Beats ("See the U.S.A. in your Chevrolet," crooned Dinah Shore)—is part of the noir story. The development of Levittown and other cheap suburbs as well as the visions of urban planners, such as New York's Robert Moses, doomed most U.S. cities, crisscrossing neighborhoods with thruways, tearing down tenements for high rises. Film noirs reveal what happened both within those evacuated, blackening cities and behind the doors of the well-kept, bleached suburbs.

PULP MODERNISM

Film noir provides a medium for understanding the peculiar ways in which America expressed its uniquely hokey modernism. The films offer a theory of its pulp modernity. Pulp, the byproduct of the timber industry that helped build the nation, is at once useless waste, clotting the landscape, and recycled goods, making possible the paperback revolution democratizing letters. By activating the world of scandal and trash and relocating it within the domestic melodrama, these films archived changing sexual, gender, and racial mores during the embourgeoisement of white working-class ethnics. Echoing Ann Douglas's assessment of nineteenth-century America, Andreas Huyssen sees modernism as staging a tough-guy fight against a femme-fatale mass culture.[10] However, modernism itself—at least as it was performed within the American frame—could never escape its stake in kitsch.[11] At this millennial moment, it seems we just cannot get enough of modernism—there's New Deal Modernism, there's Hollywood Modernism, there's Modernism Inc., there's vernacular modernism, modernism "we have wanted to forget," "low modernism and modernism of the street," Afro-American modernism, transnational modernism, among many others.[12] These many and proliferating modernisms relocate modernism onto American soil with, in Michael Denning's terms, a "plebian" flavor. Extracted from the ruins of European imperialism found in the gassed and traumized, defeated and fragile, bodies on the Western Front, modernism is reinvigorated through the stirring figure of working-class solidarity. The Depression and fascism form its background, not World War I and the Jazz Age. The twin spectres of unemployment and mass murder, and the burgeoning popular culture of Hollywood movies and other mass media are the sources for America's pulp modernism.

Salvador Dali's 1935 cartoon hanging in the Menil Collection in Houston, Texas, "Gangsterisms; or the Goofy Visions of New York," tracks the interconnections among Hollywood gangster films, proletarian culture, and modern urban settings that were also the basis for Kenneth Fearing's ominous poems from the mid-1930s. Alan Wald calls Fearing a "Marxist Noir" poet who brought a new and nasty aesthetic of the popular to the older literary radicals orbiting the *New*

Masses. Fearing's 1930s poems, especially his collection *Dead Reckon-ing* (1935–1938), like Dali's drawing, map what will become, after World War II, film noir. Film noir, in turn, charts more than post-war traumas of nuclear annihilation; it aids in understanding our current crisis and horror-stained landscape of destruction and war. Fearing wrote his poems with the nightmares of National Socialism's rise in Germany and the defeat of the Loyalists in Spain as backdrop. "C Stands for Civilization" anticipates CNN coverage of the wars in Iraq and Afghanistan: "zooming through the night in Lockheed mono-planes the / witches bring accurate pictures of the latest disaster ex- / actly on time."[13] Relying on the newly created mass-media adver-tising devices—captions, boldface type, repetition, slogans—the poems produce jarring dissonances between the cheery affect of the sales pitch and the grimness of the object being purveyed.

His jazzy, headline-poaching songs—dirges, elegies, requiems—speak the language of noir, sing their lyrics: "smoke the last ciga-rette, drink the last tall drink, go with the / last long whistle of the midnight train" ("Lunch with the Sole Survivor" 102) "Tear up the letters and bury the clothes, throw away the keys, / file the number from the gun, burn the record of birth, / smash the name from the tomb, bathe the fingers in acid, / wrap the bones in lime, / Forget the street, the house, the name, the day" ("Escape" 49). Like a scene from any number of 1940s films (perhaps *The Big Clock* from Fear-ing's roman noir, his lyric, "Memo," asks "is there still any shadow there, on the rainwet window of the / coffee pot, / Between the haberdasher's and the pinball arcade, / . . . // Is there on tonight's damp, heelpocked pavement somewhere the / mark of a certain toe, and especial nail, or the butt of a particular dropped cigarette?" (77). Death is all around "the night of love, and murder, and reckoning, and sleep" ("American Rhapsody (1)" 43). Yet the goofy settings of daily life repeat endlessly—lunch counters, and movie theaters and dime stores: "Whether we found a greater, deeper, more perfect love, by / courtesy of Camels, over NBC; whether the comics / amused us, or the newspapers carried a hunger death / and a White House prayer for mother's day" ("No Credit" 58). These purveyors of the emerging "culture of abundance," as Rita Barnard calls it,[14] serve as the backdrop for the wrecked but profoundly moving lives of men and women passing through a "city for sale, for rent" with "ghost horizons" ("Manhattan" 110) full of "shattered glass"

("Debris" 98). This gloomy image of the city—"No name, any name, nowhere, nothing, no one, none" ("Escape" 50)—returns in visual form in the post-war documents called film noir. What Fearing, with incredible prescience, scripted was the scenario for hundreds of B-movies. Fearing's intimations that fascism was both a threat from afar and from within the ghost horizons of our second-rate cities were reimagined during the cold war as nuclear annihilation and threats of a resurgent native fascism in McCarthyism or fears of communist terror from Asia and eastern Europe and from the son and daughters of their emigrants within—Jews for the most part, the supposed threat to German nationalism now seen as destabilizing America, an America that dropped atomic bombs destroying cities and gassed a mother and father for disclosing its "secrets."

Left-wing iconography from the 1930s attempts to shore up the "Hollow Men" as Mike Gold, glossing T. S. Eliot, called those intellectuals failing to join the CPUSA. The hungry bodies of unemployed men limned a crisis in American manhood as much as an economic crisis. *New Masses* cartoonist Hugo Gellert's lithographs and worker-writer H. H. Lewis's poems were terribly concerned with rebuilding the solid musculature of the working class in order to fight decadent fat cats and emaciated vampires of capitalism. It's homophobic and homoerotic overcompensation with a vengeance that has a frightening commonality with what Klaus Theweleit identified motivating the German Freikorps, the shock troops that formed the core of Hitler's SA—fear of the new woman, of modern female sexuality and mobility felt as aggression.[15] Because gendered metaphors aligning the bourgeoisie with femininity, suffrage, the unconscious, the new woman, women's education, autonomy and emergence as citizens lurk behind much of the call to fraternal arms to solidarity. Even the word "solidarity" suggests anxieties about softness, flaccidity, and so forth.

Film noir fixated on this dangerous scenario—the woman left alone to work the machinery of the homefront while her man was off fighting on the battlefront, often returning a damaged man. Demobilized vets numbed, perhaps maimed, by the horror of war they have experienced, remembering the emptiness of pre-war Depression life, come home to nightclubs glittering with bejeweled women—sisters under our minks, as Gloria Grahame calls them in *The Big Heat*—on the prowl, aggressively seeking money and sex in a new world of pleasure and commodities. A world filled with toasters and refrigerators and radios playing bebop and bulbous black cars, with supermarkets piled high with canned peaches and peas, with women sporting short tight skirts and spiked heels that clatter across the pavement like artillery fire. The terror of this place, home, yet not home—the uncanny home, was first envisioned in the surreal nightmare of Maya Deren's *Meshes of the Afternoon* and the bleak Office of War Information photographs of women in rooming houses and Washington, D.C., bars shot by the misnamed Esther Bubley (both 1943) and spread across popular culture in the iconography of noir spilling out of Hollywood throughout the 1940s and '50s. This time, *Dead Reckoning*, with Humphrey Bogart and Lizabeth Scott (1947), tracks a woman who has rubbed out her first husband and secretly married a gangster only to seduce her dead husband's army buddy as he investigates what happened to his friend. Men can be together in America only by dying together, or through the triangle with the third, the other woman, who dies instead. Bogart's saved when Scott dies in a flaming car crash. Like Barbara Stanwyck in *The File on Thelma Jordan*, like Lana Turner in *The Postman Always Rings Twice*, like Jane Greer in *Out of the Past*—and on and on.

C. L. R. James understood the connection between "the popular arts and modern society" as one in which the "characteristic of modern American life—an enormous tension" is expressed "in well-made gangster films" (126). The tension keeps building up, as it did for Algren's brunette, and pulling the trigger seems to relieve it. These works "are a form of art which must satisfy the mass, the individual seeking individuality in a mechanized, socialized society, where his life is ordered and restricted at every turn. . . . Gangsters get what they want, trying it for a while, they are killed. In the end 'crime does not pay,' but for an hour and a half, highly skilled actors and a huge organization of production and distribution have given to many millions a sense of active living, and in the bloodshed, the violence, the freedom from restraint to allow pent-up feelings free play, they have released the bitterness, hate, fear and sadism which simmer just below the surface" (127). James's insight into the connection between the world of the gangster, one that celebrates the rising, raging individual who functions within a highly organized organization, and the system of Hollywood film stars and film production suggests how film noir can offer a theory of American modernity. The crime film provides a template for its expression and experience. He cites Humphrey Bogart and Ida Lupino in *High Sierra*, but any number of films might do. In their reliance on individuating the masses—through stars, as gangsters—these popular crime films collapse the difference between example and theory, particular and general. According to James, "[O]ne after the other, these films pour out, vying with each other in bloodshed and violence, cruelty, sadism and disregard for all established standards" (132). They offered mass audiences a cogent and fulfilling entry into the workings of power: "They stamp on his face, they crush his jaw, when he is knocked out, they hold him up and beat him, they revel in violence. A succession of evil women has appeared, as cruel and ruthless as cobras" (130). This was the reason audiences lapped them up. The scenarios James outlines and the characters within them—the guy whose face is stamped and the cruel, ruthless women—repeat the classic outlines of masochistic dreams. "Disavowal, suspense, waiting, fetishism and fantasy together make up the specific constellation of masochism," notes Gilles Deleuze.[16] They suggest that while America may have emerged on top of the twentieth century—which Henry Luce had declared to be "The American Century"—in its fantasy life, America resembled a perennial bottom. America's pulp modernism continually restages the "coldness and cruelty," as Deleuze calls it, of masochistic fantasy. James and de Beauvoir commented on postwar American culture as outsiders, left-wing alien observers. They shared much in common with the many expatriate directors creating these parables of modern American life with the aesthetic hammers of Expressionism and the ideological nails of Marxism they brought with them from abroad.

They were not as appalled as some were. Observing Hollywood, Theodor Adorno, aghast at the vision of modern times it afforded, quipped: "The modern has really become unmodern."[17] The danger Adorno saw in film was precisely its ability to concretize the reactionary shift of the modern into a regressive sentimentality through the reification of subjectivity, "a mere function of the production process," in art into saleable goods that administer to the public its own inward emotions (214–15). This sentimentality was precisely what made American desire so perverse. It turned everything into "catchwords for a hit song, designed to boost it." Doubling back on itself as object and sales pitch, America's pulp modernism offers up a sloppy melodrama. "Illuminated in the neon-light switched on by these words," Adorno notes in "English Spoken," "culture displays its character as advertising" (*Minima Moralia*, 47). It is the foundation for the repetitive masochistic fantasy. Whether one agrees with James's more optimistic vision of popular culture providing an analysis of modern America to its subjects or with Adorno's sense that America's modern subjects were hopeless objects of its consumer culture is, to my mind, less important than seeing how both these theorists of American modernity turn to the popular to understand its expression. I should amend my statement—not only do Americans dream modernity through the movies, foreigners dream America in them as well. That is why, despite claims for a British cycle of film noir for instance, it is, as Alain Silver and Elizabeth Ward call it, "an American style," requiring the peculiar geographical history of the nation.[18] Great Britain is an island, too small to allow for escape, too established to enable anarchic invisibility, too accustomed to maintaining a stiff upper lip and bearing up; after all, its highway detours are called "diversions."

Jacques Tourneur's noir psychological horror film *Cat People* (1942) traces the tensions both James and Adorno refer to in the mutable body of Irene, the Serbian artist working as a dress designer whom the smitten Oliver meets while she is sketching a black leopard in the Central Park Zoo. She claims its sleek black coat offers fashion inspirations, but the crumpled paper she discards, tossing it defiantly onto the pavement rather than the trashcan nearby, belies another story. It is a picture of the leopard impaled on a sword, the masochist's vision of "Venus in furs." Oliver's work as an engineer designing ships contrasts with Irene's, although he too draws: he measures precisely and has an office full of assistants. He's an "Americano," he tells Irene, who has never been unhappy in his life until his marriage to her installs him in her dark claustrophobic studio apartment, close to the nighttime growls of the leopard, where she works at her easel alone. His assistant, Alice, ultimately reveals her love for Oliver, declaring herself to be "a new kind of other woman." As Oliver's wholesome workmate, she will not lure him into the clutches of ancient rituals associated with the violent past of another's race as Irene has. Alice may be the blonde girl next door, but she too demonstrates an aggressive mobility and autonomy. Leaving Oliver late one night to walk home alone, she tells him she's a "big girl" who knows how to take care of herself. She wants to have a sexual relationship with Oliver, while Irene, haunted by the legend of her village that demands she kill whomever she kisses, sleeps alone behind a locked door.

This blood legacy from a medieval Eastern Europe connects Irene to the anti-Semitic iconography circulating in and from Nazi Germany. She is the Jew; as such she is also the African presence in America.[19] Alice suggests to Oliver that Irene might be helped out of her shell by seeing a psychiatrist; however, the doctor's dapper urbanity in accent, manner, and dress, and his profession as a mind doctor link him to Irene. No pragmatic engineer who uses measurements to improve a ship's design, Dr. Judd, like the Viennese Dr. Freud driven from his city by fascism, knows about the unconscious and its uncanny desire for death. Forcing Irene to kiss him, Dr. Judd unleashes the deadly feline within her. A few years earlier, Rosita Forbes documenting "women called wild," had tracked women who had turned into beasts through Central America and Africa; a few years later, *Amazing Stories* featured a cover story depicting the "Tiger Woman of Shadow Valley."[20] But the American cobras, as James had called them, roaming New York or San Francisco, expected full access to the sites zoned for men—the streets at night, bars and nightclubs, jobs and apartments.

Made shortly after the United States entered the Second World War, *Cat People* crystallizes central tropes of film noir—human annihilation, female desire, racial history, social mobility, and the production and replication of objects and machinery—that play themselves out as camp in Robert Aldrich's *Kiss Me Deadly* thirteen years later. Like so many film noirs, these two films implicate art and science—both high-end concepts trying to divorce themselves from the tackiness of American life—in the big business of capitalist production. In *Kiss Me Deadly*, Mike Hammer drives through Los Angeles in his full-metal-jacket sports car searching for the anonymous woman he picked up hitchhiking. This woman, barefoot and naked under her trenchcoat, quotes Christina Rossetti and listens to opera and classical music stations on the radio and has literally swallowed the key to human survival. Hammer ultimately discovers the "big whassit" he's been tracking by interpreting the lines of poetry recited to him by his strange passenger. Literary criticism unlocks the secret bomb that annihilates the Malibu beach house where the

FIGURE 1. Isobel Beard, "Women into Beast," from Rosita Forbes, *Women Called Wild* (1937).

crooks are keeping it, and with it, the entire world. For both films, literary analysis—the talking cure of the psychiatrist, the textual study of the poem—becomes part of the violent actions of men bent on piercing the surface, solving the mystery. Strange women— aliens, asylum escapees, poets—possess dark knowledge, secrets locked within their bodies that threaten death and destruction if they are plumbed. These women are irresistible, hiding a darkness, like America itself.

My take on film noir, like James's and Adorno's, is symptomatic. This book is less about film noir as a subject of study than as a leit-motif running thorough mid-twentieth-century American culture. James Naremore's superb study, *More Than Night*, places, as its sub-title asserts, "film noir in its contexts." Instead, I view film noir *as* the context; its plot structure and visual iconography make sense of America's landscape and history. The terrifying size and emptiness of the American continent are tamed by the incessant crossings of tele-phone wires, linked by a never-ending web of female operators rout-ing calls through their switchboards, highways traversed by lone roadsters driving through the night, and road houses where a satin-sheathed chanteuse sits alone on her cigarette break. Film noir shows how communication, transportation, and entertainment shade into pulp. These systems, major industries that dominate the nation and the world, enable crime; in fact, they are criminal enterprises. Noir offers a template for analyzing how cultural formations achieve legi-bility through stable repetitions of instability, predictable renderings of chaos, sinister animations of immobile objects. The hazy smoke clouding the diner counter, hotel lobby, or nightclub suggests that the straight lines—Route 66, the Empire Builder, telephone poles ris-ing with regularity—connecting city to city and city to small town are dotted with hidden dangers. These transgressive sites provide spaces for the illicit expression of sexuality and greed. They house a restless, mobile population, dislocated by hunger, war, and desire—a popula-tion on the make, in search of a new life cut off from the past, itself long banished, though never wholly overcome, in the new world.

Film noir served for me and many women of my generation as a form of documentary reportage on the lives of our parents. Shown daily on *Million Dollar Movie*, these black-and-white lenses into the 1930s and 1940s, years of our parents youth about which they were militantly silent, cued us to their hairstyles, clothing, and home and work lives. Isolated snapshots of my parents—my mother and her sisters posing as pin-ups on tar beach, my father in cut-off sweatshirt tramping across the blankets of Brighton Beach—accrued narrative heft in the convoluted plots of these films. I understood why they could never speak about the past; it was simply too dangerous. The black Bakelite telephones, the white Venetian blinds, the curved Studebaker windshields, the brass Zippo lighters, the mirrors and doorways and hats presented a menacing world of the mundane. In her memoir of her middle-class girlhood in 1950s St. Louis, Charlotte Nekola details how she and her girlfriends attempted to live out Ida Lupino's sinister travails.[21] I too have never quite shaken this sense of film noir; no matter how wacky and contrived the plot, the films speak truths; they offer designs for living. This is precisely what Adorno was railing against and what James found so useful about popular culture. These films operate fantastically to give the feel of the real, but they also catalogue the pulpy back story that is the real America.

Black & White & Noir offers a historical and theoretical overview of the noir sensibility, expressed almost daily during the late 1990s in the pages of the *New York Times*, on Hollywood screens, in fashion, and in the cultural fascination with lurid murder trials involving white women and black men, from the case of trailer-trash mom fatale Susan Smith to that involving Brentwood confidential—O. J. Simpson's white Bronco, Bruno Maglis, and the bungled police work of the LAPD. At the MAC cosmetics counter you can buy a dark purple lipstick called "film noir"; at Pottery Barn you can purchase a black *Dial M for Murder* telephone (the dialer, however, is actually a touch tone); stiletto heels are once again available from Gucci and Manolo Blahnik, not just fetish stores; and since Quentin Tarantino's *Pulp Fiction* simultaneously resurrected John Travolta and film noir in 1994, even sugary Carly Simon got into the act; she reappeared imitating a femme fatale in her album *Film Noir*, which was used as the theme music for the American Movie Classics marathon film noir series that year.[22] As Andrew Sarris recently commented, "Everything is noir—try finding something blanc! . . . Every film is a film noir now. . . ."[23] Literary noir, from its heyday between the 1930s and 1950s, has been institutionalized with the publication of the Library of America anthology, but it also has generated a neo-noir genre of memoir, such as James Ellroy's gripping memoir of his mother's 1958 murder, *My Dark Places*, and literary trash, such as Joyce Carol Oates coming out as Rosamond Smith with the publication of *Starr Bright Will Be With You Soon*.[24] Even that Pillsbury doughboy Garrison Keillor and the jaundiced suburbanite John Updike have their noir alter-egos: Guy Noir and Beck Noir, respectively. The "effetto noir" even reached as far as the mountain town of Trento in the Italian Alps where an exhibition of films, comics, pulp fiction, and clothing was held in Summer 2000. The many forms noir has taken—movies, photos, novels—are valences of the changing racial and class makeup of urban America.[25] In the midst of Nixon's presidency, film noir's resurrection in 1974 by Roman Polanski in *Chinatown*, with its text-book screenplay by Robert Towne, captured the ways in which government intrigue, legal trials, and congressional hearings surround popular culture. The postwar moment of noir was dominated by HUAC hearings, the Army-McCarthy hearings, and Smith Act trials; the second flowering of noir coincided with Watergate, with its significant missing eighteen minutes of tape, the Vietnam War (yet another generation of traumatized veterans), the Chicago Seven trial, among many others, and, in a terribly personal way for Polanski, Charles Manson's trial for the murder of Sharon Tate, Polanski's pregnant wife, and her guests.

Film noir, rather than reflecting these changes, in my view, pre-figures them, encodes them, and makes them intelligible. Cultural sensations coalesce around the spectacles of crime in part due to the conventions film noir provides; it's a template. American political hegemony being assured, at least in retrospect, since the end of the Great War meant that as an empire the nation barely registered an external world. Of course, this is an exaggeration; numerous wars fought in Europe and Asia, as well as the pervasiveness of cold war brinksmanship, meant fears of foreign aggression were matched by military force. However, the national imagination remained fixed within interior landscapes; the terror of nuclear attack was personalized as each schoolchild was trained to "duck and cover" in the event of an attack, for instance, despite everyone's knowledge—gleaned from sci-fi movies as well as John Hersey's *Hirsohima*—that we'd all be vaporized instantly. In his argument about the rise of "imagined communities" of national identification, Benedict Anderson links the daily reading of the newspaper to monumental structures of capitalist nation building. The pervasive dailiness of the newspaper—its ability to appear every day on one's doorstep or to precipitate a daily walk to the newspaper stand—and structure each morning's activity singularly but communally is part of the mundane accession to nationalism. Anderson is not too interested in what is in the paper; however, Mikhail Bakhtin and Walter Benjamin, writing in the 1930s, considered the contents of the feuilleton—the endless accounts of murder, suicide, assault, and scandal—to be a central feature of modern social experience. The fact of their presence alters ideas about literary culture.

Film noir's obsessive return to the scene of the crime anticipates how ideas of guilt about America's violent history would emerge as crucial facets of twentieth-century politics. My girlhood fascination with my parents' past secrets was also an attempt to pry loose the mask covering the nation's brutal history. Growing up in the 1950s, if one were at all sensitive to the messages flowing over the airwaves, left one perpetually ill at ease. You knew things were wrong, even if it was unclear what that might be, no matter how insulated you were in your modern suburban house, as I was by the middle of the decade. The film noirs on your television set confirmed it. But I was watching the equivalent of reruns. These films had foreshadowed the anxieties I felt, intimately aware as I was with a father working in the defense industry, of impending destruction. Like fortunetellers, film noirs predicted the nation's future.

This is a book about film that barely mentions them. At once film and feminist theory, American cultural history, literary criticism, photography study, and political analysis, *Black & White & Noir* reconsiders the cultural politics of the 1980s and 1990s by tracing a hidden stream in 1930s and 1940s popular and leftist (often overlapping) cultures that has recently resurfaced. If one reads the credits of Hollywood B-movies of the 1940s and 1950s, it appears HUAC was right: American movies were plying the minds of average citizens with critiques of capitalism. Between August 26, 1927 (the executions of Sacco and Vanzetti), and June 19, 1953 (the executions of Julius and Ethel Rosenberg), left-wing culture permeated popular American life. The Depression ushered in a wave of working-class agitation, and World War II propelled a massive Popular Front to fight fascism; during this brief quarter century, movements to challenge state and corporate violence seemed, if not triumphant, at least legitimate. However, like the bombings of Hiroshima and Nagasaki to end World War II, the two acts of state violence against immigrant left-wing working-class people lurk as residual horrors.

Black & White & Noir offers an interdisciplinary cultural history of twentieth-century America through episodic readings of films, photographs, and literature—a history of the myriad detritus floating beyond the borders of acceptable scholarship. Tracing the dark edges of trash lurking amid our postwar political unconscious, this book views pulp as prefigurative, a kind of political theory of America's problematic democracy disguised as cheap melodrama, with origins in two submerged aspects of American modernity: the contradiction of slaveholding in a democracy and the suppression of working-class organizing. Violence is at the core of both of these strands. Noir— emerging out of German Expressionism and pulp fiction, among other sources—normalizes horror by deflecting it from the public arena into the private home. Politics in twentieth-century America becomes pulp fiction; or, more accurately, pulp fiction leads the way in matters political. A generation was raised on the dichotomous popular cultural images television offered in Ozzie and Harriet, on the one hand, and the reruns of Ida Lupino and other B-movie stars, on the other. The Nelson's neat, spacious, modern home was supposed to signal a radical break from war, fascism, and the Depression, but the ghosts around Ricky were interference from that earlier program. The dark side of 1950s culture was silently indebted to the cultural politics of the 1930s. Today's political imagination is haunted by all forms of our everyday trash, from the spent uranium bomb casings littering Kosovo to Monica Lewinsky's literary tastes, from the tons of debris from the destroyed Twin Towers to Arabic flight-training manuals. My central premise is that modernity in America is structured around two poles, each working to suppress a hidden history of state violence: racial codings (hence the black-and-white motif) and class melodrama (hence the recourse to noir sentimentality and nostalgia). These in turn are revealed in the pulpy silhouettes of the femme fatale—the dark lady who glows in the bright key lighting of B-movies.

Part I, "Black," begins just as noir makes the big time. If John Huston's *Maltese Falcon* (1941) signaled the emergence of this new sensibility, shifting Humphrey Bogart's role from the thuggish gangster in *Bullets or Ballots* (1938) toward the morally complex detective figure of Sam Spade because of the introduction of a new term—the "femme fatale," seductress and betrayer—then the war-time photographs of Esther Bubley charted what happened to Mary Astor's Brigid O'Shaughnessy. Chapter 1, "Already Framed," examines unrecognized precursors to film noir in the work Esther Bubley did for Roy Stryker's Office of War Information (OWI). Her photography projects in Washington, D.C. rooming houses and across bus and train stations throughout the country found a nation of solitary, determined, dreamy, rootless women. Bubley, one of the last photographers hired by the Farm Security Administration (FSA), stayed on when the department became the OWI. She continued to train her camera on the disrupted lives women experienced during and after the war. On her long bus trip across the Midwest and South during the war years, her images of women alone and of segregated waiting rooms revealed a dark underside of the war that would find its way into noir. After the war, she worked for corporations such as Standard Oil, TWA, and the pharmaceutical company Ciba, continuing to take disturbing images while under their sponsorship. Her troubling images belie the consensus forming around postwar corporate liberalism. Her haunting photograph of a lone woman waiting to pick up a sailor in a Washington, D.C., bar, like Marion Post Wolcott's defiant shot of two couples drinking rum and Coke in a juke joint, push the 1930s images of ruined, yet noble, womanhood into the terrain of noir.

The lone woman surviving the city, like Lutie Johnson in Anne Petry's novel *The Street*, are also relocated daughters of the Depression's "Migrant Mothers." Set in geographical and social motion by World War II, they end up singing in a *Road House* (like Ida Lupino) or looming up *Out of the Past* (like Jane Greer), packing a pistol if they are white. But if they are black, like Lutie, they find themselves cleaning these bad girls' rooms. Chapter 2, "Domestic Labor," looks at the racialized sexuality of the maid in pulp fiction and film noir in order to examine how African-American women's left-wing literary culture fed into, yet transformed, the stereotypes of black female sexuality. Writing in the 1940s and 1950s, Petry and Gwendolyn Brooks pick up the femme noire to revise her depiction in that classic melodrama, Fanny Hurst's *Imitation of Life*. Each considers how race, ethnicity, and class are detected on the female body, especially those of various fatal moms of 1930s to 1950s popular fiction, such as *Mildred Pierce*.

Chapter 3, "Double Cross," reads Richard Wright's 1953 novel, *The Outsider*, as a film noir. Reversing many film noirs that "rip their stories from the headlines," Wright lifts dozens of plots and scenes from the movies he saw in late 1940s Paris. Moreover, the 1952 rewriting of his own life story in Ralph Ellison's *Invisible Man* (resulting in the National Book Award for Fiction) spurred Wright's own revenge plot. Both novels owe much to 1930s detective fiction and 1940s film noirs' unconscious charting of the changing racial make-up of postwar cities, the absent presence in their depictions of urban space. These two African-American authors used the genre's conventions to expose the Communist Party's racism, in much the same way as other left-wing writers had used the gangster story to expose capitalism's exploitation of workers. They rewrite the passing narrative into one of amnesia and changed identities and pulp America's racial melodrama (and the theme of the "tragic mulatto") through noir.

Where part 1 maps noir across the wretched spaces where a restless population dwelled—waiting rooms, hotel rooms, kitchens— part 2 ties noir to a nostalgia for America's past. "White" returns to some overlooked sources for noir from the 1930s—Farm Security Administration photography, labor iconography, and radical social workers' accounts of Depression privation. Chapters 4, 5, and 6 address how pulp modernity is expressed through pictures of rural white poverty, nostalgia for the heroic "working stiff" of proletarian culture, and literary investigations of prostitution and domestic chaos, respectively. Quite paradoxically, representing the pockets of 1930s poverty paved the way for the homogenous 1950s, enabling an amassing of a white urban middle-class culture by offering it images of what it wasn't. Chapter 4, "Blanc Noir," begins with *Fargo*, the Coen brothers inversion of film noir and its city locales, to argue that America became a modern mass nation not during 1920s modernism—marked by its gleaming skyscrapers and efficient assembly lines—but later, during the 1930s, when an urban, middle-class audience could consume images of white rural poverty—a dystopian pastoralism—through the mass media.

Chapter 5, "Melodrama/Male Dramas," considers how the tradition of labor documentary is suffused with melodrama (especially 1930s proletarian melodramas of the unemployed "working stiff") to express working-class masculinity. This historical investigation turns to two recent labor documentaries—*Roger & Me* and *American Dream*. Each film demonstrates how so-called postindustrial labor relations in which corporations must become "lean and mean"

mimic the sleek muscular working-class body of the idealized proletarian man. At the same time, unemployed workers slacken because
the new labor solidarity requires hiring media consultants rather
than picketing to counter corporate hegemony. This feminized labor
force takes up noir melodrama to narrate its story.

Chapter 6, "Not 'Just the Facts, Ma'am'," reads the history of
debates about welfare through the social work novels written in the
1930s and 1940s by Caroline Slade. Slade's female social workers
investigate the deviant bodies of poor white women to show the
deep connection between pulp aesthetics and left-wing politics in
the United States. These social workers resembled detectives; however both their gender and their relation to the state meant they had
little autonomy. Instead Slade's social workers mirrored the many
women reporters, like Martha Gellhorn, who had toured the nation
and the world documenting the crises of war, fascism, and the
Depression. This reportage and fiction often verged on a tabloid
noir. It was cleaned up in the layouts of *Life* but splayed across pages
of *PM*. Margaret Bourke-White's first assignment in the town of
New Deal, Montana, (in *Life*'s first issue) sanitized the sensational
photojournalism of Weegee, both of which, like Slade's novels, wrap
class conflict in racialized sexual perversions.

Part Three: "Noir" muses on how the ominous trappings of
women's daily lives that circulated in film noir coalesced into feminism. Chapter 7, "Barbara Stanwyck's Anklet," connects the case-
hardened steel persona of the femme fatale to the various solid
objects surrounding and enclosing her. How to dress and accessorize
the femme fatale? Phyllis Dietrichson descends her staircase in anklet
and spiked slippers; Thelma Jordan stands in District Attorney Cleve
Marshall's doorway in her black pumps. Stanwyck's iconic poses in
this footwear, as well as in her black shades or with her black Bakelite
telephone, are accessories to the crime of female desire. The chapter
analyzes how gender creates difference in and through objects by
tracing philosophical, political, and psychoanalytic discussions of
footwear. Objects tell stories. In the 1960s, when feminists argued
against women's position as sex objects, demanding subjectivity,
objects acquired a lousy reputation. But in commodity culture, as
Marx suggested, they have something to say. Film noir highlights
their sinister nature as consumer goods meant for women's use.

The concluding chapters argue that just as 1950s popular culture

refers unconsciously to 1930s political culture, recent popular political culture gestures continually to noir. This section pulps postwar
America by linking aspects of culture not usually thought of as
pulpy—documentary (with its serious attempt to expose crises) and
avant-garde (with its communal, visionary ecstacies) and literary fiction, especially its middle-brow magical realism—to this pattern of
deflecting racial horror and class tension onto scenes of privacy.
Chapter 8, "Medium Uncool," shows how indebted second-wave
feminism was to the 16mm black-and-white movie culture of the
1960s. It finds in women's experimental cinema made during the
Vietnam War an uncanny domesticity akin to film noir's unsettling
post–World War II views of household objects and the city. Chapter
9, "Mapping Noir," concludes the book with a trip through recent
women's fiction and a history of literary "dark ladies." It describes
how American fiction has performed political theory through sensational narratives. The two chapters thus draw a larger picture of
postwar American suppression of the Left within various strains of
popular political culture, explaining, in part, why Hollywood
bankrolled "neo-retro-noirs" in the 1990s.

Black & White & Noir risks appearing eclectic and incoherent.
Yet, precisely because the book ranges among seemingly disparate
fields of inquiry, it demonstrates the wild totality possible through
interdisciplinary work. Only by stepping out of bounds, like the
doomed characters in a film noir, can one link film noir to FSA
photography or to social workers' reports, or investigate Richard
Wright's debt to film noir. Just as a prism's many facets refracts
white light into the full range of colors—ROYGBIV—the chapters
of this book break apart the constituent elements within, behind,
and emerging from noir. By arguing episodically for the presence
of a noir sensibility—a pulp politics—throughout twentieth-century America, I improvise a method for theorizing its peculiar
modernism, not as seamless grand narrative, nor as tightly focused
case study, but as the chaotic repetition of the familiar. The title plays
on the various forms of black-and-white circulating in modern culture—newspapers, pulp fiction, photographs, B-movies, 1950s TV,
underground films—and, of course, indexes the racial system superintending American life. Symbolically, there is a connection. This
book frames it; that's what noir is all about.

PART I

BLACK
ROOMS AND RAGE

CHAPTER 1

ALREADY FRAMED: ESTHER BUBLEY INVENTS NOIR

ROOMING HOUSES

There comes a moment in many film noirs when the bad girl emerges snarling with anger as she ensnares the dimwitted doomed guy. The appropriately named Ann Savage turns on hapless, guilty Tom Neal in *Detour*, her face transformed from forlorn innocence after he picks her up hitchhiking into vicious rage when she reveals to him that she recognizes his clothes and car as belonging to another man, the dead one Neal has dumped along the highway. Jane Greer, dressed like a nun, turns on Robert Mitchum in the final moment of *Out of the Past* after she kills her gangster lover Kirk Douglas, leaving Mitchum dead and framed for a number of murders. So too Barbara Stanwyck in *Double Indemnity* sneers at Fred McMurray when he starts getting cold feet about their plans to murder her husband. By the time she appears in *The File on Thelma Jordan*, Stanwyck can turn on her former pimp with such fury she blinds him with a cigarette lighter. Gloria Grahame laughs at Jack Palance when he slaps her face in *Sudden Fear*, reducing him to her sex toy after she threatens to alert his rich wife, Joan Crawford, that he is already married. Lizabeth Scott in *Too Late for Tears* reveals her greedy murderous desire for the cash hurled mistakenly into the

FIGURE 2. Esther Bubley, "A picture-taking machine in the lobby at the United Nations service center," December 1943.

convertible she and her husband drive. She viciously gets rid of one man after another until she lands in Mexico alone with the money. These scenes repeat themselves again and again as if it is not enough that the women's morbid sexuality already marks them as bad. They must also mutate into animals. Simone Simon in *Cat People* literally turns into a seething black leopard stalking her competition, her husband's assistant, and killing her psychiatrist after he kisses her. This early noir horror film sets the image of sexual allure as animality. Because it is literalized, we never see Simone Simon's face transform; it is her body, which is never actually seen either. Instead, we hear the rustle of her paws amid the leaves, see the shadow of her form, discover the slashes of her claws. Good girl "Kansas" in *Phantom Lady* dresses up as a femme fatale to get drummer Elisha Cook Jr. to admit to seeing the elusive woman in the hat accompanying her boss. When she goes with him to the after hours jam session, she lures him with her orgasmic responses to his drum solo. The image of the woman turning into wild beast is a code for the impossible: to see the moment of female orgasm. Its terrifying ability to alter the woman's face is perhaps what these moments of vituperation are really about. Rather than the laugh of the Medusa, we see her fury at men's irrelevance.

This view of triumphant female rage—refusing to look pleasing, to be the soothing and demure helpmate—inevitably results in death. Both she and the man are doomed, but for a tiny instant her desire and its expression have trumped social conventions about femininity. We watch Jean Wallace in Joseph H. Lewis's *The Big Combo* as her lover Richard Conte slowly goes down on her. The camera remains focused on her face as it fractures following her orgasm. By this time when the genre had entered its baroque period, with films as different as Robert Aldrich's *Kiss Me Deadly* (1955) or Samuel Fuller's *The Naked Kiss* (1963), the moments of female rage—when Lily Carver points her gun at Ralph Meeker's Mike Hammer and begs "Kiss me, Mike" or when Kelly grabs the phone receiver and beats Grant to death after she discovers his pedophilia, repeating and mirroring the first scene where she beats her pimp with a leather handbag—had entered the realm of domestic sit-com camp. During the mid-1940s, however, these scenes still had the air of tragedy clinging to them because they revealed anxieties circulating within the culture about women's wartime mobility and participation in heavy industry. Women's seething rage could burst forth without logical antecedent; it's somewhat confusing to the man why the femme fatale explodes at the moment she does. The plot motivation is never quite enough to account for it; only her unpredictable and invisible sexuality explains it. A mystery to the ordinary men attracted to these women, it is always transparent to the women who meet them; yet, knowing who they are, the women rarely condemn their demonic sisters. As Gloria Grahame insists in *The Big Heat*, "We're sisters under our minks."

This dangerous autonomy, visualized in the snarl that comes invariably at the moment when the female takes control of the man and the situation, indexes the changing position of women accelerated by the Second World War. Women had experienced a different kind of mobilization during the 1940s when many left poorly paying jobs as domestics or clerks in search of more lucrative employment in factories and in federal government offices. Many of these women ended up living in rooming houses full of other single women with whom they shared meals and chores and movie dates. Marjory Collins's April 1943 shot of women massing a downtown block for an evening movie documents a female takeover of urban space, one that Giuliana Bruno revealed had occurred in Italy during the rise of fascism and throughout the war.[1] Crowds of "Thursday night shoppers [stand] in a line outside a movie theatre" in Baltimore, Maryland, as neon flashes above them a huge exclamatory: NEW.[2] Louis Faurer's photograph of working women waiting for a bus on Broadway before a poster advertising a Barbara Stanwyck movie (clearly misdated as 1948, because the movie is the 1950 film *No Man of Her Own*) details how women could move through the city at night dressed much like the actress (in that film she assumes the identity of a dead woman she befriended on the train to San Francisco just before it wrecks). In 1948, the Kinsey Report had opened up discussions of Americans' sex lives. As Andrea Fisher observes in her ground-breaking look at the women photographers working in the FSA/OWI, "[T]hese images from the 1940s . . . cast suspicion on their promise of a visual presence, their fascinations turn on an offering of sexuality."[3] That offering could be had, in part, because women could live alone, occupying single rooms. If the film noir femme fatale rarely possessed this kind of domestic isolation—she's usually a kept woman—her snarl set her apart from proper domesticity. She didn't need to work a job, like the women flocking to war work, but she was their sister nevertheless.

Photographer Esther Bubley was among the last members of the extraordinary crew of artists hired by Roy Stryker to document government programs aimed at ameliorating poverty during the Depression and, when the nation entered World War II, to record the efforts undertaken by citizens to support national defense. Hired as a negative cutter, Bubley stayed on after the Farm Security Administration had become the Office of War Information. Her large body of work focused on these uprooted working women. Bubley tracked the private lives of young women, such as her sister Enid, who lived in boarding houses or in a series of furnished apartments, as Esther and her other sister, Claire, did, while they worked government jobs. Her many photographs, intimate moments of pri-

FIGURE 3. Marjory Collins, "Thursday night shoppers in a line outside a movie theatre." Baltimore, Md., April 1943.

FIGURE 4. Louis Faurer, "Barbara Stanwyck Movie Poster, Broadway NYC, 1948." Miriam and Ira D. Wallach Division of Art, Prints and Photographs, The New York Public Library. Astor, Lennox and Tilden Foundations. Silver gelatin print. Permission by David Ferber.

vacy—daydreaming out a window, napping on a couch, thumbing a magazine, arranging personal objects on a dresser—offer a sense of stasis, of lives held in abeyance waiting alone for an uncertain future. In her most famous image, captioned, "Girl sitting alone in the Sea Grill, a bar and restaurant, waiting for a pickup," Bubley anticipated the signature icons surrounding the femme fatale: a lone woman sits at the end of long booth, a glass of beer almost empty, smoking, framed by Venetian blinds. Behind them the night is black save for the neon letters above her; but a man's head is visible outside the window behind her, peering at her back. She waits under surveillance, explaining: " I come in here pretty often, sometimes alone, mostly with another girl, we drink beer, and talk, and of course we keep our eyes open you'd be surprised at how often nice, lonesome, soldiers ask Sue, the waitress to introduce them to us."[4] Like Ella Raines in *Phantom Lady*, who sits night after night watching bartender Andrew Tombes Jr. until she finally follows him through the dark streets one night aggressively chasing him, not for companionship but for information, Bubley's girl also "keeps her eyes open" for men. In her impassive availability, she signals her desire; yet hers is a figure in relative repose, arms crossed, not in defiance but resignation. For the young women in the rooming houses and bars of Washington, D.C., in 1943, nightlife is spent usually alone or in the company of other lonely women; they wait, but they are free. The sequence of pictures from the Sea Grill contains some of the most detailed captions written by Bubley. They constitute a pulp narrative about how to pick up soldiers. One image notes a "Girl and a soldier came into the Sea Grill separately, but are developing a beautiful friendship."[5] Another zooms in on "A slightly inebriated couple at the Sea Grill."[6] These women, as Bubley makes clear, are poised in a 'strange contradiction. Alone and mobile, they are free from family scrutiny and control; yet their availability is limited by the absence of men who have deserted this and other urban spaces for war.

Hints of lesbian desire appear everywhere in Bubley's images as the women curl up together to read or listen to the radio, but the overriding sense is of a deep malaise. All dressed up and nowhere to go, these women wait—for men. No wonder the films made immediately upon the war's conclusion feature a new brutal kind of female sexual aggression. Phyllis Dietrichson in *Double Indemnity* doesn't

FIGURE 5. Esther Bubley, "Girl sitting alone in the Sea grill, a bar and restaurant waiting for a pickup. 'I come in here pretty often, sometimes alone, mostly with another girl, we drink beer, and talk, and of course we keep our eyes open you'd be surprised at how often nice, lonesome, soldiers ask the waitress to introduce them to us.' " Washington, D.C., April 1943.

just await Walter Neff after he arrives at her bungalow door to sell her an insurance policy. She shows up later at his door, hair coiffed and perfumed in sweater and slacks, asking for a drink. Although she is housed in a tidy bungalow complete with step-daughter, husband, and maid, and the year of the film's action is 1938—before the war had even started in Europe—thus seeming to have little in common with Bubley's sisters and their roommates, she too appears poised for something to happen. As does her step-daughter, Lola, whom we find playing Chinese checkers a few nights later with Phyllis when Neff shows up to have Mr. Deitrichson sign the insurance policy, biding her time until she can go downtown to meet her boyfriend, Nino Zachetti. After her father's death, Lola moves into her own apartment: "Four walls and you just sit and look at them," as Neff characterizes it. Filmed in 1943, the movie locates these two women—the murderous stepmother and the grieving, alienated daughter—who live out a solitary female existence, dependent upon, yet divorced from, men.

Although the rooming houses Bubley was documenting seemed wholesome enough in 1943, the rooming house remains, in fiction, film, and art, a sinister place filled with wild women and brutal men. Cornell Woolrich's novel (which became the Stanwyck film *No Man of Her Own*) *I Married a Dead Man* tracks Helen Georgesson as "she climbed the rooming-house stairs like a puppet dangling from slack strings. A light bracketed against the wall, drooping upside-down like a withered tulip in its bell-shaped shade of scalloped glass, cast a smoky yellow glow. A carpet-strip ground to the semblance of decayed veg-etable-matter, all pattern, all color, long erased, adhered to the middle of the stairs, like a form of pollen or fungus encrustation."[7] This dreary space, home to the rejected, pregnant nineteen-year-old girl becomes an iconic zone of danger and defeat; Gloria Grahame, her face hideously scarred when her gangster lover scalds her with hot coffee, holes up in tough cop Glenn Ford's room in Fritz Lang's 1953 film, *The Big Heat*. In Robert Siodmak's *The Killers*, Burt Lancaster (Swede) awaits his murderers in his small dark room with stoic calm; double-crossed by a woman, he has simply given up the will to live. More recently, the Coen brothers made the hotel where *Barton Fink* suffered Hollywood writer's block a central character in their parodic, moody film noir. Ed and Nancy Keinholz's *Pedicord Apt.*, an installation in the Weisman Art Museum in Minneapolis, reconstructs a seedy 1940s rooming house, letting us enter its claustrophobic hallway and eaves-drop on the domestic melodramas behind each grim door. Just those sorts of doors had been the actual inspiration for one of the greatest works of twentieth-century America fiction. Living in and managing the rundown hotel his family owned, Nathanael West watched its long-term residents who lived out a desperation during the Depression. They became the basis—along with a cache of real letters he was given—for his brilliant dissection of transience, *Miss Lonelyhearts*.

What distinguishes Bubley's images of the rooming-house young women from Helen Georgesson or *Miss Lonelyhearts*, for that matter, is the way her camera has opened the doors finding behind each rather clean, well-lighted spaces often cluttered with friends, magazines, pictures from home, and drying hand laundry. These women have made this zone of violent transience homelike, inviting, quite unlike the noir vision of enclosure. In the typical film, a woman (or man) is trapped in the rooming house, like Tom Neal and Ann Savage in the apartment they share in Los Angeles; its walls close in upon the inhabitants, whose only escape are endless cigarettes and cheap booze. The opening sequence of Jean-Pierre Melville's homage to American film noir, *Le Samourai*, begins in the dark room where Alain Delon lies absolutely still on his bed. The slow pan from one desolate object to another tracks a bleak existence enlivened only by his pet bird. The noir rooming house barely provides cover much less shelter; it is a space of waiting and death. These were the places New York crime photographer Weegee (Arthur Fellig) frequented in his work as freelance photographer for a number of daily newspapers during the 1930s and as staff photographer for *PM* in the early 1940s. Weegee's tabloid images of murder and accident victims, or of apprehended criminals, always held an aura of intimacy about them; he knew his subjects, hanging out with them in the Bowery restaurant Sammy's. Bubley's rooming-house images seek to portray another side of transience, one that might make single life possible for middle-class women. But they shade into discomfort with the dullness attendant upon the working life. Margaret Bourke-White, on assignment for the first issue of *Life*, photographed the men and women filling up the transient housing of New Deal, Montana, as they built the Columbia River dams. These pictures of hard-drinking men, women, and even children suggest an unsavory element to the search for employment. Weegee's images make nighttime New York look like a lurid zone crawling with lowlifes, cops, and high-society dames. However, Bubley shows a more middle-class world, a world of sisters and friends who carefully wash their nylons every night in preparation for work the next day. These women might have been the spinster aunts of a generation before. However, they are not at home. Instead they circulate within the rooming house entertaining men or at the bars on the lookout for soldiers or just lie together dreamily listening to the radio. Unlike Woolrich's Helen, who finds an envelope tucked under her door containing a five-dollar bill and a one-way railroad ticket back to her

FIGURE 6. Esther Bubley, "Listening to a murder mystery on the radio in a boarding house room." Washington, D.C., Jan. 1943.

hometown San Francisco, Bubley's rooming-house women have settled in, even if they would eventually leave for acceptable marriages.

At the same time, however, there is a darker side to the rooming-house pictures. Bubley frames many of the images through open doorways. She finds the woman staring out the window, or reflected in her bureau mirror. These solitary women, dislodged in their lodging house, languorous, in limbo, which, while not filled with incipient dangers, like those awaiting Gloria Grahame in *The Big Heat* for turning on the gang, suggest at once a radical dis-ease and a stubborn revelry within their solitude. In picture after picture, women are caught sleeping while a card game goes on in the background; they sit alone smoking while listening to the radio. Beautiful rebellious Pearl Ginsburg "refused to have her boarding house rent raised;" yet she too sits alone on her bed staring pensively, averting her eyes from the camera.[8]

34

FIGURE 7. Esther Bubley, Washington, D.C., 1943.

FIGURE 8. Case-hardened and hard-boiled Barbara Stanwyck stands behind Fred McMurray's door in *Double Indemnity* (d. Billy Wilder, 1944).

Each of these scenes reactivates the gangster movie sequence of the hole-up, when, on the lam or in the midst of gang warfare, a group of men, reconstituted as a family (think of Michael Corleone being instructed by his elders in how to make a sauce in *The Godfather*), huddle together waiting out the heat. In other images, glanced from the hallways into rooms with doors left open while a man visits, the deep focus hints at the possibility of a sexuality central to noir.[9] In one of Bubley's images, a single hall light glows behind two partial silhouettes of a man and a woman who stand talking in the darkened foreground. Between them and framing the woman's face is a sliver of her lighted bedroom glimpsed through the open doorway. Here erotic lighting clashes with the codes of respectability enshrined by the open door. This 1943 image anticipates a scene from *Double Indemnity* in which Phyllis stands behind Walter's open door hiding from Barton Keyes. In the shot, the door itself separates the two, who are starkly-lit: Neff stands against his dark apartment; Phyllis against the spot-lit hallway. Mystery and eroticism are performed within the space of iconic objects—open doors and light fixtures—Bubley had scrutinized. In another of her photographs, two women lounge together—one dreamily staring into space, the other smiling warily at her—on a bed separated by a bare light bulb that burns between them casting deep shadows across their faces. Is this seduction? It's faintly in the air, especially as the eye travels up between the two women's faces to the bare bulb encircled by a halo of wire from the missing shade and the Degas print of a nude woman reading taped to the wall above it. Again, the bare bulb and the line of the door on the far edge of the picture reinforce the curve of the barred bed frame, all details of desire.

Another photograph of two women together, which Bubley captioned "Women gossiping in a drugstore over Cokes. Washington D.C., 1943," places the women, again lit from behind, conspiratorially together across a wooden table. Smoke hangs in the air between them as one woman partially covers her mouth seeming to gesture behind her with her hand while speaking to her rapt friend. Only the paper cup and the women's heavy coats keep this from looking like a much seedier bar. These interior shots by Bubley all conspire to define a sense of enclosure and desperation, even as they portray daily mundane spaces and activities: women sitting together or alone talking on the phone, listening to the radio, playing cards, writing a

FIGURE 9a. Esther Bubley, "Pearl Ginsburg refused to have her boarding house rent raised." Washington, D.C., Jan. 1943.

FIGURE 9b. Esther Bubley, Washington, D.C., 1943.

FIGURE 10. Esther Bubley, "Women gossiping in a drug store over Cokes." Washington, D.C., 1943.

letter. These often grim moments are supplemented by the occasionally tense, intimate visits by men. Even with the front across the oceans, the war takes its toll.

Bubley's photographic portraits of single working women living in rooming houses or picking men up at bars, included a series of women working at their government and industry jobs. At the Western Union telegraph office, women are shown operating all manner of the machinery of communications. Miss Ethel Wakefield sits at a PBX board; Miss Genie Lee Neal reads perforated tape; Miss Helen Ringwals works with pneumatic tubes; Muriel Pare commands the switchboard.[10] These images of serious and competent young women, almost all of whom Bubley identifies as "Miss," in control

38

of the inner workings of the system wiring the nation together during a time of war, became staples of film noir iconography. The repeated presence of telephones and telegraphs in so many films, and the important role these devices play in the plots, signal, like the empty dark highways or train tracks crucial to so many of these films as well, a new sense of women's mobility, freedom, and power through their essential labor for the war effort. Women like Kathie Moffet in *Out of the Past* call the boss when the caper collapses; women like Leona Stevenson in *Sorry, Wrong Number* rely on the telephone to protect them; women like Vera in *Detour* die of strangulation by a telephone cord. Bubley's work among these young women in Washington, D.C., incarnated the iconography so central to film noir's sense of dislocation: the lonely aggressive female who can adroitly use a series of mundane objects—telephones, cigarette lighters, radios—with deadly results and who inhabits and works in a world full of others like her. Bubley's photographs remained largely unpublished during and after the war years, unusual for the project whose purpose was to broadly underscore a national sense of purpose. Her disturbing intimations of female eroticism, authority, and autonomy were perhaps too unsettling. Nevertheless, looking at the photographs now, it seems clear that she was inventing the icons of female pulp modernism—on the one hand, a kind of sleepwalking existence of endless sexual deferral; on the other, eventual economic self-sufficiency.

Bubley's rooming-house photographs oscillate between varied images of the nondomestic domicile, the house that is not a home, the uncanny. One aspect derived from half a century of pictures of Bowery flophouses, like those Alfred Stieglitz found in 1892 at Five Points, which became the basis for the one Lillian Gish inhabits in D. W. Griffith's *Musketeers of Pig Alley* (1912), and that Weegee was splashing across the New York papers every day. His two solo exhibits at the left-wing Photo League were entitled *Murder Is My Business*.[11] The other developed from wholesome images of young female co-eds lounging in college dormitories flooding many mass-circulation magazines.[12] While she was in Washington, D.C., Bubley's other projects included following the lives of students at Woodrow Wilson High School, who were busy decorating the gym for the prom, checking new fashions, and hanging around the cafeteria. These images of stable middle-class normalcy, coupled with a

FIGURE 11. Esther Bubley, "Miss Helen Ringwals works with the pneumatic tubes through which messages are sent to branches in other parts of the city for delivery." Washington, D.C., June 1943.

FIGURE 12. (*Opposite page top*) Esther Bubley, boarding house, Washington, D.C., 1943.

FIGURE 13. (*Opposite page bottom*) Claire Trevor on display for Dennis O'Keefe in *Raw Deal* (d. Anthony Mann, 1948).

series of photographs of GIs sightseeing in the nation's capitol, stressed that the nation was, like the well-appointed home, still a safe haven; they helped allay fears of enemy invasions.

ROAD TRIPS

Rooming houses offer temporary solace and privacy for the city's poor or unattached workers. The rural version is the motel, the inn, or the roadhouse, whose utilitarian rooms allow anonymous bodies temporary rest after a long day on the road. The opening shot of the Coen brother's *Blood Simple* (1984) plays on the classic noir scene of the couple driving through a rainy night, stopping at the neon sign calling their restless bodies to "Dew Drop Inn." The noir sensibility is based both on the black-and-white aesthetics of cities and on the open stretches of gray asphalt, telephone wires looping along their shoulders, fleeing them.[13] But as with so much of the noir effect, it had origins in earlier movements. During the late 1930s, a number of women published book-length sagas about their travels among the world's downtrodden. Women photographers were mobilized during the Depression years to take their cameras with them on the road in search of "the trouble I've seen," as Martha Gellhorn called her book-length reportage. Reversing the plaint of the blues song, Gellhorn and, even more insistently, photographers such as Margaret Bourke-White, working for *Life* magazine, and Dorothea Lange, working for the FSA, sought to make sure everybody'd seen the trouble they'd seen. Bubley's photographs of her bus trip throughout the midwestern and southern United States are part of this tradition. In fact, Bubley cited Margaret Bourke-White's 1936 *Life* cover spread on New Deal, Montana, as inspiring her to become a photographer.[14] Like them, she recorded a nation of women beaten down by or making do with whatever raw deal they'd cut.

In many ways, the "bus story," as she called her assignments, made Bubley's career as a photographer.[15] Although Bubley had worked briefly for *Vogue* during their busy pre-Christmas season in 1940, she left New York to return to Washington, D.C., for a job at the National Archives in early 1941, where she took pictures of her sisters' rooming house. A word from her supervisor to Roy Stryker landed her a spot in the darkroom at the OWI lab, and thus

Stryker licensed her study of single women, which became part of the file even though it had not been formally assigned. After he left the OWI, Stryker hired Bubley to work on the huge Standard Oil of New Jersey project he was coordinating, and she became known for her industrial photography and worked not only for "slicks," such as *Redbook, Life*, and *Ladies Home Journal*, but for numerous corporations, including TWA, Ciba, and Pepsi.

Writers, such as Ruth Gruber, Ella Winter, and Anna Louise Strong, had marked out the entire globe for inspection. Offering politically observant versions of traditional women's travel narratives, these women found other women in Soviet Russia or on the Long March through Hunan Province who were shock-workers and soldiers. British writer Rosita Forbes detailed her excursions among *Women Called Wild* with sensational stories of sex slave markets in Arabia, Stakhanovite women window washers in Leningrad, women opium addicts in Java, Foreign Legion camp followers in Morocco, and prostitutes in the " 'Waste Spaces' between 'Buenos Aires' and 'Shanghai' " in Algiers: in short, the usual salacious Orientalism found traditionally in these.[16] But like her left-wing sisters, Rosita Forbes embarks on her journey as a participant observer, one of the wild women who lurk the jungles of Yucatan disguised as cheetahs. It appears from Forbes's telling that "cat people" can be found the world over, not just in the "delicious" novel she cites entitled *Lady Into Fox*.

Women on the road through slave markets and harems, through China and the Soviet Union, through bus terminals and rooming houses, were called "wild." Those who recorded what they found often did so with a kind of uninhibited mania, even as they might abhor what they found. Going on the road in search of misery, hoping to expose and thus to ameliorate it, was one of the effects of 1930s movements' goals.[17] Of course, it was also part of American self-mythologizing, from Huck Finn's "lightin' out for the territories" to Horace Greeley's call to "go west, young man"; now the automobile and burgeoning highway system made it possible for most anyone, not just rebellious boys. Commenting on her road trip through the nation in 1947, Simone de Beauvoir notes "the gas stations, roads, hotels, and solitary inns . . . these things are profoundly part of America. The landscapes of the Far West [she was] driving through exist essentially for the sake of tourists." De Beauvoir distains the way in which the stark landscape has been transformed because of tourism; yet she herself, like so many, participates in the experience of national space via the automobile. She revels in it: "Night is falling; it has fallen," she comments as if narrating a film noir, "A luminous wheel turns in the darkened sky: a hotel sign" looms up from the desolate highway connecting Las Vegas to Los Angeles promising "a martini and a hearty dinner. . . . We've still got four hours on the road."[18] Amazement at the vast spaces of this country give way to a sense of claustrophobia as de Beauvoir boards a bus to travel through the South observing Jim Crow first hand.

Esther Bubley had already made this trip in 1943 for the OWI, whose photographers, she explained to Tony Van Witsen, "did the war effort. They did shipbuilding and I did buses. I traveled through the country riding on a bus."[19] Another FSA/OWI photographer, Marion Post Wolcott, shot the gleaming silent snowed-in streets of Woodstock, Vermont, in March 1940, the halo glow of the streetlight sanctifying this zone of peaceful America. Wolcott also commented visually on Jim Crow. Her October 1939 photograph is captioned: "Negro man entering movie theater 'colored' entrance. Belzoni, Mississippi, in the Delta area." Its stark shadows indicate the distinctions between black and white, the sign pointing to "Colored Entrance" just one of many crowding the side of the building. Two years later, she was making portraits of blacks and whites in the Florida Glades relaxing at their "juke joints." In one photo, two young black men stare sullenly at her camera, beer cans on the table between them and an advertisement for Cobbs Creek whiskey featuring a white bespectacled judge slamming his gavel to declare "judged *mild* 43 million times!" In another, two young white couples drunk on whiskey and Cokes (the empty pint of whiskey lies on its side between them) lean hotly into each other under a hand-painted sign announcing "Rooms/ By-Nite or Week/ Ask - at - Bar." These images play on the disjunctures between the efforts of self-presentation and those of documentary disclosure, on the one hand, and on the secrets kept hiding behind images of America's economic recovery, on the other. Within a year, neither peaceful Vermont nor steamy south Florida would resemble itself; war altered everything. Wolcott's attention to architecture exposed racial tensions that Bubley found in the restless yet drowsy women living in "a waiting room."[20]

Like Wolcott, Bubley subtly notes the discrepancies racism fosters between blacks and whites during a time of national mobilization.

FIGURE 14. Marion Post Wolcott, "Two couples in a booth in a juke joint." Near Moorehaven, Florida, 1939.

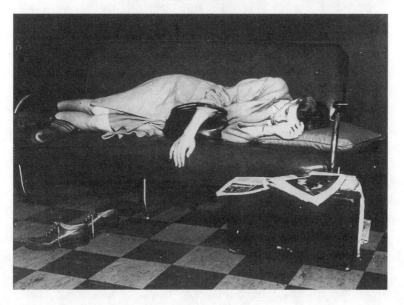

FIGURE 15. Esther Bubley, "A girl who is waiting between buses in the ladies' lounge at 4 AM in the Greyhound bus terminal." Chicago, Ill., Sept. 1943.

Her trip began by heading through Pennsylvania to the Midwest. She is attentive, as she was in the Sea Grill, to evolving sexual dynamics opened up by the war. Her pictures of young women sleeping in bus stations across America detail the tedium of commercial transport—"a nation of zombies."[21] In Chicago, she finds "A girl who is waiting between buses in the ladies' lounge at 4AM in the Greyhound bus terminal."[22] Stretched out on a wooden bench, her purse strap linked around her arm, shoes on the black-and-white linoleum below her feet, she dozes after reading the newspaper opened on her small suitcase. These women, coiled in exhaustion, are, as curator Andrea Fisher notes, open to inspection; yet, lost in sleep, they maintain their dignity. They are wholly isolated even as they are on public display. This sense of separation is powerfully conveyed in one image of a young woman wearing a tailored suit getting off a bus in the middle of an empty field. Self-contained, she strides off through the brush, her clutch purse firmly locked under her arm, but it is impossible to see where she is headed.[23]

FIGURE 16. Esther Bubley, "Girls sleeping in the waiting room of the Union station." Washington, D.C., March 1943.

FIGURE 17. Esther Bubley, "A girl getting off the Macon bound Greyhound bus in Georgia. Passengers can get off at any place they wish along the road." Sept. 1943.

The world of the bus is also set apart, maintaining its own ecology. Sleeping women are curled up against wooden booths everywhere in Pittsburgh and Indianapolis and Cincinnati and Louisville bus terminals. They are living along the highways with their families in converted gas stations left empty because of wartime gasoline rations, leaving the place, as the sign in front announces: "Closed Nothing For-Sale."[24] Noting the items available to travelers in the Chicago Greyhound bus terminal's ladies' restroom, she finds a culture and commerce of daily life on the road: "Items ranging from soap and nail polish to soda for upset stomachs may be rented from the maid on duty, who owns her own stock. Her business is usually

FIGURE 18. Esther Bubley, "Bus passengers in the Greyhound bus terminal's ladies' restroom. Items ranging from soap and nail polish to soda for upset stomachs may be rented from the maid on duty, who owns her own stock. Her business is usually brisk." Chicago, Ill., Sept. 1943.

very brisk."[25] Bubley, like many FSA/OWI photographers, was an inveterate list maker; objects fascinated her.[26] Walker Evans surveyed the belongings of the three tenant families he and James Agee had documented in *Let Us Now Praise Famous Men*; Bubley depicted the shelves and dressers of the women in the Washington, D.C., rooming house.

These images, glanced from her bus window or stolen in waiting rooms or disclosed as she followed bus drivers and charwomen into their rooms, reveal a nation on the move yet strangely caught, stuck in limbo. In one caption of a picture of bus driver Clem Carson, Bubley lists the contents of his suitcase: "a cigarette package with

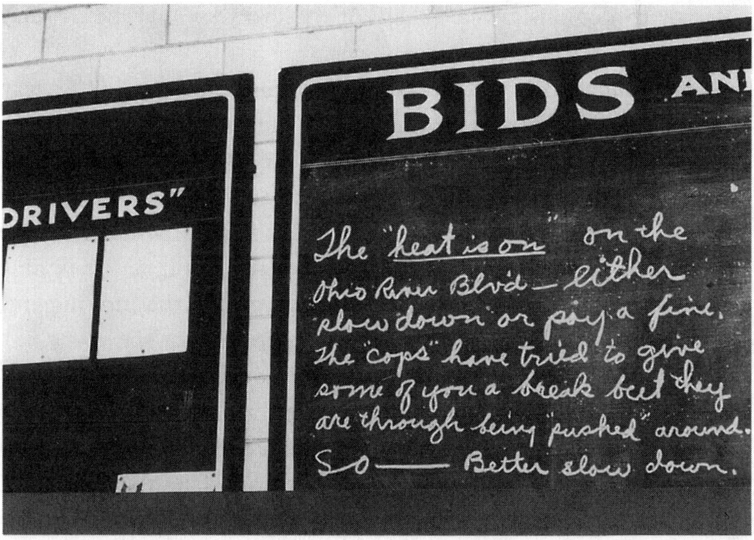

FIGURE 19. Esther Bubley, "A warning on a blackboard in the drivers' room of the Greyhound garage." Pittsburgh, Penn., Sept. 1943.

one cigarette, a pay sheet signed by the dispatcher, a flashlight, extra batteries, cash fare pad, form for cutting transfers, 1 look magazine, 1 Pic magazine, 1 small can shaving powder, 1 baggage crank, 1 knapkin [sic], shaving lotion, razor, shaving cream, work gloves, baggage checks, comb, 1 black address book, envelopes, trip reports, hair tonic, two packs of gum, name plate, whiskey ration card, pliers, screw driver, soap, pencil, 1 red address book, bus schedules, towel, 3 handkerchiefs, toothbrush, 2 pairs sun glasses, a washcloth, 1 shoe-string, ammonia inhalant, ticket clamps, witness pads, company rule book, tarriff [sic] sheet, shirt, tie, socks and underwear, old pay sheets, and 1 cockroach with which buses are frequently infested. This was removed."[27] It's a Whitmanesque catalogue singing of the modern body electric. Driver "Bud" Carson lived at the Southern Hotel in Columbus, Ohio, explaining how he and another driver doubled up in the room; then he revealed to Bubley his anger that he had received a "checker's" report accusing him of smoking and eating a candy bar and stopping too long at a rest stop. The mundane intimacy of this list and of the items kept for women passengers by the restroom attendants was part of the Office of War Information's attempt to demonstrate a quality of the everyday to workers' and travelers' lives during the war.

Bubley, like most of Roy Stryker's field photographers, had a wry sense of humor and was ever on the look out for contradictions. She included a synopsis of "Us on a Bus," the novel-in-progress by a driver who detailed how he bought a bottle and nipple and milk for a young mother only to be told he'd make a good father; a soldier who jumped up and "loudly announced to the world . . . 'Memphis is God's country' "; an old lady who "unscrewed a thermos jug and took a drink explaining to the public in general that she was a frequent traveler from Texas to Nashville, that she like to drink when she liked it"; and many young women on the lookout for, or being hustled by, soldiers.[28] Her picture of "an eating place near the Greyhound bus stop" in New Bedford, Pennsylvania, shows a giant coffee pot that serves as the café.[29] This emblem, like those de Beauvoir stopped at a few years after the war, "exist[s] only for the tourist and

FIGURE 20. Esther Bubley, "An eating place near the Greyhound bus stop." New Bedford, Penn., Sept. 1943.

because of the tourist," according to de Beauvoir's assessment;[30] however, Bubley places it firmly within a landscape of work—the bus driver's job necessitates stops for the passengers' comforts, who, like one woman, is on her way to Nebraska to study nursing—and housing shortages. The café is connected to a home and serves, like the gas station-turned-house or the bus itself, as a reconstituted family living space. It domesticates the vast and savage emptiness of the nation's landscape; it's cozy in its hokey absurdity.

These images, like the rooming-house pictures, preserve a sense of continuity, even as they track endless mobility, by emphasizing everyday life. When Bubley went on the road to photograph Standard Oil workers while working for Roy Stryker after the war, she kept a diary that listed objects and their associated activities, images she intended to record. Running down the page for the week of January 22–26, 1948, they read as a protofeminist poem about women's invisible, intimate labor:

Beating rug	scrubbing porch
canning	vacuuming
washing windows	wheeling baby
on Ladder	bubbling baby
cooking	baking
~~canning~~	gardening
hang out wash	painting screen door
waxing floor	piano lesson
sewing	defrosting refrig
mending	waxing floor
taking children out	painting sashes
dishes	making aprons
feeding older kids	
ironing	
dressing child	
cooking meal	
putting child to bed (story)	

Her accounting includes the names of the Texas women whom she had photographed, as well as the hours they spent doing each of their various tasks. The focus on women's domestic labor, performed within the suburbs springing up around Standard Oil's

Texas refineries, contrasts with the images Bubley had been recording in Washington, D.C., of single, urban women operating the
machinery of communications. This bus trip uncovered a new stability and predictability to women's daily lives.

Yet it was the same year Hollywood was churning out *Raw Deal*,
Kiss the Blood Off My Hands, *Road House*, *They Live by Night*, and
The Lady from Shanghai among many more that featured tough
women fleeing domesticity and traveling in pursuit of pleasure and
cash. In fact, the images from Texas are unsettling. The houses
crammed together, dwarfed by enormous television antennas, are far
less hospitable than the gas stations, waiting rooms, or coffee-pot
café. By the end of the year, Bubley was living her own domestic noir
melodrama. In November, she was busily working a job at
Doylestown, Pennsylvania, shooting enough for her to underscore
that she "used 2 cases bulbs" on Wednesday, November 10, 1948.
The next day, she recounts the following entry: "Doylestown—
worked all day—Ed [Locke, her husband] called—sounded very
sorry for himself—also drunk—I got sorry for him too but I don't
like being pushed around. Garage .75 Br. L. D. 3.50."[31] Throughout
the next year, her journals record a series of jobs—including the
amazing *Ladies Home Journal* assignment series on mental illness—
and the dollar amount she had given Ed with notations that he was
drunk again. Her 1950 passport, issued under the name Esther Bubley Locke, has a handwritten line crossed through her married name.

Even before then, Bubley's eye had already differentiated a postwar aesthetic from the kinds of socially concerned documentary
images taken only a few years earlier. Where Wolcott records the
lonely climb by a single dignified man up the colored-only stairs of
a Mississippi movie house in 1939, Bubley suggests that the war had
altered the racial landscape considerably. Her shots of the Memphis
bus station, with their pointed focus on the signs designating "White
Waiting Room" dominating the frame above masses of black and
white men and women crowding onto the waiting buses, stage a
sense of frenetic activity. The bodies mix together, jamming their
way forward to the open bus door, and tell a story of conflict and
change rather than the enduring legacy of Jim Crow. Certainly she
includes a stark image of the "Colored Waiting Room" sign found
in Rome, Georgia, which she captioned with damning simplicity: "A
sign at the Greyhound bus station." But there is something about

FIGURE 21. Esther Bubley, "Waiting for a bus." Memphis, Tenn., Sept. 1943.

FIGURE 22. Esther Bubley, "A sign at the Greyhound bus station." Rome, Ga., Sept. 1943.

the composition, with the phone wires running just below the sign, connecting the brick building behind it to the rest of the world that offers a sense of impending change. Where the pictures of the South taken by Dorothea Lange, Walker Evans, and Margaret Bourke-White challenged the nation with the images of an enduring racial caste system little distinguished from that of Reconstruction, despite the automobiles occasionally found lining the streets, Bubley's bus trip limns a glimpse of the nascent civil rights movement in the sheer physical movement of a restless population.

MENTAL ASYLUMS

Shortly after her Texas assignment, Bubley was offered a number of assignments for *Ladies Home Journal*. *LHJ*, like the Italian *Enciclo-pedia delle Donne* which could be bought monthly at newspaper stands, was designed in part to facilitate the rise into middle-class suburbs of a postwar rural and urban working-class population in the United States. (In Italy, its job was to help teach peasants and labor-ers to become urbanized national citizens of the new democracy.) With popular fiction by such middle-brow writers as John Marquand and extensive hints on fashion, homemaking, gardening, as well as features on marriage and childrearing, it also included political commentary and art criticism. In the April 1949 issue, Esther Bub-ley's photographs illustrated a serious examination answering "What *Is* Mental Illness?" The special and general features sections include an essay by Eleanor Roosevelt, a reproduction of El Greco's *Virgin with Saints*, a discussion of "American and Un-American Social Security," advice on moving "From School to Job," and on "Mak-ing Marriage Work," as well as a "Diary of Domesticity." Bubley's photograph of a young schizophrenic woman "being treated with electric shock" depicts a pained woman in hospital dress hunched over and covering her face with her hands. Behind her, framing her, is a large window crisscrossed with many panes suggesting bars. Off to her side and behind her sits another patient staring out another window; her hand also covers her face. "Mrs. Templeton—that's not her real name, of course—is not unusual." She is one of the 3,000 women admitted annually for "involutional melancholia, an emo-tional illness to which women in the change of life are particularly susceptible," which "shock and hormone treatments have proved

FIGURE 23. Esther Bubley, "Paranoid Schizophrenic," from *Ladies Home Journal* (March–June, 1949). Property of Jean B. Bubley.

tremendously fast and powerful in treating," claims author Joan Younger.[32] The image is chilling; a cropped version, with just the girl in the foreground, became a standard depiction of schizophrenia in psychiatry textbooks.[33]

It is the image Hitchcock uses to conclude his noir "docudrama," *The Wrong Man.* After finally being cleared, Manny (Henry Fonda) visits his wife Rose (Vera Miles) in the mental hospital where she retreats from the tensions accruing from his arrest, trial, and conviction. Her final comment to him: "That's fine for you," contradicts any sense of a Hollywood happy ending. Hitchcock had meticulously researched this film, making sure that the Queens and Manhattan locations were accurate, even visiting Riker's Island jail to observe how inmates carry their bedding to their cells. It seems logical that he would have found an authentic image to portray Rose's descent into madness so he could avoid the Hollywood clichés of "the snake pit" imagery of insanity.[34] Bubley's image of a schizophrenic woman codified film noir iconography. The caption for Bubley's photograph asserts, "She is being treated with electric shock and there is hope for her recovery," but her gestures, like Rose's comment, suggest otherwise. Bubley's image, like that of Hitchcock, lends a caveat to this hopeful scenario, exposing the potential detours of danger and desire sending anyone veering off the road.[35]

Because of the *Ladies Home Journal* article, Bubley worked again in mental hospitals documenting the effectiveness of Ciba Pharmaceuticals's antischizophrenia drug Serpasil. Her work appeared in a promotional booklet for the drug that lauded its benign effectiveness. Bubley's before and after photographs of a young black schizophrenic woman who "displayed marked denudative tendencies" show the positive effects of this "drug which the Indians had claimed for centuries could aid the mentally ill." In the top picture, a solitary naked black woman kneels on her stripped bed, her head pressing down on the mattress ticking. The contrasting bottom image, just one day after her first injection, shows her sitting up in a made bed in striped pajamas drinking a glass of water with a prim white nurse looking on. In this image, the nurse stands in a flood of sunshine coming in the room through an open window; however, the top photograph includes only the bed partially in dark shadow.[36] It is an eerie vision of induced normalcy. Even under contract to promote Serpasil, Bubley managed to disturb the images and cast noir overtones across them.

In their attention to the enclosed spaces of solitary women living in institutions with others, these photographs extend the projects she had begun in Washington, D.C., and continued in Texas as she tracked the daily work routine of Standard Oil workers' wives. Like the images shot for the federal government and big industry, they have a disturbing element of celebration for capitalism and conformity, even as they also hint at rebellion just below the surface. One set of photographs from March 1949 focused on the emerging new technology of television and concentrated on "TV Antenna," "TV FAMILY," "TV Home," "Parent TV." These images tracked a further move into the confines of a claustrophobic domesticity in the postwar period. An undated set of contacts, entitled "Black Star Girls," suggests this refashioned domesticity was an on-going interest. These pictures of B-girls taking bubble baths or standing on a bathroom scale, range across their possessions—spiked heels and baby dolls. Perhaps they figured as the back story to the *Ladies Home Journal* feature "How America Lives" that Bubley also worked on during the late 1940s. To some extent, these and the 1949 assignment for the "Profile of Youth" series continue her OWI project on Woodrow Wilson High School as they focus on the lives of five high-school girls from Maine's "potato empire"—three are "still hanging on the thin edge: Phyllis Donaghue, whose lumpy exterior covers some driving dreams; Leona Pryor, a dynamic young beauty with a restless urge; and Loretta Lannigan, a little 'nobody' who can't make up her mind what she wants to do." Bubley "personally found more interesting the struggle of the children who were determined to stay in high school no matter what odds were against them, [so she had] thrown in two more stories—the story of Dorothy Lynch and Muriel Breuer, both of whom are working their way through high school . . . the only possible ticket to the outside world. All are in the lower third of their class."[37] These girls present a new generation of young women whose lives, despite the postwar

FIGURE 24. Esther Bubley, "A boarding house rule forbids men guests to come into girls' rooms and vice versa." Washington, D.C., Jan. 1943.

FIGURE 25. Esther Bubley, "Riding on a street car." Washington, D.C., March 1943.

prosperity, seemed headed for trouble, or at least boredom, without the possibility of escape from small-town life. The opportunities for sex and anonymity provided young women by the Venetian blinds in the Sea Grill have collapsed into grueling tasks, like those of the oil workers' wives, alleviated by television. No wonder involutional melancholia was epidemic.

Bubley framed the changing experiences of young women between the onset of the United States's entry into the Second World War and the nation's emergence as a world power by concentrating on the melodramas of daily life. Her pictures, made for the federal government and major corporations—both intent on advertising and marketing their triumphant goods and services, perhaps reflecting her own life's experiences, focused on a certain unmistakable darkness "behind Washington's marble fronts."[38] These girls, with names straight out of Hollywood's B-movies— Loretta, Leona, Phyllis—were already framed, their faces about to break into a raging snarl at any moment. After all, they were featured in a *Ladies Home Journal* "profile of youth" article called "Teen-Age Cruelty" as examples of "poison personality girls," like "the super-sophisticate" who "wears black whenever possible, likes lots of jew-elry, uses a cigarette holder," and is "too utterly bored by every-thing."[39] Notwithstanding her surname, Esther Bubley could be counted on to photograph lives already framed by the boredom, routine, restrictions, and despair that was lurking everywhere across a nation supposedly teeming with frenzied war (and postwar) pro-duction. Someone who worked constantly, with "a pride of craft,"[40] and was an avid movie-goer, she also spent time in a Brooklyn box-ing gym working out, after a visit to it on assignment convinced her this was the solution to the backaches she suffered carrying around her equipment on her 5'4" frame.[41] Like her own refashioning of her body during an era when women did not work on their biceps, her images of seductive women alone in bars, of single women on the road, of anguished women isolated in asylums, of bitchy girls claw-ing their way out of small towns belied America's postwar vision of femininity. Her photographs had already framed the femme fatale.

CHAPTER 2

DOMESTIC LABOR: FILM NOIR, PROLETARIAN LITERATURE, AND BLACK WOMEN'S FICTION

On the trail of the missing Kathie Moffett, private investigator Jeff Bailey begins Uptown, in a Harlem nightclub, by interviewing Kathy's maid, Eunice. In this minor scene in Jacques Tourneur's *Out of the Past* (1947), Bailey enters the smoke-hazed, jazz-filled club and is escorted by the maitre d' to a table with two couples; he asks which woman worked for Kathie. Bailey seems at ease in the club; like many private eyes, he's used to interacting with African Americans, and after one couple leaves for the dance floor, he inquires about Kathie. Elegant and sly, Eunice says she has no idea where she went, Miami perhaps—she got some vaccinations and took off. Bailey buys the table a round of drinks and leaves, commenting, in his detective voice-over narrative that you don't get vaccinated to go to Florida. Kathie took off to Mexico. James Naremore describes this scene and others like it depicting encounters between beautiful, sophisticated black women and the white detectives in film noirs as crucial to the noir hero's/detective's "aura of 'cool' . . . his essential hipness," because the integrated nightclub is an iconic transgressive location within film noir.[1] As Kathie's maid, Eunice served a dark woman *but* she is herself a black woman; moreover, her visual position between two men—one white, the other black—is critical to understanding the different complexion of the femme fatale.

Coded through dress, lighting, and mise-en-scène as a femme fatale in her own right, Eunice is Kathie's aura—another type of literal femme noire. The dark lady of film noir is a woman with a past, a kept woman who performs no useful function other than sex. Her body is available, draped in mink and diamonds, for display and desire. She is free to meet men at night or in the afternoon because she is unencumbered by the usual trappings of domesticity. She is free in part because she has a housekeeper to clean up after a long night of drinking, to fix the drinks and make the coffee, to help her dress. The "aura of cool" blacks impart to the white detective occurs through a transference: as authentic bearers of alienation, African Americans are, in Richard Wright's term, the original outsiders. Both the white detective and the white woman he pursues acquire their abilities to pass into the underworld through their encounters with and knowledge of darkness found beyond conventional work and marriage (both of which, because of slavery's legacy, have been denied to African Americans). Like the "authenticity" of the original possessing an "aura," according to Walter Benjamin, Eunice stands before Bailey as the "prerequisite" of another woman he has never seen.[2] Eunice holds no metaphoric status as femme noire. She embodies it. In this, she resembles Benjamin's notion of the "original" work of art, which remains fixed within "tradition," while its copies, endlessly available, are mobile and potentially destabilizing.[3] She vibrates sexuality—a sign hanging around black women's necks since they unwillingly arrived shackled together on this continent— and thus allows us to know Kathie through her. Yet Eunice resists Bailey; she is straightforward in her lie, and Bailey can see through her because she is the original woman of the dark. She points up Kathie's double duplicity. The white femme fatale has the potential to disturb the "tradition" of racism, especially its economic and sexual effects. However, her rupture with conventional white femininity is limited because, as a "mistress," she still remains dependent on this tradition.

While Eunice never reappears in the film, her presence hovers behind the white femme fatale in this and many film noirs. Out on a date in Harlem, dressed as Billie Holiday did in the 1940s—upswept hair coiffed with a veil of white camellias, black dress accented with

FIGURE 26. Theresa Harris (Eunice) on a date in Harlem dressed like Billie Holiday in *Out of the Past* (d. Jacques Tourneur, 1947).

white trim—Eunice, stylish and independent, assuredly resists a white man's authority; she defends herself and her former boss in a gesture of female solidarity, which extends to her look. The two women are erotic cross-dressers, as the white femme fatale will inevitably wear the clothes of the torch singer and the maid may acquire her boss's hand-me-downs. Her deception parallels the deceit embodied by the object of desire, in this case femme fatale Kathie Moffett. Eunice's loyalty is to her employer, whom she knows has had a rough time with men. Presumably, as a single woman kept by those same men, Kathie doesn't require too much work from her. When Eunice aids Kathie, it's an isolated incident within the film. Yet, in Max Ophuls' *The Reckless Moment* (1949), Lucia Harper's (Joan Bennett) black maid Sybil (Frances Williams) appears as a central figure in her boss's cover-up.[4] Like many domestic melodramas that rely on the household presence of a maid, Sybil helps Lucia, who hides evidence (a body) that her daughter has killed a blackmailing gigolo. In so doing, she also allows Lucia access to an underworld and its erotics. In this film, as in the classic melodramatic vehicle in which a black maid's domesticity facilitates a white woman's business, *Imitation of Life* (1934, 1959), the maid participates in the maintenance of middle-class white family economic order, helping to support it when there is no man around, and acts as confessor for the white woman she serves.[5] The black maid, like the detective or the femme fatale, by occupation, slides between two worlds. As a black woman in racially segregated America, she lives on the margins of white America; as a servant to the bourgeoisie, she inhabits the bedrooms of the white middle class. As entertainer, cook, and servant, the black woman is rarely the center of the action in film noir (see Jean-Pierre Melville's *Le Samourai* (1967) with an impassive Alain Delon as the hitman for a post–civil rights and French exception to this), but her presence appears necessary to the complex postwar sexual and racial dynamics that film noirs track by linking domestic melodrama to hard-boiled proletarian culture.

What kind of work does the maid perform in film noir? Her service to the femme noire, as an overt femme noire, is more complex than simply that of the loyal employee in Hollywood melodrama. Her ability to understand and function within alien worlds makes her more of an equal to the female protagonist; yet she does little more than protect her, lying and covering up for the white woman. Because the dark lady of film noir is a rebellious white woman— glowingly white in her initial key-lit scenes—the black domestic worker of film noir crystallized racial and class issues raised by the Left during the 1930s when domestic labor debates resurfaced after disappearing with Charlotte Perkins Gilman's powerful 1903 tract *Women and Economics*. She shows up the bourgeois house as little more than a brothel whose sole purpose—now that even the housewife is freed from housework and childcare—is sexual and reproductive. Racial erotics, tracked throughout the 1930s in reportage, poetry, and short fiction, became the focus of postwar novels by black women. Ann Petry's *The Street* (1947) and Gwendolyn Brook's *Maud Martha* (1953), two novels by authors connected to the Left, were both published during the heyday of Hollywood's film noirs. Like the films' concerns with the new kinds of social relations forged during the Depression and World War II, each locates black women's labor within proletarian literary culture by linking domestic melodrama to female Bildungsroman. Each also revises the image of the black domestic from mammy to maid, recasting a symbol of antebellum racial hierarchies into an urbanized form of labor.[6]

As a popular medium, albeit often in its "B" form, postwar film noir began to visualize many of the issues lurking within proletarian literature—city life, the organization of work, social mobility, cross-class desire. Noir films borrowed 1930s proletarian narratives, themselves hybrid revisions of socialist realism and domestic fiction. They also generated new literary concerns. *The Street* owes much to Stephen Crane's *Maggie, Girl of the Streets* and American naturalism, but it also taps fears haunting Jacques Tourneur's *Cat People*.[7] Gwendolyn Brooks structures *Maud Martha* like the jazz orchestrating film noir as she revises a coming-of-age story to reveal why the black femme fatale cannot be visualized in racist America. Alan Wald and Michael Denning have recently argued that the radical novel, or the cultural front in American literature, exceeded the bounds of 1930s proletarian culture.[8] For many writers, especially black writers, the themes and concerns central to 1930s fiction—the experience of collective subjectivity within social relations formed by economic and racial stratification—appeared after the Depression had ended. *Invisible Man* is a 1930s novel, even if it didn't appear until 1952; so too is Margaret Walker's *Jubilee*, begun in the 1930s and completed in the 1960s.[9]

Focusing on the difficulties black women faced in supporting themselves and their families, analyzing the racial and sexual dynamics of black domestic workers in white women's households, these two novels deepened the domestic labor debates central to women in the American Left. They pushed the discussion beyond analyzing one's own housework as a "double burden" for the working woman employed outside the home to consider what it meant to maintain two homes—one's own and another's of a different class, race, and neighborhood.[10] This contradiction became a focus of Toni Morrison's first novel (set during the 1940s) *The Bluest Eye*. Pauline Breedlove travels between the white family, doting on the blonde daughter of her employer, and her own, where she ignores her dark-skinned daughter Pecola (whose names echoes that of Peola in *Imitation of Life*) with tragic consequences. Richard Wright's *12 Million Black Voices* graphically displays the social differences between the maid's workplace kitchen and her own. In a two-page spread, pictures of the dank kitchenette are contrasted with the uniformed maid in a sparkling kitchen. This image of a black mother tending white children is among the only recognition of a black woman's labor by Wright whose first-person plural nar-

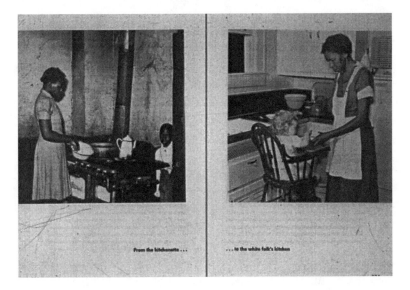

FIGURE 27. Two-page spread from Richard Wright, *12 Million Black Voices* (1941). Left: Russell Lee, "Mother and Son." Chicago, Ill. Right: Marion Post [Wolcott], "Maid." Georgia.

rative "we" does not include women who are pointedly spoken of as "our women." Nevertheless, the racial dimensions of domestic labor had been an on-going concern of writers throughout the 1930s; the pages of the *Crisis*, the *New Masses*, and the *Daily Worker*, among countless little journals sponsored by the Communist Party, explored black women's double life under white supremacy and capitalism; but these were often works of short reportage, poetry, or short fiction. They never attained the recognition that a novel did.[11] For instance, Belle Traub "Discovered: A Modern Slave Block!" and interviewed one of the many black women lined up on the street corners of major cities waiting for day work as a domestic during the 1930s. Mrs. Rose Johnson described her day as follows: "I get up at six each morning. Get breakfast for my three children. Wash the dishes, fix sandwich lunch for them, and send them off to school. Then comes a bit of family work. All this, before coming out on the block . . . and then to stand around on a street corner for hours waiting" for the same work in another woman's house.[12] Ella Baker and Marvel Cooke went underground to detail the workings of "The Bronx Slave Market" in the *Crisis*. Here, on Jerome Avenue, black women line up waiting for day work within the mostly Jewish households of the neighborhood. "Paradoxically," they note, "the crash of 1929 brought to the domestic labor market a new employer class. The lower middle-class housewife, who, having dreamed of the luxury of a maid, found opportunity staring her in the face in the form a Negro women pressed to the wall by poverty, starvation, and discrimination."[13] The work appears especially onerous, for in addition to the usual window washing, scrubbing, laundry, dusting, turning of mattresses, and chasing off the wandering hands of the son, to wash dishes Orthodox Jews required "a different dishcloth for everything they cook. For instance, they ha[d] one for 'milk' pots in which dairy dishes are cooked, another for glasses, another for vegetable pots, another for meat pots, and so on," according to their informant Millie Jones. As late as 1940, Louise Mitchell decried the "Slave Markets" where "Negro women wait[ed] for employers to come to the street corner auction blocks to bargain for their labor."[14] The authors advocate self-organization among the women, castigating "organized labor's limited concept of exploitation, which permits it to fight vigorously to secure itself against evil, yet passively or actively aids and abets the ruthless destruction of Negroes," and citing the hopeful signs of an "embryonic labor union . . . in the Simpson avenue 'mart' . . . [where for] the recent Jewish holiday, habitués of the 'mart' actually demanded and refused to work for less than thirty-five cents an hour."[15] While the strains between black workers and Jewish petit bourgeois entails a legacy of anti-Semitism and racism lurking within the *Crisis* exposé, the description of the housework, with the exception of the extra dishwashing for Orthodox Jews, is typical, with the white woman expecting immense labor—weekly window washing for instance—from the black woman for a pittance—five dollars a week and carfare. Millie Jones lost her position when she took Sunday off because her boyfriend was visiting.

Gwendolyn Brooks's "Hattie Scott," one of the residents of *A Street in Bronzeville* (1945) also resists her employer's demands on her time to pursue her own desire. Nora, "a butter-colored maid with the hair on the 'riney' side" and resident of Marita Bonner's "Frye Street" in Chicago rejects her lover Sam when she decides to enroll in City College to study law at night, only to die of pneumonia brought on by exhaustion. But Hattie Scott daringly seeks pleasure with a black man, leaving the white woman and night school behind.[16]

> If she don't hurry up and let me out of here.
> Keeps pilin' up stuff for me to do.
> I ain't goin' to finish that ironin.'
> She got another think comin.' Hey, you
> Whatcha mean talkin' about cleanin' silver?
> It's eight o'clock now, you fool.
> I'm leavin.' Got somethin' interestin' on my mind.
> Don't mean night school.[17]

Again, petty domestic chores—polishing silver, for instance—interfere with the speakers' sexuality and romance. The title of the poem, "the date," suggests that Hattie Scott plans not only to make love, "somethin' interestin' on my mind," but to go out in public (perhaps to a nightclub like Eunice) first. As the "Queen of the Blues" sings, the point of domestic labor in a white woman's kitchen is to support the man she loves and get his loving in return: "I was good to my daddy. / Gave him all my dough / . . . Scrubbed hard in them white folks' / Kitchens / Till my knees was rusty / And so" (58). This story is repeated almost verbatim by Lutie Johnson in Petry's terrifying novel *The Street*. Lutie abruptly leaves domestic service when she learns her husband is living with another woman. She eventually becomes a nightclub singer in the Harlem club owned by the gangster Junto, who expects to pimp for her. As historian Jacqueline Jones points out, during the Depression, "it was the entertainment field that fueled the dreams of black girls who yearn[ed] for a life's work of glamour and triumph" as nightclubs, radios, and records featured the voices of Billie Holiday, Bessie Smith, Ella Fitzgerald, Lena Horne, and others.[18]

This plot trajectory, from domestic work to entertainment to prostitution, was typical: "A young girl from North Carolina came to New York City in 1936. Unable to find work in a respected capacity, she sought domestic work. Here, her relations with her employer were not entirely moral, but at least raised her income. Finally domestic work becoming odious, was forgotten, and another prostitute was created."[19] The link between domestic labor and prostitution—sexualizing housework and racializing sex work—is central to the image of the femme fatale's maid who can keep the house of a woman not known for her domestic virtues because she, too, exchanges her body for pay. Lutie Johnson runs up against this continually as a live-in maid in Lyme, Connecticut. Overhearing conversations among her employer, Mrs. Chandler, and other women friends, neighbors, and relatives, Lutie learns that these women fear her as an attractive, young (and therefore obviously sexually available) black woman: they all assume she is a "whore." "Apparently," she realizes, "it was an automatic reaction of white people—if a girl was colored and fairly young, why, it stood to reason she had to be a prostitute."[20] Chester Himes inadvertently endorses this connection between young black maids and prostitution, discussing his work as a hotel bellhop in Cleveland during the 1930s, he recalls: "Black women were easy to pick up and made exciting bedmates; maids were the easiest and good-looking whores were the hardest."[21] This continual sexualizing of the young black female body in the employ of white middle-class families is directly connected, as Himes notes, to the history of slavery, which made the bodies of black women available to the white master to, in the words of Frederick Douglass, "make a gratification of their wicked desires profitable as well as pleasurable."[22] Moreover, it shrouds the sex work of the white housewife, whose livelihood as a legal prostitute is covered by displacing it onto the maid.

Jacqueline Jones points out that for the black woman, the "forces that shaped the institution of human bondage in the American South endured, albeit in altered form, long after the last slave embraced freedom . . . [as she] toiled . . . in the kitchen of a Chicago white woman" (3). During the Depression, urban black women's labor was restricted to domestic work and laundry work; even during World War II, when factory jobs opened up, they were janitorial. Seeking to expose this, the *Daily Worker* routinely decried women's work, especially domestic labor, as slavery, seeing even female industrial workers as "slaves" whose bodies were being destroyed by brutal work.[23] A typical page lists the following headlines: "Rubber Workers Paid $2 Daily for Slavery," "High Maternity Death Rate Under U.S. Slavery," "Women Slave in Steel Mill."[24] In this they echoed the complaints of Bessie Smith's 1928 "Washwoman's Blues": "All day long I'm slavin' / All day long I'm bustin suds . . . just to make my livelihood . . . rather be a scullion / cookin in some white folks' yard / . . . wouldn't have to work so hard."[25] Historian Phyllis Palmer finds that in the South "service was a job for slaves. After emancipation that imagery of service remained intact. White Americans," moreover, "were trained in or learned from the southern models after the Civil War, and northern beliefs in the housewife's duty to supervise labor meshed with southern beliefs in leisured ladyhood."[26] Thus black womanhood was associated with domestic service, or slavery, while white women were seen as supervisors of domestic labor, not as workers themselves.[27]

This continues a curious history of the use of "slavery" as a metaphor for wage labor. As historian David Roediger notes, in antebellum America, "[t]o be a slave, even a white slave, was to be associated with degradation. Genteel factory women who rejected the term knew this, and knew that slavery implied sexual exploitation as well. To be a slave also implied a connection with blackness."[28] During the Depression decade, the American Communist Party portrayed workers as strong virile examples of democratic men; the image of the robust factory worker standing tall in interracial brotherhood against he forces of decayed, effeminate capitalism appeared in prints, poems, novels, and essays.[29] So it appears surprising that the *Daily Worker* relies on the imagery of slavery to describe workers, but not so strange when one realizes that these workers are female. Moreover, among female workers, racial differences still encoded the black woman as a slave, while her more revolutionary white sister has understood "that we have a government of murderous bandits, parasites and oppressors" and thus could excoriate her black sister as insufficiently politicized. For instance, Fannie Austin exhorted:

Negro working women! When you go to look for a job you find it very hard to get, and, when you do get it, you only obtain ten or twelve dollars for a big week of *slavery*. You are very much oppressed and exploited for a little nothing and you are looked upon by the bosses as *not human*. You are handled by the exploiting parasites as if you are *sold to them*. They hire and fire you any time they feel like it. Are you going to let those fat-bellied bosses fool and *enslave* you forever? Are you going to be pressed down and stepped upon forever—or are you going to unite with your white working women sisters in struggle, in battle against the capitalist oppressive system—against the *wage slave, lynching system?* Negro and white women workers!

she concludes, should join the Communist Party: "Show your solidarity, show your strength! don't sleep—wake up!"[30]

These metaphors of the slave mart and the slave block to describe domestic labor and women's work in industrial labor indicate the long history of invalidating women's labor by sexualizing it as reproductive labor, differentiating women workers from those members of the "producing classes."[31] Presidential candidate Al Gore's use of the term "working families" called forth this ambivalence about the nature of work and class conflict within America.[32] On the one hand, trying to appeal to the so-called gender gap, "working families" feminizes labor as service done on behalf of family, (all work is thus domestic labor); on the other hand, by insisting, as Gore did in late August 2000 to a rally of workers, that they needed to ask "which side are you on?" he signaled an association with the tradition of masculine workers fighting the boss. The next line of Florence Reece's, 1930s song answers: "you either are a union *man* or a scab for D. H. Blair."[33]

The dynamics between the white female employer and the black maid cannot be seen as merely about economics. As Baker and Cooke note, domestic work barely registers as labor by union organizers; its location in the privacy of the home and the intimate nature of the work—cooking, cleaning, caring for children—blurs the lines between workplace and home. Domestic workers might organize (as they did) across households, but that still did not alter the private day-to-day engagement with the employing woman who is often home alone with the maid.[34] Lutie notes the bizarre change that occurs in her dealings with Mrs. Chandler, who often confided in her when the two were alone, even chatting amiably on the train down to New York "about some story being played up in the newspaper, about clothes or some moving picture. But when the train pulled into Grand Central, the wall was suddenly there. . . . There was a firm note of dismissal in her voice so that the other passengers pouring off the train turned to watch the rich young woman and her colored maid; a tone of voice that made people stop to hear just when it was that the maid was to report back for work. Because the voice unmistakably established the relation between the blond young woman and the brown young woman" (51). Trudier Harris points out that "[i]n moving from her home to that of the white woman, the black woman connects two racially and spatially distinct worlds in one direction—she goes into the white world."[35] Lutie's public train travels with Mrs. Chandler back into New York City imply a reversal of this racial/spatial direction; it is this threat to the white woman's social location that must be contained. Yet this is the awkward intimacy film noir broaches as it revises domestic melodrama to enable a new kind of pulp modernism embodied within unencumbered female aggression and sexuality.

Lutie had noticed that the tensions over sexuality were racial not class based, as the young white women hired to serve meals at the Chandlers never became the object of women's jealousy or men's desire, nor did they receive the intimate outpourings or the cast-off clothes of the white woman employer. In public, the blonde woman oversaw the brown one; employer controlled employee. In private, Lutie fed the bored bridge club a ladies lunch and watched Mrs. Chandler kiss a friend's husband on her couch. In fact, she watched Mr. Chandler watch her watching Mrs. Chandler. The two women were intimately connected. Of course, the history of the British novel is a history of tales of domestic labor. From *Clarissa* to *Jane Eyre*, the domestic novel recorded the plight of the serving girl whose isolation in a large, empty household sparks gothic stories of lust, terror, and surrender through letters and diaries. For eighteenth- and nineteenth-century British novelists, the consolidation of the bourgeoisie could best be tracked through the travails of the female domestic servant, governess, or teacher alone in the home of a wealthy man. Her body and her bedroom became the intimate locus of desire driving the narrative.[36] What Petry had done was to take the American version, which racialized the class conflict of the domestic novel, and use pulp fiction to modernize the naturalistic settings of urban horror so that the nightclub and the train station replaced the attic and the cellar, thus moving gothic domestic settings into sleazy noir public spaces.

With the exception of the insistence on interracial solidarity among black and white women's auxiliary workers in steel mills, auto plants, and rubber works celebrated by the Communist Party as a vital aspect of its antiracist work, in popular culture, black and white women were routinely portrayed interacting only in private through domestic service: a white woman employed a black woman to tend her children and fix her meals and clean her home and laundry.[37] In Fannie Hurst's novel, *Imitation of Life*, this intimacy is reinforced by the different kinds of work the two women perform: Bea pounds the pavement drumming up orders for maple syrup; Delilah turns the extra syrup into candies to be sold, eventually becoming the basis for B. Pullman enterprises. In the 1959 Douglas Sirk version, the white mother Lora's career as actress and singer takes her out at night. Annie, the black mother and Lora's maid, stays home and supports her two families. Through the perfect waffles she makes, first for her two charges—her daughter, Sarah Jane, and Lora's daughter, Susie—and then for an ever-expanding public, she eventually runs a domestic business, while Lora lives the high life of celebrity. Not only is there a connection in the political unconscious linking domestic service to prostitution through the bedroom and living room couch, this connection is transmitted by staging entertaining and performing as housework. Sarah Jane's passing eventually leads her to "imitate" in a debased form (as nightclub singer) Lora's imitative profession (as actress), as Lora's house begins to resemble a stage set.[38]

In the film version of *Mildred Pierce* (1947), Mildred (Joan Crawford) relies on Lottie, her black maid (Butterfly McQueen), to expand Mildred's pie-baking expertise into a booming business, primarily as domestic servant but also as her assistant.[39] However, once Mildred makes it, Ida (the tough white woman who first hired Mildred as a waitress) replaces Butterfly McQueen as a sidekick. In James. M. Cain's novel, the lower-middle-class women of Glendale understand that service, whether as domestic or waitress, is essentially prostitution. When Mildred finally confesses to her neighbor, Mrs. Gessler, that she has taken an unspecified job, her cynical neighbor quips: "I hope you picked a five-dollar house. You're too young for the two-dollar trade." Mildred provides the details that she is a waitress, to which Mrs. Gessler comments: "It rhymes up the same way," something Mildred quickly learns as she hustles tips from businessmen who run their hands up her legs.[40] As a single woman, the femme fatale employer offers a kind of solace from the sexual harassment of sons and husbands. The two dark ladies are alone together, sometimes conspiratorially, as the maid becomes protective of her employer and the employer needs the maid's confidence.

In the melodramatic noir film version of *Mildred Pierce*, Eve Arden plays this sidekick role, and it is clearly meant to be understood as a lesbian role: the lover and consort of an increasingly butch Mildred, who moves from waitress to freelance pie maker to restauranteur, eventually owning a string of franchises and, in the process, like Lora, conspicuously upgrading her house. Thus she has converted domestic labor into a small business by moving domestic functions out of the house and making public her private acts of fixing drinks, meals, and desserts previously done for her family. Lutie also moves out of her home into a nightlife offer by the Junto Bar and Grill on her street corner when her causal singing along with the jukebox lands her an audition with Boots Smith's band. But, as she has already surmised from her neighbor, the madam Mrs. Hedges's, offer to fix her up with a white man, "on this damn street you're supposed to want to earn a little extra money sleeping around nights" (84). As usual, there's more to the job than fronting the band. After accidentally killing Boots, who pimps for Junto, and his white bankrollers, who run everything in Harlem, Lutie ends up on the lam. She had tried to get money off Boots to hire a lawyer to pry her son from the child welfare agency, where he was taken for mail fraud. She surmises that Bud's life would be better off in reform school, because as a murderer she'd lose custody anyway. Finding herself thinking and acting like a criminal, she rifles Boots' wallet for money, hides her bloodied gloves, takes the stairs rather than the elevator down from the apartment, and heads for Penn Station. There, she buys a one-way ticket to Chicago, where she could disappear, slide into the anonymity of the Southside, maybe get a job singing at a nightclub, hustling drinks.

Lutie's poverty and race have sent her on the trajectory prepared for her by the jealous wives of Lyme, Connecticut; she's on the way to being the femme fatale of film noir. Yet, as a black woman, all she can hope for is the bit part as her maid, the one who covers her trail, helps cover up her crime, backs up her alibi, sings her torch song. The black femme fatale cannot be visualized within film; she is not going to be discovered in Chicago and end up packing a road house as Ida Lupino's Lily in Jean Negulesco's *Road House* did. Her presence remains located aurally in recordings of blueswomen's voices. Ultimately, however, she finds her way into these novels. We can watch Mildred Pierce and Lucia Harper, as overly devoted mothers of noir melodrama, cover up crimes committed by their ungrateful daughters. Both depend on the domestic servants they employ to get them out of a jam; but no one can come to Lutie's or her son's aid; nor can she expect to be picked up from the two-bit bar where she might end up singing in Chicago to star in a *Road House* (1948).

The classic femme fatale, Ann Savage in *Detour* (1945) for instance, moves from the street to the bedroom. She ensnares the doomed noir hero first by her freedom to move alone through the urban landscape, then by her outspoken desire for sex, and finally by her dead body. The femme fatale possesses a power offered by the street that is never available to the maternal woman of postwar Hollywood films who has planted herself in the kitchen. The domestic white woman appears to be denied erotic power because her function is solely reproductive. However, her domestic servant, as Lutie learned, produces an economy out of the invisible reproduction of the home.[41] Living at her work site, having a bedroom in her employer's house, resexualizes the reproductive labor of housework. The maid turns into an object of desire who appears as mobile as the femme fatale pacing the sidewalks nightly, like Ella Raines in *Phantom Lady* (1944). Because she is from elsewhere and will eventually also return there, she too has a double life, one never of interest overtly to her employers but nevertheless hanging as a veil between them. She cannot be wholly owned. As free labor, rather than wife, she is able to dismiss herself. Even if "The *Mistress* terminates the *interview*, Mildred," as Mrs. Forrester reminds Mildred Pierce when she comes for the job of housekeeper, the "servant" can always take off: "Mrs. Pierce, if you don't mind. And I'm terminating it" (43). Mildred's assertion suggests her connection as a servant to black women. In Langston Hughes's "Madam" series, Alberta K. Johnson declares: "My name is Johnson— / Madam Alberta K. // I do cooking. / Day's work, too! /Alberta K. Johnson— / *Madam* to you."[42] Each may end up running her own business. "The Madam stands for business." Usually, however, as Lutie Johnson discovers, except for work in a laundry or prostitution, no other employment is open to a black woman, even though Lutie manages to land an underpaid civil servant's job that allows her to move to the disastrous street.

Mildred Pierce, as a self-sacrificing suburban mother and a respectable white woman, can scoff at the haughty Mrs. Forrester, herself a kept woman recently installed as the second wife of her wealthy husband. A black maid, even if she too were a self-sacrificing mother as Lutie is, is subject to suspicions about her sexuality, and her job possibilities are far more limited than even Mildred's. Baker and Cooke correctly called the Jerome Avenue "mart" a slave block because domestic work recalls, as Phyllis Palmer notes, antebellum racial and sexual divisions of labor. Myra Page's *Gathering Storm* (1932), a novel about the Gastonia, North Carolina, textile mills strike, tracks the tripartite class and racial divisions in the milltown of Greenville. In it, Martha Morgan dies fighting off a rape by "that young massa" Elbert Haines. Her family is murdered and lynched after her fiancé avenges her death.[43] Page's novel directly links the Gastonia strike to the Scottsboro case and makes clear the remnants of white supremacy in the South, with black workers living as tenants on the plantation and with black female servants at the mercy of white men. Because a domestic servant lives in a bedroom of her employer's house, her intimate connection with daily life reinforces her sexuality. While the image of maternal labor seems at odds with sexuality, when that labor is performed by another, it opens the domestic to exploitation and fantasy. She is at once maternal and sexually available. Moreover, she also makes her female employer sexually available as she frees her employer from domestic drudgery. For the single, white female employer, the black domestic becomes the surrogate mother. She allows the white woman access to the streets where she can conduct business and have affairs.

In Fannie Hurst's *Imitation of Life*, Delilah moves into Bea Pullman's house, freeing Bea to spend days hawking maple syrup up and down the Atlantic City boardwalk, using her dead husband's business cards announcing simply "B. Pullman."[44] Delilah tends Bea's ailing father and her infant daughter as she cares for her own daughter, Peola. She cooks, cleans, takes them for walks, then gives Bea nightly backrubs. Eventually, her cooking skills become the basis for Bea's business success. Like the train car whose name Bea assumed with marriage and whose porters were organized into the most powerful black union, "[s]o it was from a going household of Delilah and three babies that Bea plugged every morning into the territory for the day."[45] Bea walks the boardwalk, "with her vigorous, honed-down contours," as an anomaly, "a woman salesman" (78). In *The Reckless Moment*, Frances Williams stays home tending the children while Joan Bennett, left alone to manage her family when her husband gets a commission overseas, travels to downtown Los Angeles from their Balboa Island beach house. She wanders the streets trying to borrow money from pawn brokers and loan sharks for the blackmailer hounding her murderess daughter. Walking the streets is an essential element of the white femme fatale's deadly eroticism, as is her "honed-down" phallic presence.[46] She may end up in the bedroom (or more typically the living room couch) of her doomed lover, but she got there by stepping out of the bounds of home. By contrast, the black domestic alters the contours of the white bourgeois home, making it into a fit home when her employer is a single mother, co-conspiring with her single, white woman employer, and becoming the object of sexual desire when her "mistress" has a husband.

Gwendolyn Brooks directly takes on this erotic "epistemology" in the chapter of *Maud Martha* bitingly entitled "the self-solace."[47] In horror, Maud Martha watches as Miss Ingram, the white woman salesman of beauty products, tires to sell Maud's beautician, Sonia Johnson, a new product line for "dark complexions," including a lipstick called "Black Beauty" (279). Critic James Smethurst notes that Brooks's ambivalence about popular culture, including products that remake African-American women's physique advertised daily in the black newspaper *Chicago Defender*, reflects Brooks's engagement in a debate within the 1930s black Left about the relationship of the masses to popular culture, which had altered from the Third Period to the Popular Front.[48] Where Langston Hughes, unlike Richard Wright, found in American popular culture the possibility of a jazzy voice to indict its racism, Brooks's sensitivity to gender exploitation made her far more skeptical of its subversive potential. For instance, when Maud Martha and her husbnd, Paul, travel to downtown Chicago to see a movie at the World Playhouse and find themselves "the only colored people here," it's clear that American popular culture is racially restrictive. Not everyone is part of the masses supposedly participating in mass culture (214). Lutie Johnson discerns the emptiness of the Chandler's lives, "learn[s] all about Country Living," by skimming "the pages of the fat sleek magazines . . . *Vogue, Town and Country, Harper's Bazaar, House and Garden, House Beautiful*" (50). Maud Martha's disdain for Miss Ingram's failure to discern black differences—"in the 'Negro group' there were complexions whiter than her own, and other complexions, brown, tan, yellow, cream"—grows into raw fury at her casual racism (279). Complaining of her working conditions, which force her into "walking the streets" in all kinds of weather, the saleswoman comments, quite unconsciously, "I work like a nigger to make a few pennies. A few lousy pennies." (280–1). Even when targeted for black women, mass-marketed beauty, offered in movies, magazine, and make-up, excludes and ultimately degrades them.

Like the private battles between white female employers and black domestics, this rare interaction between a white woman and black women occurs over work. Again, the work is about intimacy: here, refashioning the body; there, the home. The white woman walks the streets, but it's not Jerome Avenue and she's not in search of a "slave" to bring home to do her housework. In this case, she enters a black businesswoman's shop as supplicant. In a role reversal, she must please the black woman. Mrs. Johnson notes that some black beauticians were "glad to have the whites at their mercy, if only for a few moments. They made them crawl. Then they applied the whiplash. Then they sent the poor creatures off–with no orders. Then they laughed and laughed and laughed, a terrible laughter" (278). Their job as beauticians to redo black women's hair was now vengefully aimed at refashioning the white woman into a "poor creature" dependent upon them for her economic survival. Is Miss Ingram reasserting her racial superiority by referring to herself as a nigger before these two dignified black women? Or is she seeking to align herself with them in a misguided attempt to name herself a "slave"? For Maud Martha, the answer is clear; the woman is a racist and should be called on the carpet for insulting Sonia Johnson in her own shop. However, Mrs. Johnson declares: "Now 'nigger,' for instance, means to them something bad, or slavey-like, or low. They don't mean anything against me. I'm a Negro, not a 'nigger.' " (283). Sonia Johnson's assertion of racial pride misses the echoes of the nineteenth-century mill girls' refusal to be called "wage slaves" that Maud Martha clearly discerns. Just because streetwalkers were also called "white slaves" doesn't excuse Miss Ingram's reimposition of racial superiority (especially if it comes through an invocation of gender solidarity).

Smethurst argues that during the 1930s, African-American poets were engaged in a project of reclaiming folkloric images of the black masses that could bridge rural southern and urban northern vernaculars. To some degree, the figure of the domestic servant in the novels and films I describe is connected to this ambivalent location within and outside of modern political economy and commodity culture. For Lutie, domestic service opens a pastoral zone skewed by racism and loneliness. It ultimately destroys her own family when she must live with the white family on their tree-lined street. For Page's Martha Morgan, domestic service differs little from slavery. For Baker and Cooke, the women on the slave blocks of northern cities link domestic service in the urban industrialized north to servitude in the antebellum south. Bea Pullman's marketing scheme for her sweets business is to photograph Delilah as a stereotypical mammy; her big breakthrough comes when she dresses her in white toque and apron to cook waffles in her boardwalk stall. Joan Crawford puts Butterfly McQueen to work on her pies in Glendale, California, just as Vivien Leigh had relied on her to midwife Olivia de Havilland's baby a few years before in *Gone with the Wind* (1939). In the novel, the maid Lettie, like Ida and Mildred, is white, so that when Veda discovers Mildred's uniform hidden in her closet and insists Lettie wear it when she accompanies her two charges to the swimming pool, it confirms Mildred's connection to service and her potentially aggressive sexuality but maintains her whiteness. Lettie takes the girls to the pool daily to flirt with the lifeguard. But when Butterfly McQueen (as Lottie) is seen wearing Mildred's clothes, it suggests another trajectory: like Marlene Dietrich emerging in blonde wig from the gorilla costume in the "Hot Voodoo" number of *Blond Venus* (1932), it points up the camouflage of racialized sexuality. Underneath the costume of blackness—gorilla suit and voodoo, uniform and domestic service—lurks a white movie star, whose value is in maintaining racial purity (and so the bourgeois home). Lutie takes pride in never wearing any of the hand-me-downs she receives from Mrs. Chandler that were "Designed for Country Living," sending them instead to her father's girlfriend to be worn "nightly in the gin mill at the corner of Seventh Avenue and 110th Street" (50). These Connecticut clothes serve as a kind of drag to stabilize white bourgeois femininity. Luties's revenge against her employer lies in revealing their function by ripping them out of their context as benign charity and placing them in a site of transgressive pleasure. The idea that Butterfly McQueen could support Joan

Crawford's shoulder pads adds comic relief, but it also undercuts Mildred by linking her to servitude, destabilizing her value as broad-shouldered star.

In both versions of *Mildred Pierce*, Veda's shame that her mother wears a uniform in public is deflected by forcing the maid, hired to help Mildred take care of her growing pie business, to appear as a servant. Crawford's voice-over narration begins by intoning that her life had been little more than service, wearing an apron forever cooking, cleaning, baking. "I was always in the kitchen. It felt as though I'd been born in a kitchen and lived there all my life. . ." But the crucial distinction is over the public display of her service, which connects her to Lottie. In Ramona Lowe's devastating rebuttal to *Imitation of Life*, "The Woman in the Window," a short story published in the Urban League's journal, *Opportunity*, Mrs. Jackson endures the humiliation of publicly dressing as "Aunt Jemima . . . a ol' Southern mammy" (the very image of Delilah Bea had concocted to help sell her maple sugar candies) to fry chicken in the window of a restaurant of the same name. Mrs. Jackson, like Mildred Pierce, cannot hide her uniform from her children, who discover her one day while walking home from school and are shamed when the white kids call her "nigger." Mrs. Jackson lets her children know that "[s]ome work's dignified 'n' some ain' so dignified. But it all got t' be done. My work's cookin' 'n' there ain' nothin' wrong with that." Like Maud Martha, she insists on confronting white racism: "*'N' son, doan you never let me see you run no more when a body say nigger. You turn roun' 'n' give 'm such a thrashin' they woan never forget.*"[49]

As David Roediger and Lauren Berlant point out, questions of labor, racialized as they are in American history, are always questions of citizenship.[50] During the 1930s, membership in the Communist Party, or at least, as Michael Denning has argued, allegiance to the Popular Front, became a vehicle for a group of "plebeians," European immigrants, and southern migrants and their first-generation urban children to participate, albeit oppositionally, in American culture.[51] Film noirs, based so often on fiction from the 1930s, visualized this racial and class dynamic. Central to the femme fatale's position as a mobile figure on the landscape was the Depression and the War and the shifts in populations and work opportunities it provided women. This is, in part, what allows Lutie Johnson to disappear to Chicago—the massive migrations of African Americans to industrial cities, coupled with her essential anonymity. She is an "invisible (wo)man."[52] Within the film noirs of the 1940s, like many of the 1930s novels, there lurks a figure of questionable race or ethnicity— Mexican, Spanish, Italian, Jewish, Greek—dark, but never black, who moves near the femme fatale. The femme fatale, like Kathie Moffett, can establish an identification with her beautiful maid, Eunice, because she has no place within bourgeois domesticity; yet her visual presence in popular culture is overdetermined.

Gwendolyn Brooks's two volumes of poems from the 1940s and her 1953 novel, *Maud Martha*, all conclude with the end of World War II and its ambivalent effect on black Americans caught within the racist United States. Maud Martha notes the returning soldiers parading maimed, but alive, in contrast to "the Negro press (on whose front pages beamed the usual representations of womanly Beauty, pale and pompadoured) [which] carried the stories of the latest of the Georgia and Mississippi lynchings"(321). Brooks expressly links color stratification within the black community to the racist lynchings of black Americans by whites. This is the violent underpinning of America tracked by film noirs, many of which were made by left-wing directors from fiction by left-wing writers. Kathie could flee to Acapulco; Lutie only makes it to Chicago, where, like Maud Martha, she'll find her "type is not a Foxy Cat favorite," her "color" also acts "like a wall" (Brooks 223, 229). What appears to adhere to the surface of the black woman's body in popular culture is "the plight of the black woman (which is, precisely, a problem of nonrecognition)."[53] In postwar Jim Crow America, she cannot be seen; thus her narrative might be sung or written, but not filmed.

When Eunice resists Jeff Bailey's entreaties to help him find Kathie, she underscores, through her deceit, a loyalty that Kathie will inevitably betray. The white femme noire double crosses white men because she can get away with it; she's never had to clean up her own mess. Lutie Johnson and Maud Martha, keen observers of their cities' grimy streets, recognize her type immediately; they've seen her, read about her, even worked for her, many times before. Perhaps she sings in dives in Harlem or Chicago's Southside along with Ida Lupino. But they also would recognize Eunice out on a date, like Hattie Scott or Lutie or the other "[y]oung women coming home from work—dirty, tired, depressed—[who] looked forward to the moment when they would change their clothes and head toward the gracious spaciousness of the Junto . . . because they couldn't bear to look what they could see of the future smack in the face while listening to radios or trying or read an evening paper" (144–45). Like the radio and the newspaper, proletarian literature and film noir, in part, also dimly outlined their unrecorded stories. Once again, these dark visions of mid-century America provided a template for sketching an alternative to either Betty Crocker or Aunt Jemima. Lutie and Maud Martha know exactly what happens to the femme noire; she gets out anyway she can.

CHAPTER 3

DOUBLE CROSS: WRI(GH)TING
AS THE OUTSIDER

THE NOVEL AS FILM NOIR

Most film noirs began first as text—novels, short stories, plays or scripts, screenplays, treatments—but as soon as they appeared, they began generating prose. Just as the films depended on the kinky nighttime police shots of *PM* photographer Weegee, whose book *Naked City* became the basis for Jules Dassin's film of the same name,[1] or the eerie bus ride series from Esther Bubley's OWI assignment, so too did they generate new photographic obsessions in Robert Frank's and Diane Arbus's street photography that captured in a single frame what the films took an hour and a half to spell out: America was a nation of loners and misfits. The films also created new works of prose. Much popular 1930s fiction included hard-boiled, tough-guy detective and police procedural novels—often written by those connected with left-wing literary radicalism.[2] These were part of an emerging pulp literature that, with the paperback revolution, crossed the boundaries of respectable literature and sleaze. What is one to make of Pocket Book's 1941 edition of Emile Zola's *Nana* with its lurid cover of a torch singer in a transparent white dress? Its back-cover blurb declared, "she squandered fortunes, ruined lives with sublime contempt and abandon—yet her last disease-ridden days were spent in squalor and oblivion." Is this art or trash?

Moreover, many 1930s novels, such as Ralph Ellison's *Invisible Man*, didn't get published, or even written, until long after the decade was over. Vicissitudes of politics and culture kept these works out of print. Richard Wright's wildly popular and disturbing sociological roman noir *Native Son* launched his career as literary superstar; however, its popularity and his political disillusionment with the United States and with communism took its toll on his ability to get another novel into print. He was traveling and living in France, Spain, and Africa, participating in black expatriate political culture in each place, writing some of his best work. But it was nonfiction, and in the minds of mid-century literati, this was second-class material. As Georgia O'Keeffe would later comment about the "city men" of the late 1920s and early 1930s: "They talked so often of writing the Great American Novel—the Great American Play—the Great American Poetry."[3] O'Keeffe was definitely not speaking about literary radicals, much less black intellectuals, but the sentiment against nonfiction prevailed in all quarters. It would not be until James Agee smashed the boundaries of narrative, fiction and nonfiction alike, that reportage/journalism/memoir would achieve critical stature, but this happened in the 1960s, decades after he had written and published *Let Us Now Praise Famous Men*. Wright's struggle with himself over the scope of his second novel plays itself out in the ultimate form it assumed. Full of violent battles, the narrative of *The Outsider* enacts a contest with itself over its own philosophical and aesthetic legitimacy by recreating iconic visuals from film noirs.[4] Much as the 1943 zoot suit riots in Los Angeles had pitted hip Latino teenagers against uniformed sailors, *The Outsider* plays out its internal and external conflicts through dueling styles. In Wright's case, literary style, like fashion, signals political and philosophical affiliations that set its user apart from dominant culture as it advertises its subcultural allegiance. Subcultural style, according to Birmingham Center critics Angela McRobbie and Dick Hebdige, describing a theory of British punk style, visually maps class and ethnic and gender clashes of Thatcherite Britain onto the bodies of its victims.[5] Richard Wright's novel falling into the midst of McCarthyite America—it was published just months before the Rosenbergs were executed—exhibits how literary style also maps racial and political conflict.

BLACK & WHITE AND NOIR

This chapter reads Richard Wright's second novel, *The Outsider*, as a literary version of film noir—a reversal, in more ways than one, because, for the most part, film noirs began as prose. Much has been written on the spider women who gleam white as snow in their low key-lit frames and in turn frame guys who should know better—but don't; or on the visual style that foregrounds negative space. But practically nothing has been written on the "blackness of blackness," the racial codes of these films.[6] Typically, film noirs picture lower middle-class WASP horror. Set in Los Angeles, the garden suburb revealed as hell, many film noirs look back to New York or sometimes Chicago, as places apart, zones of difference, where a man could lose his identity and pick up another for a small price. Within the standard plot—a regular guy works a regular job (say he sells insurance like Fred McMurray playing Walter Neff in *Double Indemnity*), gets hooked by an evil woman (say she wears an anklet like Barbara Stanwyck playing Phyllis Dietrichson), and commits murder—maybe gets away with it—but then she's got something on him, so, most likely, he kills her; but she gets him anyway, because there's another guy (say he's a cop or investigator like Edward G. Robinson playing Barton Keyes), who's a pal, likes him too much, can't see the forest for the trees because "He's close, too close"—"Closer than you know, Walter."

Within that dark woods also lurks a minor character—usually a gangster, but sometimes a hot-headed youth, always coded ethnically: dark, with names that are Greek or Italian or Spanish or Jewish, who is out of place in the world of daylight, preferring to slide out from behind thick shrubbery or stand on corners late at night for a secret rendezvous. This character has something on the guy, and on the spider woman, and often on her "other"—the innocent maiden who stumbles into the plot when she falls for the doomed guy. He is not central to the plot, but he is always there. And because he is, and because of what he becomes in the late phases of the style (*Touch of Evil* and *Crimson Kimono*) and in its second (*Chinatown*) and now third reincarnation (*Devil in a Blue Dress*), and because, in America, the play of light and dark, as Toni Morrison reminds us, is always about race relations, these films, which barely feature black faces, signify race and its meaning within postwar American urban imagination.

Richard Wright took this cinematic variation on melodrama, inverted it, and pushed its implications to the limit—outside it really. He did so, because, in true noir style, it provided a means to "take care" of three "problems": racism in the United States, the Communist Party of the United States (CPUSA), and his literary protégé-turned-rival Ralph Ellison. The plot of *The Outsider* trails Cross Damon, a brainy and well-read black postal worker from Chicago's Southside, on the lam for numerous murders, theft, and fraud. Fortuitous accidents and clever aliases land him among New York's circle of Communist Party intellectuals, where he commits still more murders until finally caught by the tenacious hunchbacked district attorney, Ely Houston. "A crime story in a newspaper evokes a sense of excitement far beyond the meaning of the banal crime described, a meaning which, in turn, conjures up, for inexplicable reason, its emotion equivalent in a totally different setting and possessing a completely contrary meaning," wrote Wright.[7] Michel Fabre notes that Wright's first story, "Suspicion," based on the "gothic detective stories" found in pulp periodicals, was a rewriting of an Edgar Allan Poe tale, and that both "The Man Who Lived Underground" and "The Man Who Killed a Shadow," like *Native Son*, were based on Wright's perusal of true crime reports.[8] Margaret Walker recounts how she clipped the news items from the *Chicago Tribune* on the Robert Nixon case and sent them to Wright after he left for New York.[9] Wright was always on the lookout for intriguing stories to probe the absurdities and horrors of the racial system governing America. His friends contributed anecdotes. For instance, sometime during the mid-1940s, the city of San Francisco was terrorized by a serial rapist, a light-skinned black man who targeted white women. After the man was arrested, tried, convicted, and sentenced to the die in the gas chamber, a police officer got interested in the case of "Green Gloves," as he was known, and discovered he was actually white.

Knowing Wright's interest in this kind of twisted plot, psychologist Horace Cayton wrote a long detailed account of the case, which included a deep Oedipal fixation—because his mother had routinely punished him by saying she would send him back to "the black people"—and intense rage at Negroes. Eventually, "something happens (mothers death or violent argument with her) which . . . causes him great emotional distress . . . he falls into fancicy [sic]" and concocts a "history" that his father had been lynched by white racists who accused him falsely of raping a white woman. Thus he decided to seek revenge on them as a black man by himself raping white women. He refused to acknowledge that he was not black, going to his death as "a Negro rather than undo the great harm which he had done the Negro community," which had endured a vicious race-baiting mayoral election, police sweeps of thousands of young black men who "were put in jail and lost their jobs," and a near race riot. Along with the story, Cayton even supplies a title: "You could call it 'Black Blood' or 'The Man Who Turned Black' or facetiously, 'Mind over Matter' or 'What Ho!, The Oedipus.' Seriously I hope the plot interests you. I will send you all of the material I have on it if it does. It might fit into your series like 'The Man who lived underground.' "[10] Cayton knew that Wright relished true stories on which to base his fiction, partly because Wright felt he was inventing a realist tradition for African-American literary history.[11]

Fabre's careful tracing of Wright's earliest literary sources begins with a perusal of the crime pages of the Memphis *Commercial Appeal* and *Flynn's Detective Weekly*, but he notes in passing, one need also look at more than these "gothic detective stories," because "the weekly billings of the Strand, the Majestic or Loew's Palace could be checked with profit to map Wright's early movie culture" (13). Moreover, Wright's education in Parisian existentialism, after his 1946 expatriation, also included "other domains of true aesthetic expression, films in particular," running twenty-four hours at the Cinematheque.[12] Going to the movies is a central pastime for both Bigger Thomas and Cross Damon, who spies among Gil and Eva Blount's belongings and finds in her diary that she too spent her time in postwar Paris watching American movies: "a horrible gangster film with a tense, melodramatic atmosphere" (*The Outsider*, 209). By 1951, Wright had written the screenplay for (and even acted in) a film version of *Native Son*. This immersion in movie culture and true-crime plots, spurred by the rave reviews of *Invisible Man*, unleashed a flood of prose between February and May 1952, that became the 650-page manuscript of *The Outsider*.

For the most part, *The Outsider* is viewed as a failed novel; the reviews neatly clipped and collected for Wright repeatedly refer to it as a sloppy "melodrama."[13] While this feminizing epithet is bad enough, the critics often go on to compare Wright's novel to cheesy pulp fiction reminiscent of Mickey Spillane.[14] It is characterized as a "thriller," "a surrealistic cops-and-robbers story," "a cheap drugstore whodunit."[15] Perhaps the most galling of the reviews were those that directly linked the novel to Ellison's as did the critic for the *Nation*. So too did Granville Hicks, writing in the Sunday *New York Times Book Review* on March 22, 1953, and Harvey Curtus Webster in the April 6, 1953, *New Leader*. What scholarly criticism has been written tries to salvage Wright's name by discussing, as many of the original reviewers did (with sneers), its Dostoevskian nihilism, or Kirkegaardian dread, or Christian existentialism, or Freudian psychoanalysis, and of course his disillusionment with communism, to deflect attention from its awkward trashiness. In fact, the novel fits perfectly within the contours of what James Naremore, quoting Graham Greene, calls "blood melodrama," a modernist "interest in popular stories about violence and sexual love."[16] So it is not surprising that Fabre reads it as a "novel of ideas disguised as a melodrama" (*Quest*, 367). However, Wright's contemporary reviewers relished the novel for what it displayed about him. "His almost psychopathic lust for violence," wrote the reviewer for *Jet*, " his story becomes as completely phony and unreal as a cheap drugstore whodunit."[17] Whodunit, indeed. Wright is out for vengeance and not just against the Party and the nation he felt had so betrayed him.

His rivalry with Ellison, whose *Invisible Man* is the mirrored backdrop for the novel, becomes a second frame for the plot. In a letter to Ellen Wright written a few weeks before its publication, Ellison asks her to "[t]ell Dick that I hope that I haven't let him down since it is the best I could do."[18] Still anxious about his status in relation to Wright, Ellison appears as supplicant.[19] However, within a year a radical reversal of fortunes would occur. At the bottom of a long typed letter, dated January 21, 1953, the last one it seems that Ellison sent Wright, in which he notes "I will be right at the bookstore on the 18th [the scheduled date of its release] to get a look at *The Outsider*," is a handwritten addition: "Perhaps you've heard by now that lightning struck me, leaving me standing amazed with the 1952 National Book Award for Fiction."[20] No more letters from Ellison, who had had a long and voluble history of letter-writing to his former patron, exist in Yale University's Beinecke Library files, as if the lightning that had left Ellison standing had taken its toll on Wright. Wright had predicted according to Ellison's recounting that "Negroes will not like it [*The Outsider*]," to which Ellison had reassured him that Roy Ottley, who had been "going around discussing me as simply 'a disciple of Dick Wright's'," and Ben Burns in *Jet* hadn't liked *Invisible Man* either; but this could hardly offer solace to Wright who was clearly anxious about his reputation.[21] Ellison's long discussion of Chester Himes's new 1948 novel in many ways prefigures the criticisms that would be lodged against Wright's novel. "I believe," he remarks, "that when one writes of politics one is called upon to do more than cull a few terms from *Materialism and Empro-criticism* [sic] and scatter them dialoguewise between episodes of a cops and robbers plot."[22]

Despite claiming that "the hard-boiled stance and its monosyllabic utterance" of stripped down 1930s prose could not work for an African-American writer steeped in the "alive language" of the blues, the dozens, and gospel preachings, Ellison brilliantly employs the genre's first-person narration to tell his noir tale of descent.[23] Moreover, his letters to Wright read like a series of revenge plots in which a group of disaffected former gang members bicker among themselves. They are filled with jousts lodged at the insider world of estranged African-American [former] communists, as if a constant battle to be on top required vigilance about what one said or did in each other's company. Noting that Chester Himes had not been to see him, Ellison speculates, "Could he fear that I might put him in *my* book?" After all, he notes "The character referred to as 'Ellsworth' who argued with Lee concerning the material character of certain class divisions of the Negro family, actually refers to me and a conversation I had with Chester last year."[24] "The Party boys around Harlem," including Abner Berry, who "wrote an attack in *The Worker*, calling me the standard names and saying that I had 'sold out' in writing *Invisible Man*" simply confirmed Ellison's and Wright's understanding of the CPUSA as another gang.[25] It could only have enraged Wright to find an article entitled, "Native Doesn't Live Here," which complained that "While Wright sits out the threat of totalitarianism in Paris, an abler U.S. Negro novelist sees the problem of his race differently. Says Ralph (Invisible Man) Ellison: 'It's a big wonderful country.' "[26] Maybe so, if you win the National Book Award. However, in his biographical remarks, Wright describes his novel about an outsider, not an invisible man, as a response to the cold war. "The message to the West 'the game is up.' "[27]

While Cross Damon does not narrate his story retrospectively, the novel has, as Wright wrote his agent Paul Reynolds, "four murders, a suicide, an ambush murder, which ought to be enough blood. There is a kind of love story in it, but rather a dark and tortured one" (quoted in *Quest*, 366). The early drafts of *The Outsider*, however, indicate that Wright began the book by writing it as a first-person testimonial: "Wherever possible, I shall present facts, documents, rather than my own words to substantiate this record, for that is what it is: a record." Using this device that was so prevalent in the film noirs he was attempting to reshoot in prose, his narrator reveals that instead of being underground, he is speaking from "beneath the water-line of this city." Like so many film noirs, the hero of this earlier draft is a disillusioned veteran, "here in this damp cell . . . sit[ting], brood[ing] and think[ing]" in his ship's brig.[28] Wright's original idea for the novel came from a story he had followed about a black soldier who faced court martial for refusing to go to the front. To his General Court Martial Order Number 20 issued by Headquarters 69 Infantry Division 4th Signal Battalion April 5, 1945, Corporal John Jones had simply declared himself, "Not guilty please." Wright also notes another case of a soldier court martialed for not guarding mail bags in 1946. These apparent acts of defiance against the United States Armed Forces intrigued Wright as he struggled to find a story to fit his proposed title "Cornering a Man" during the mid-1940s.[29] A would-be author, asking Wright's help and advice, grasps the difficulties ahead for anyone wanting to take on World War II: "I know by now that nothing—nothing is as dead as World War 2—any phase of it. Not even pulp magazines will touch it. I've check [sic] many sources of information in the publishing field on that point and the consensus of opinion is that not even a Tolstoy could sell a ms. on it. . . . If one wrote of WW3—a nice juicy, red-baiting, witch-hunting job dripping with blood from Communists' heads on pikes—ah—that's magic; *that* would certainly sell."[30]

Not even pulp magazines would touch the Second World War directly; however, both Wright and Ellison used the conventions of pulp to dissect race, postwar America, and the CPUSA, including the pseudophilosophy conveyed in long speeches that is also one hallmark of the more literary forms of the genre. In the final pages of *The Maltese Falcon*, for instance, Sam Spade explains to the back-stabbing Bridget, the woman he loves, why he has to turn her in. It is long lesson in the credo and ethics of living private eye: "Listen, this isn't a damned bit of good. You'll never understand me, but I'll try once more and then we'll give it up. Listen . . .," he says before listing the attributes of a PI that make him both someone with no use for the police yet someone with a moral stance.[31] Like Poe's detective Dupin a century before them, Sam Spade and Philip Marlowe and the other noir detectives dismiss the police and the DAs who prosecute and investigate criminals as inept cogs in the wheel of a corrupt system; yet they share their work. Occasionally the DA crosses over, as does Wendell Corey after he falls for Barbara Stanwyck in *The File on Thelma Jordan*, or he is too close to the frame, as is insurance claims investigator Barton Keyes in *Double Indemnity*. So, in *The Outsider*, DA Ely Houston, a man "crammed with guilty knowledge," solves the murder cases because as a hunchback he lives in the shadows of normal life too; but, because of this, he fails to see that Cross actually committed them.[32]

The formula for noir—guilt, knowledge, desire, deceit, vengeance, a past weighing heavily on the present, and a lone man, an outsider, who, like DA Ely Houston, is "crammed with guilty knowledge"— provides a frame for understanding African-American experience.[33] As Houston tells Cross AKA Addison Jordan AKA Lionel Lane, paraphrasing W. E. B. Du Bois: "Negroes as they enter our culture, are going to inherit the problems we have, but with a difference. They are outsiders and they are going to *know* that they have these problems. They are going to be self-conscious; they are going to be gifted with double vision, for being Negroes, they are going to be both *inside* and *outside* of our culture at the same time. . . . They will become psychological men . . .; they will be centers of knowing" (129). Wright's position as the foremost African-American literary figure of the mid-twentieth century, a center of knowing, who remained outside of his nation's borders, embodies the identity he has cast for Houston.[34] Cross agrees, relishing in the delicious irony that he is talking to a white DA as a black fugitive—a man presumed dead who has just gotten away with murder—a man "haunted" by desire, "desire for desire": "I desire desire, he told himself. . . . And then there came to his mind the memory of the many sultry, smoky nights when he had been drunk with his friends in cheap dives and seen girls like this (25)." Du Bois had argued that Booker T. Washington's program for advancing the race amounted to a suppression of desire: "Mr. Washington distinctly asks that black people give up, at least for the present, three things,—

First political power,
Second, insistence on civil rights,
Third, higher education of Negro youth."[35]

After setting off this list like a poem or chant, he goes on to note the peculiar characteristic of racist logic. Without some sense that "spiritual strivings" will be fulfilled, any African-American citizen "must more and more brood over the red past and the creeping, crooked present, until it grasps a gospel of revolt and revenge and throws its new-found energies athwart the current of advance." (80) The African-American condition of "double consciousness . . . ever a twoness" provides an understanding of social and psychological, historical and private, political and individual subjectivities (2). Richard Wright had traced his own version of the great migration in *Black Boy*, his poetic account *12 Million Black Voices* and his introduction to *Black Metropolis* explored how his personal story was part of a mass history. "The problem of the twentieth century is the problem of the color-line" depicted in film noirs in the stark black-and-white Venetian blind slats crossing the faces of the femme fatale and her doomed fall guy. African Americans already lived the noir world, guilt and betrayal the central theme of their American experience.[36]

Nelson Algren had characterized *Native Son* as a "threat . . . a personal threat. . . . I don't think any white person could read it without being either frightened or angry at the end." Algren went on to detail how the novel should be read: "It's the best detective story I ever read. It can be read like somebody'd read *Serenade* also—just for reading a tough book. But *Serenade* is tough for the sake of being tough, just as Poe is full of horror for its own sake. Moreover *Serenade* ends so damn cold, yours ends warmly. It could be read for its sociology much more convincingly than *Studs Lonigan*. And it's readable as a political novel as well. I read it as a horror story, and kept going on that to the end, where he's alright [sic]. Then I realised [sic] that it was, above the other things, to be read as an humanitarian work." Algren understood just how significant linking racism to horror and detection—to the "tough" writing of James T. Farrell and James M. Cain—was to evincing the proper emotional response in America's readers: "It's the first book I ever came on wherein gruesomeness served a social purpose . . . simply to scare whites into thinking about Negroes."[37] Where Farrell, following Dashiell Hammett in *Red Harvest*, had relied on tough-guy prose, though without the detective per se, to expose the rottenness of lower-middle-class white society, Wright retrieved the horror story and connected it to the crime plot to lay bare the psychology and social pathology of racism. Wright's unraveling of Bigger's "lava-like waves of cultural hunger which reside in the souls of the slow moving men who walk the streets!" was designed to show Bigger "*just as white America had been taught to expect him.*"[38] Racism was a racket corrupting everyone in its orbit—black and white, businessman and Communist.

Yet Wright had been severely criticized for this by Ben Davis in *The Daily Worker*. Wright penned a long response to Mike Gold that ends with a direct comment to Davis, who wrote that in keeping with International Labor Defense (ILD) policy, Bigger should have pleaded not guilty to his crimes: "Ben, all of us who live in the world today and want peace, bread, and freedom are *guilty!* Bigger was *guilty* because he wanted to live. The Germans who work in Underground Germany are *guilty!* The French workers who conspire for peace are *guilty!* The English worker who is against Chamberlain is *guilty!* The American who fights for democracy is *guilty!* You see, Ben I'm using guilt in a much deeper and more suggestive sense than you suspect. Today the world is *guilty!* With the doom of fascism hanging over our heads, we are all *guilty* if we want to live!"[39] If *Native Son*, written while Wright was an active member of the CPUSA, was all about investigating guilt, *The Outsider*, written after his disillusionment, was predicated on the refusal of guilt: 'Because in my heart . . . I'm . . . I felt . . . I'm *innocent.* . . . That's what made the horror," Cross finally tells the District Attorney (440). Refusing to acknowledge, much less accept, the guilt of crime and desire makes Cross Damon an outlaw more despised than Bigger Thomas, who claims his guilt because he wanted to live. But Wright ends *The Outsider* on another note: "He was dead." In this Cross Damon follows Eva Blount, who commits suicide to escape the clutches of the Party, which would "destroy" her because she was "guilty not because of what I've done, but because of what I know" (209). It is knowledge itself that is dangerous in the noir world of American race relations.

DETECTING RACE

In her stunning 1929 novella, *Passing*, Nella Larsen uses the devices of popular pulp fiction and true detective stories collected in 1920s

FIGURE 28. Book jacket from first editon of Richard Wright, *The Outsider* (1953).

dime periodicals like *Black Mask* to retell the classic African-American tale of the tragic mulatto.[40] Since William Wells Brown's 1853 novel, *Clotel*, and especially after the 1896 *Plessy v. Ferguson* decision, racial confusion and its detection have been a central theme in American literature, allowing writers as diverse as Mark Twain and Charles Chestnutt to expose the mysteries of racial categorization that persisted in Jim Crow America. For instance, Melville's "Benito Cereno," anticipating Twain's *Pudd'nhead Wilson*, turns on the problem of race and investigation. And, like Poe's "Purloined Letter," the solution to the mutiny lies in plain sight—but because race codes knowledge so powerfully in American imagination, Amaso Delano can barely detect it. *Passing* updates these nineteenth-century narratives and makes clear that urban life (like *The Outsider*, the novel moves between Chicago and New York) provides further opportunities to transfigure the African-American self. Passing, Clare hides in plain sight of her husband; even her former friend Irene, the "race woman," is not above passing when she needs to escape the hot, dirty streets of downtown Chicago in August to the airy tearoom atop the Drayton Hotel.

The Chicago of Wright's *The Outsider* by contrast is a snow-covered, wind-blown tundra, frozen and icy, the whiteness of its winter setting off Cross Damon from his environment, even as he himself has set himself off from his community. This is a community of betrayed women—his mother, his wife, his lover, a prostitute— and of well-meaning coworkers who sort mail during the night shift at the post office. Wright sets the scene of an urban wilderness, of neon staining the dirty snow, of smoky bars smelling of old whiskey, as Cross listens to his friends chide his "quadruple A program" "*Alcohol. Abortions. Automobiles.* And *alimony*" (3). FDR's Triple A program had been "plowed under" in defeat. Like so many doomed guys haunting noir, Cross is mired in the residues of the Depression, trying to extricate himself from a past that includes a series of women who want things from him he can't provide. Plagued by his inability to control these scheming women—and underestimating their ability to work the system of sex and money exchange—Cross tries to appease first one, then other, of his women: women once desired, who now represent stale legacies, desire's fulfillment. He knows very well that there is always a morning after.

Cross's entanglements with women, his debt, his dislocation set the stage for the noir plot. Double-crossing, two-timing, drinking and self-pity characterize the noir hero—Walter Neff in *Double Indemnity*, Wendell Corey in *The File on Thelma Jordan* are just two classic examples—white-collar workers bored with their routines, drinking too much, caught up in the machinations of women— wives, lovers—who need (or sometimes have) money, their mas-culinity eclipsed by their desire for these scheming female bodies. Wright describes a woman Cross meets slinging hamburgers at a lunch stand by focusing on "her sloping hips . . . her plump arms, her protruding breasts, the gently curving shape of her legs, and the width of her buttocks." In "the bluish haze of tobacco smoke" this girl becomes "woman as body of woman"—pure physicality, and dangerous too . . . "an intractable bitch" (24).[41] In the white city, what begins in desire ends in death—the only end for desire—as the novel begins with dread and ends with decision.[42]

In its African-American retelling, the noir city appears covered with snow and ice—a white out. In *Passing*, Irene (perhaps) murders Clare in the midst of a terrible snow storm; Cross gets away with tossing Joe's murdered body out a cheap hotel window when it lands in a snow drift. Ellison's invisible man, almost killed making "optic white" at Liberty Paints, wanders Harlem's snow-covered streets until he collapses. Where the white noir hero lurks the black night streets of steamy (or more often rainy and foggy) cities; the black noir figure is alone in a bleached landscape devoid of color, his body in constant contrast. The *blanc* world in which Cross Damon lives is no asphalt jungle—more like Siberia. The heart of darkness for an African American is frozen—white as a snow-covered pavement, as a blonde's neckline. It is a city simultaneously full and empty, affording the possibility of invisibility and of chance encounters. Cross Damon, like Melville's Captain Ahab, must confront the horror at the vacuum, the cipher, of whiteness itself.

Like Ellison's invisible man, Cross Damon changes names throughout the novel. Supposedly dying in a fiery train wreck, only to be resurrected as anybody riding a train to New York, Cross reverses the usual drift west. These noir noirs travel north or east, fugitives in search of a presumed freedom. Cross takes the name Addison Jordan when he introduces himself to the radical sleeping-car porter and the hunchback DA who ponders black psychology whom he meets on the train east, then renames himself Lionel Lane to enter the Party. As one who feels a form of outsiderness, his deformed body leaving him a man alone, living behind a kind of veil, Ely Houston, like the detective in *Laura*, lives on the edge of crime, obsessed with its logic and its possibilities. We know he will return. Chance meetings on a train, as in Hitchcock's 1951 *Strangers on a Train*, set the plot in motion for many of these movies. In *No Man of Her Own*, the film version of Cornell Woolrich's novel *I Married a Dead Man*, Barbara Stanwyck, pregnant and deserted on her way to California in pursuit of her lover, survives a train wreck and assumes the identity of a wealthy young wife sitting near her because she has slipped on her wedding ring.

In the classic noir world, the femme fatale—almost always a gleaming blonde hiding a dark past and a cold heart—is coded as noir. She is dark, despite her blonde hair, because of her steaming sexuality. Often, as in *Out of the Past*, she is opposed to the peaches-and-cream blonde whose all-American wholesomeness dims her sexuality. Because the femme fatale moves in the night world, the border world of the underground, she uses her sexuality to acquire wealth, power, and control. She has contacts with the dark ethnically marked men of crime; she figures in the equations of gangsters and mobsters, sings in their nightclubs—like Rita Hayworth in *Gilda*, or Lauren Bacall in *The Big Sleep* or Lizabeth Scott in *Dark City*—gambles in their Mexican casinos—like Jane Greer in *Out of the Past* or Lizabeth Scott in *Too Late for Tears*—and, of course packs a pistol. In Richard Wright's inversion of film noir, white women offer black men the transgressive power of the femme fatale.[43] Like the femme fatale, she is desirable because she is trapped. Jenny, the Chicago prostitute, and Eva, the abstract expressionist in New York, are caught by systems controlling their desire; pimps and brothels, on the one hand, and the CPUSA, on the other, resemble the gangster world. However, these women are truly victims, not scheming, two-timing bitches. These roles Wright reserves for black women. In an early draft of *The Outsider*, Jenny tells Cross her story—and it's straight out of James M. Cain and Horace McCoy: "I got into trouble with a boy and had an abortion. . . . You wouldn't think it, but 'til two years ago, I didn't know where babies came from. . . . I ran off and came to Chicago. The first week I worked in a Greek café; like a dope, I went out with the Greek. He raped me. Sounds crazy, hunh? . . . I want to go to California." To which Cross can only respond: "Movies?"[44] But, as Maud Martha and Lutie Johnson know, running off to Hollywood to star in the movies was not an option for the black women Cross encounters; their roles are circumscribed by race to that of the loyal maid. Recognizing this, however, does not make Cross sympathetic; instead it infuriates him because he is dependent on these same women. Despite the greater obstacles within black women's lives, the nasty femme noire role is appropriated for the black women in Cross Damon's life: his wife, who will never question the circumstances of his death because she can cash in his insurance policy and thus walk away with the house and car paid up and some cash; his lover, who uses her pregnancy and her threats of statutory rape to blackmail Cross into marrying her or paying her off; the "bitch" at the lunch counter who turns her back on Cross. Cross's vengeance against these women paradoxically raises them to central billing.

Cross Damon's rage against black women, like everything else in this novel, is exaggerated, over the top. Cross cannot decide where he stands with these women whom he at once desires and detests. First expressed so acutely in *Native Son*, Wright's fictional violations of African-American women occur in the "white city." The access Chicago provides to white women's sexuality inexorably pushes Wright's African-American men to transgress the racial divide in American culture; crossing the color line violates the spatial and sexual order of America, and cities foster this circulation. Where film noirs recognize the threat of urban white women's mobile sexuality to the middle-class family, Wright also understands how it destabilizes Jim Crow social conventions as well. Knowing beforehand of her betrayal, the white noir hero still cannot resist the enticements of the white femme fatale; his revenge is doubled because he is betrayed and because he knows it. Like the femme fatale, Cross is a knowing betrayer, but of black women as well as white men. His rage is turned on them because they know the nature of his betrayal—desire for the white woman's body. This desire sends America into its pulpy modernity. In Ellison's novel, the crazed veteran warns the young invisible man on the bus north to New York not to seek symbolic freedom in a "dance with a white woman" (136). In phrasing his warning, he admonishes the boy to "learn to look beneath the surface" (137). Racial differences appear only skin deep; however, their imbrication in virtually every aspect of American life, from sexuality to economics, makes them profoundly significant. The fact of depth—that the surface masks hidden, profound, secret, truths—is central to noir sensibility. That not everything can be immediately discerned at first sight became the basis for Ellison's play on invisibility, for Wright's use of the outsider, for Larsen's anatomy of passing. The obsession with racial differences and their subsequent confusions in postwar urban America left DA Ely Houston "wonder[ing] why [he] couldn't detect this feeling of the outsider in the Negroes [he] met" (133). Detecting race—seeing the passing woman as a black woman, as Clare's husband finally does at Irene's Christmas party, or seeing nothing but a black man, as everybody does who meets Ellison's invisible man—is the standard American plot. Like film noir, it always results in catastrophe.

GOING UNDERGROUND

B-movies gave American left-wing writers a venue to reveal the underside of American consumerism and postwar homogeneity.

They pried open the inside of the bungalows in Los Angeles, the crooked deals in the DA's office—"The Story on Page One," as the title of one of the (mercifully) rare Clifford Odets directorial efforts declares—as sources for the noir world that was hiding in plain sight. John Dos Passos and Kenneth Fearing used the bizarre quirks of American news headlines to fill their chronicles of twentieth-century America, commenting by citation on the perversities of daily life. Wright, following his close friend, Ellison—answering Ellison, upping the ante—took the headlines he found in the *Herald* and, using the pulpy plots of postwar true crime and film noir to shape his memory, rewrote his Communist Party story, his city-life story, and turned a genre that Ben Maddow and other Party members had used to expose capitalism to unmask racism in the CPUSA.[45] Chance run-ins with agents from the past, deals and double deals, assumed names, amnesia, changed identities, undercover meetings, over-heard conversations, innuendo, loyalty, and treachery: all are the fantastic plot twists and series of coincidences at the heart of noir. They were also aspects of the secret world, the noir world of the CPUSA, traced deftly by Ellison and turned utterly campy by Wright. The Party, especially as Cross Damon encounters it in New York, begins to resemble the numbers racket that novelist Ira Wolfert had detailed in his 1943 novel *Tucker's People*, which became the source for Abraham Polonsky's *Force of Evil* (1948). It constitutes an alternative, double cross, an underground organization that defies, yet duplicates, the legitimate one on the surface.[46]

When the invisible man first travels with Brother Jack to meet Emma at the skyscraper Chthonian, he notes the "uncanny sense of familiarity" about the soundproof elevator, the doorman, the bronze door knocker, and, most tellingly, the "smartly dressed woman . . . a clip of blazing diamonds on her dress . . . her perfumed softness. . . . I had somehow been through it all before. I couldn't decide if it were from watching some similar scene in the movies, from books I'd read, or from some recurrent but deeply buried dream" (260). For the invisible man, the dream quality of popular fiction and film becomes the central trope describing the increasingly surreal aspects of his situation, even though he reminds us on the first page of his narrative that he is "not a spook like those who haunted Edgar Allan Poe; nor . . . one of your Hollywood-movie ectoplasms" (7). Ellison seems drawn, despite himself, to the very hard-boiled scenarios he claimed to eschew for the "alive" African-American vernacular. But Wright, whose first story was a rewrite of Poe, self-consciously responds to Ellison's call with dozens of scenes from those same Poe stories and Hollywood movies. Cross Damon, already a dead man in contrast to Ellison's invisible man who's still waiting underground, acts out the plots of any number of the "spook" films he saw in "the consoling shadows of movie houses" where he spent time working out the details of his disappearance and new life (140).

The "party" to which Cross Damon is invited—like the one at Emma's, and like any gangster organization featured in noir night-club scenes—offers a complete world equipped with its own logic, its own structure, its own language. As a counterinstitution, it can offer Cross a new name, a new identity, a new residency in the down-town underground of Greenwich Village. Where (white, often Jew-ish) left-wing writers had used the intricacies of criminal enterprises to expose capitalism as the gangster underworld, Wright and Ellison flipped the genre and used it to decry the underworld of the CPUSA, as the counter-institution that mirrors society but is even more ruthless, particularly in its betrayal of African Americans.[47] In the 1940s film noirs spilling into Paris after the wartime embargo was lifted—such as *Criss Cross, The Killers, Out of the Past*, and the gang-ster movies of the 1930s Wright had watched in Chicago, home of Al Capone, "where every 3 A.M. corner looks hired"—gangsters know not only how the system works, but how to work it as well.[48] Armed with a theory of capitalism and a disciplined organization, this is also how the CPUSA operates in these two novels. The gangster world is an urban phenomenon, born in the poor, ethnic ghettoes to coun-teract the traumas of U.S. capitalism and discrimination, paradoxi-cally by taking advantage of the negative model they afforded peas-ant immigrants. This is the essentially American story behind the rise and fall of Little Caesar (with Jewish Edward G. Robinson playing Italian Rico Bandello), Scarface (with Jewish Paul Muni playing Ital-ian Tony Camonte), and that totally Irish Public Enemy (Jimmy Cagney as Tommy Powers) which Francis Ford Coppola revived so magisterially in *The Godfather*. In many ways, during the 1930s, the CPUSA resembled this organizational model as well, comprised of close-knit neighborhood- or workplace- (which usually meant eth-nically-) based units that ironically provided an alternative entry into American culture.

The picture of the Communist Party that Wright paints, like that offered by Ellison, is one of venal deception and raw exploitation. When it needed a black face, the CPUSA was willing to take on a stranger and provide a new identity. But should that stranger question the discipline required of him, he would be left dangling— offered up to rivals, including the police, to protect the organization. Mark Naison claims that despite Harlem Section leader James Ford's antipathy toward him, Wright's status as a Party "influential" meant he was protected from severe discipline by "cultural commissar" V. J. Jerome and others.[49] Naison's reading of Wright's two "Party-inspired" works finds them at odds with official lines about black-white relationships and about class alignments among African Americans during the 1930s. This picture of openness was certainly not the one offered by Wright in his testimonial "I Tried to Be a Communist" and far from the portrait of CPUSA dishonesty animating *The Outsider*. The excesses of betrayal by the CPUSA's leadership—mirrored in the excesses of violence Cross revels in, Gil Blount's abasement of Bob Hunter, his seduction of Eva, his blatant use of Damon, Hilton's insinuations to Houston, Blimin's revelations to Eva—become the excuses for Cross's series of murders. Once Cross was officially declared dead, he lived under an assumed identity, gleaned from a tombstone, a technique he learned from newspaper reports about "underground Communists" (145). Where changing names for African Americans might represent deassimilation, a refusal of a past that had obliterated their past, assuming an Anglicized name, meant, for the immigrant Jews in the Party a chance to assimilate and forget Europe.

Cross also found an organization that could give him access to American culture, not its democratic and egalitarian aspects but rather its seamy and pulpy history. He had found an organization premised on vengeance, betrayal, and lies that freed him to act on his theory that "Maybe man is nothing in particular. . . . May not human life on this earth be a kind of frozen fear of man at what he could possibly be?" (135–6). As a "god [that failed?]," he could commit his series of murders, fall for the white girl, and converse with his nemesis Houston, listening attentively as the D.A. recounted how the double murder of the Communist Party leader Blount and the tellingly named fascist, Herndon (after Angel Herndon who was a cause célèbre for the ILD), were the act of a third man, an outsider,

FIGURE 29. Richard Widmark (Henry Fabian) on the run from Greek gangsters through the ruined streets of postwar London in *Night and the City* (d. Jules Dassin, 1950).

like Cross Damon, like himself. This is what the noir city offered Wright, a space to transgress proper form, including literary form. The postwar city is a ruined zone full of gangsters seeking revenge, in which the lone man who tries to beat them at their own game—like Richard Widmark's Harry Fabian in Jules Dassin's 1950 *Night and the City*—will be tracked down and murdered at dawn because the entire underworld has been mobilized. Pursuit paradoxically afforded Cross Damon an odd freedom.

Toward the end of the novel, Houston increasingly takes on the noir hero's role, tracking Cross Damon as Damon flees his pursuers. Like the gangster's underworld business practices and the CPUSA, structured as a hierarchy, with many layers of subordinates beholden to the boss or central committee, whose power is total, a big city DA's office also operates by intimidation and psychological threat. Where the gang or the CPUSA is a total system that requires a discipline impossible to the noir hero, ironically the New York Distract Attorney's office provides Houston the kind of independent operation necessary for his type. He can maneuver within its confines, finally eliciting a deathbed confession from Cross; but Cross had not escaped the relentless organization—it covered the city and like his life "it was . . . horrible" because it always worked as a system (440). Like the gangster whose Tommy gun shoots up both his rivals and the symbols of legit society, spraying bullets across storefronts and billboards, Wright's pen had become a weapon turned at once against himself, his personal rival (Ellison), the CPUSA, and the system of American racism. A decade before finishing *The Outsider*, he had written critic Mike Gold that "we must use our pens to beat down this wall behind which people are hiding from reality . . . our pens must be cruel towards ourselves. Our pens must become a lash. . . . If some are hurt in this fray, then ship them behind the lines; let them take ether!"[50] Writing as an outsider, from exile, was possible because American culture permeated Wright's world. Its crimes, its movies, its racism, relentlessly followed him across the ocean. Like the noir detective, he was obsessed with the sleaze spreading across the nation, hidden yet quite obviously there. Wright's noir city, a dreamlike city of memory, pried open the workings of two submerged cultures in the United States, African-American intellectual circles and the CPUSA. These two arenas were seemingly off limits to American popular culture and mutually sustained by tense antagonisms; yet, paradoxically, they inspired much pulp fiction in the 1940s and 1950s, such as Chester Himes's *If He Hollers, Let Him Go*, Ed Lacy's *Lead with Your Left*, Ira Wolfert's *Tucker's People*, and A. I. Bezzerides's *Thieves' Market*, the later two themselves inspiring two great film noirs, *Force of Evil* and *Thieves' Highway*. Left-wing pulp truths about American politics were found in the phantasm of the city and its underworld. The city noir and the city of noirs posed a challenge to postwar American middle-class prosperity and racial consensus, revealing the shades of violence still walking the mean streets.

PART 2

WHITE
WORK AND MEMORY

CHAPTER 4

BLANC NOIR: RURAL PULP AND DOCUMENTARY MODERNISM

CON/FRONTING NATIONAL CULTURE

In the wake of the 1995 bombing of the Alfred P. Murrah Federal Building in Oklahoma City, the popular media echoed the sentiments of the city's residents—This sort of thing doesn't happen here; maybe in New York or Los Angeles, but not here in the heartland. Mirroring a belief that the large cities of America are somehow un-American—filled as they are with the poor, minorities, immigrants, gays, and artists—which fueled the defunding and depopulation of urban centers during the three decades between 1960 and 1990, this idea of America's heart as rural, untainted by the ills of the other half, persisted in the American imagination, even when New York, Chicago, and Detroit were centers of commerce, industry, and capital.[1] In the national imagination, America dreams itself as essentially pastoral; the center city cannot hold. Now viewed, an absent space ringed and crossed by expressways zooming suburbanites in and out of their jobs, its emptiness a sign of dangers inherited from the past, the city resembles the nightmare of postwar ruin caught in Jules Dassin's *Night and the City.*[2]

The week following the Oklahoma City bombing coincided with the closing of an important show of documentary photographs at

New York's International Center for Photography. Two exhibits—one of Dorothea Lange's photographs from 1930s through the 1960s, and the other of Joseph Rodriguez's recent multimedia documentary of East Los Angeles gang members' lives—etched divisions not only temporal, but spatial, and ultimately ideological as well. Critic Sarah Boxer contrasted Lange's depictions of noble suffering rural poor (women), whose demeanor spoke of dignified defeat, to the glaring hostility emanating from the stances of Rodriguez's urban (male) gang poseurs.[3] Rodriguez's show included long textual passages by his subjects, the room assaulted the viewers with a wall of sound as gangsta rap pulsed within. For Boxer, the gaping divide between these two shows exposed the limits of the documentary project today. It no longer holds a place in the public imagination, not merely because both observers and photographic subjects are such savvy image mongers, but primarily because, as she says, nothing is to be done for these defiant poor who refuse the pose of noble defeat and seem to aggressively challenge the viewer. (This despite the statistics indicating that many of the faces on the walls were those of the dead—victims of gang warfare and police brutality, of disease and disaster.) Lange had worked for the Farm Security Administration, which used her and others' photographs to persuade the nation of the need for drastic efforts to overcome the devastation of the Depression and the Dust Bowl. Amelioration, a central conceit of documentary, implies the *New York Times* critic, only works for some documentary subjects, not all. Why? To trace how Boxer can assert documentary's failure today to effect change, it is necessary, I believe to go back to the 1930s and follow the contours of its spectacular success.

This chapter examines the residue of documentary rhetoric clinging to various artifacts of noir popular culture in America. But it also looks at the ways in which documentaries during the 1930s—which condition everything we know of the documentary since then—were encrusted with the pulp of fiction. A national popular culture developed from the intermingling of documentary forms and popular (front) sensibilities, most spectacularly through the images of poor rural Americans—the migrant farmers forced off their land who hit the roads West, occasionally banded together huddling in Hoovervilles to share meager wares, or lined up to join work teams digging ditches and building the dams and bridges sponsored by the

Works Progress/Projects Administration (WPA). This image of rural poverty—defeated Southern whites (and occasionally blacks) stalwartly moving across the ruined landscape—provided the content for tens of thousands of photographs coming from the Farm Security Administration (FSA) project, a number of important documentary films funded by the Resettlement Administration (RA), and millions of words in pamphlets, novels, and book-length accounts of the devastation. These government-sponsored visual and literary records covered those left behind in America's quest for modernity. Ironically, this mournful retrospective of a people dispossessed, wandering in "An American Exodus," as Paul Schuster Taylor and Dorothea Lange called it, provided the substance for a modern national public culture that has lasted to this day. In the shock that terrorism happens in the "heartland" of Oklahoma City, we heard again a version of this national fantasy—that good, pure, innocent victims of social and natural catastrophes only reside out there, somewhere recognizable as America's wide open spaces.[4] The terror of city life makes those places outside the centers of media (New York and Los Angeles) or culture (Boston and San Francisco) or industry (Chicago and Detroit) appear at once more American and less violent, as if the two terms were not intimately united.[5]

Joel and Ethan Coen's blanc noir *Fargo* (1996), like their first feature *Blood Simple* (1984), troubles this image of rural purity. Playing with Karl Marx's characterization of "the idiocy of rural life," and with the sensational noir journalism of Truman Capote's *In Cold Blood*, these neo-noirs focus relentlessly on the seeming emptiness and stasis of the mid-American landscape. Roads cut through vast expanses of uniform flatland covered by prairie or snow that resist efforts to alter them. Motels, bars, even giant statues of Paul Bunyan and his blue ox Babe cannot change what Michael Lesy called the "Wisconsin Deathtrip" of small-town life. In fact, even the city itself, gleaming glass-encased Minneapolis, sitting uneasily on the open land, like Oz shimmering just beyond the poppy fields, fails to effect any changes on the horrors of rural homogeneity. However, the two films also track the ways in which the rural is suffused with a modern urban sensibility; in fact, it is a creation of it and, in turn, helps to produce it. Like Marx, Capote, and Lesy, the Coens produce a vision of the rural gothic from the safety of urban zones: Minneapolis, where they come from; Hollywood, where they work.

What *Fargo* instructs us about is the very disingenuousness of claims to an anti-urban rural space. If modern urban centers like Minneapolis or Oklahoma City can turn themselves into Fargo and become far-gone zones outside contemporary culture, it is only because the image of the heartland, as a pastoral space exempt from urban crime, violence, and social upheaval, has been thoroughly appropriated by residents of these urban centers.

In characterizing middle America as a zone apart, both the cynics in the media centers of New York and Los Angeles and the naïve dwellers of the heartland, the residents of Oklahoma City, like Frances McDormand's intrepid pregnant cop from Brainerd, Minnesota, add a melodramatic dimension to the tragic deaths. Oklahoma City's residents become a premodern people, living close to the land, despite highrises, televisions, and freeways. The rural is ever imagined as the last outpost of American exceptionalism where the histories of land development and industrial labor are denied and repressed. Thus it is somehow more disturbing for the country-side—or for cities that define themselves as rural spaces, as the heart-land—to face economic or political or social crises, because modern culture dreams the heartland as the site of unalienated labor and pastoral bliss. The rural, which signifies the last zone of an original white protestant culture in America, is supposed to be an antidote to the problems of modern urban life, with its racial and ethnic minorities, its poverty, grit, and crime, but this very dichotonmy is itself a profoundly modern notion.

Imaging 1930s rural poverty and its devastation paradoxically brought a respite from the traumas of urbanization—a crisis that foregrounded labor unrest, immigration, black migration, and the sense that WASP hegemony had been severely dislodged by the 1930s. The images of tenant farmers surveying their dried-out garden patches from tar-paper sheds provided a familiar narrative through which to mediate the enormous economic and social upheavals following the in wake of the Depression. This tale resonated equally well with such diverse groups as the Communist Party's Popular Front, corporate liberals, New Dealers, and nostalgic populists. By contrast, the image of an urban underworld linked America to a decayed European modernity. The United States, reinvented as a modern industrial space, could ill afford its isolation from global politics; but rural poverty contained within it a vision of democratic vistas from the past—the tenants seemed lifted from another era, as writers such as James Agee "praise" the subtle beauties of kerosene lamplight and the pleasures of a late-night trip to an out-house—even if it were littered with human wreckage.[6]

An earlier documentary impulse, also tied to social reform, ferreted out poverty lurking behind the cities' tenement doors in reeking rooms stuffed full of dark people working day and night in airless spaces. These uses of documentary—to expose poverty and filth in urban America—reminded Americans that New York was little better than the London of the 1840s recorded by Henry Mayhew and Charles Dickens, or the Manchester where Friedrich Engels earned his living and then described in *The Condition of the Working Class in England*. Those nineteenth-century documentaries could rely on first-hand testimony and newspaper accounts to convey the horrors of the industrial town. The invention of the mercury flash brought Jacob Riis into the squalid tenements of the Lower East Side of New York to reveal "how the other half lives."[7] This "other half," ethnic and poor, did not possess the true faces of America; they were foreigners, "street gypsies," as Riis called them. However, by the 1930s, the one-third of a nation—ill housed, ill clad, ill nourished—imaged by the FSA and *Life* photographers would assume a thoroughly American visage. Even the grotesques Margaret Bourke-White pictured in her book *You Have Seen Their Faces* looked disturbingly American, its "pure products" as William Carlos Williams called them: their lives, like their gaunt faces, molded by the contours of this continent's physical geography; its plains and rivers. Documentary rhetoric in the 1930s reworked the form into a vehicle for creating a national popular culture, securing the city, or letting it languish, as grist for pulp fiction, a space apart from the location of political truth, until Hollywood returned to the city in the postwar years with film noir.

Thus I am tracing three divergent but intimately linked exchanges in the 1930s public imagination that set the ground for the film noirs of the 1940s and 1950s: the links between documentary rhetoric and popular imagery; those separating rural from urban America; and the one superintending femininity and masculinity. Left-wing film scriptwriters and directors brought documentary rhetoric, made possible by technology and necessary for ideology—e.g., mobile camera, voice-over narration, melodramatic stories—into the pulp-fiction films of the 1940s and 1950s.[8] At the same time, the Popular Front

FIGURE 30. Dorothea Lange, "Destitute pea-pickers in California, a thirty-two year old mother of seven children." Nipomo, Calif., 1936 [Migrant Mother].

refigured Jefferson's yeoman farmers who had been denied the fruits of democracy by forces of nature and capitalism into a virile working class, and thus knit the Left into a nation drained by economic depression. Each helped to create a corporate- and government-sponsored public sphere.

It is virtually impossible to hear the word "Depression" and not conjure up Lange's iconic "Migrant Mother." Conversely, seeing the image of maternal suffering signifies Depression: ever after a woman holding a near-naked infant and surrounded by vacant-eyed children will sum up human catastrophe.[9] This feminized and rural picture of privation is barely balanced by the more masculinized image linking the Depression to the urban breadline Lange offered America in "White Angel Breadline" in 1933. This powerful rhetorical slippage between image and word is central to my contention that documentary photography, its overabundance, meant that the images circulating of rural poverty escaped no one's view. During the 1930s, over 77,000 photographs were made by the FSA, now held in the Library of Congress; popular phototextual magazines such as *Life*, whose first printing of 380,000 reached 650,000 readers by the seventh week, were widely distributed. America became a modern nation, in a sense, through nostalgia, but its view backward could not find a rosy past in the hollowed out children of migrant mothers.

Images of American rural poverty, especially white rural poverty, worked to convey a national identification with New Deal projects, and thus worked to achieve a coherent picture of America, by foregrounding want and the tenacious efforts of people of the land, often photographed as solitary figures, alone against the elements, to survive with dignity. The images of individual faces, of unique bodies, served to knit together a national public culture through conventional devices of heroic portraiture, landscape, and still life. Looking at privation, at the heart of darkness within the American dream, undid, by avoiding, the xenophobic and regionalist mentalities of an earlier era, precisely because these migrant poor people were neither urban nor ethnic. America became modern, became a mass society, by looking at those whose lives had escaped modernity.

TRUTH-TELLING AND POPULAR MEMORY

In his 1942 Yenan Talks on art and literature, Mao Zedong took time off from the Long March to consider the role of art in the revolution. His prescription for good art was simple yet fraught with the contradictions he sought continually to bring into relief. Art must both "expose" and "extol": first disgorge the horror of oppression, then sing the possibilities of liberation. This was a distillation of the aesthetic platform of the Popular Front, the broad-based coalition forged by the Communist Party to combat fascism. Ironically, Mao's dualism has structured virtually all contemporary political rhetoric about culture from both the Right and the Left (think of the National Endowment for the Arts debacle or the panic generated by gangsta-rap lyrics, on the one hand, and the uproar among gays and lesbians over *Silence of the Lambs* or *Basic Instinct*, on the other) precisely because variations on Popular Front culture remain dominant. They provide the basis of much fretting over positive images and role models and declaiming over the loss of innocence in America's heartland. The didacticism Mao called for assumed art's instrumentality; it is supposed to *do* something. Mao thus rejects the modernist sensibility claiming "l'art pour l'art." However, the effects of the Popular Front, of which Mao's Yenan Talks are a cogent summation, were paradoxically thoroughly modern.

This call for purposefulness, for useful art, which appears so utilitarian, so modern, if not modernist, slips into an antimodern sentimentality when its form is documentary whose explicit purpose is rhetorical. Documentary seeks to convince you that what you see is what you get: the truth. In truth-telling, or in posing as truth tellers, documentaries, however, appeal to raw emotion. Their often naked and direct calls for our engagement are blatant and disturbing. Documentaries are always a bit unseemly. They come about because someone has crossed the line of decorum—snapping pictures of the worst moments, cruelest situations, most extreme events—snatching a bit of another's miserable life and parading it for all to see. It is this perversity that is so fascinating and so disturbing, and that evokes from even the most nostalgic documentary project a pulp modernist effect.

Usually what we consider documentary seems far removed from popular culture. Yet the interpenetration of the two forms has a longstanding history, made most explicit in the 1930s when various technological and economic changes made possible the widespread dissemination of images for practically nothing.[10] In a segment of the PBS series *American Cinema*, B-movie director Joseph H. Lewis (*Gun Crazy*, *The Big Combo*, and other great trashy noirs) noted that the techniques of film noir—mobile camera, location shooting, night-for-night shooting—were the direct result of technical innovations brought about by World War II and the experiences film directors had shooting military footage for night reconnaissance with lightweight 16 mm cameras and new faster film stocks invented during the war. What he failed to mention, however, was a further connection to the documentary expression of the 1930s (as William Stott called it) in the many screenplays written by left-wing proletarian writers, such as *Force of Evil*, Abraham Polonsky's 1948 film of Ira Wolfert's novel, *Tucker's People*; or *Theives' Highway*, Jules Dassin's 1949 film of A. I. Bezzerides's novel *Theives' Market*; or *Body and Soul*, Robert Rossen's 1947 film from Abraham Polonsky's screenplay.

Film noir, that quintessential pulp-fictional style, relied on documentary rhetoric and methods. These, in turn, resulted from new technologies, most spectacularly the ability to print photo and text on the same page and the push to blend short story and journalism in reportage. John Steinbeck's 1939 best-seller, *The Grapes of Wrath*, began as a piece of reportage on California migrant workers written in 1936, which was reprinted in 1937 as a pamphlet to accompany Dorothea Lange's FSA photographs. Richard Wright's publisher, Viking, rushed *12 Million Black Voices* into print after the success of *Native Son*. Wright's poetic documentary text was culled from his personal experience, as well as fieldwork and archival research conducted by the Good Shepherd Community Center in Chicago and accompanied by a selection of FSA photos chosen by Edwin Rosskam. Wright's 1940 novel, *Native Son*, followed a sensational murder trial reported daily by the Chicago papers and clipped for Wright by the young poet and WPA writer Margaret Walker.[11]

These borrowings back and forth between documentary and fiction and, among proletarian and pulp fictions, crossed genders as well. Not only were proletarian writers connected by style and politics to "tough-guy writers," but women's proletarian fiction, because it saw sexuality as central to female experience, reworked romance. Hope Hale Davis remembers writing *True Stories* serialized "confessions" during the 1930s to make ends meet and appeal directly to working-class women by inserting political messages into the softcore pulp.[12] Occasionally women authors were castigated for inserting "smutty vulgar sex stories" or "pornography" into what should have been wholesome tales of proletarian struggle.[13] The commingling of genders, genres, and forms is central to the cultural coworking of 1930s documentary and Hollywood films. Documentary images circulate a rhetoric of truth that has powerfully shaped our ideas about public life, political action, and popular culture by relying on, yet denying, sentiment. The rhetoric of truth so important to documentary is didactic—documentary tells the truth for a purpose; it has become the means to bring previously forgotten men and women into view by objectifying their faces and provoking their political subjectivity. Because its mode of truth-telling so conforms to Mao's "expose and extol" thesis, it is also the prevailing aesthetic for much popular culture.

PULPING NATURAL HISTORY

In a famous piece of rhetorical analysis, Kenneth Burke parses a speech by Franklin D. Roosevelt, who declares to his audience: "You are farmers. I am a farmer too." Burke describes the powerful rhetorical gesture FDR has made by inserting himself—upper-class New Yorker—into the frame of reference of his listeners by invoking a commonality between worlds so vastly separated as to constitute two nations.[14] FDR's design to slip into a rural, even pastoral, ideal in order to persuade his listeners of his sincerity so that he might form a united front with them is part of a long history that reinvents the nostalgic rural past from the vantage of spoiled urbanized present as a response to changing economic and social formations. In the summer of 2001, President George W. Bush enacted his own version of pastoralism when he moved to his ranch in Crawford, Texas, during August to pursue his "working vacation" chainsawing brush, dubbed "Home to the Heartland." Early in Raymond Williams's magnificent study of the changing relations between "the country and the city," he posits the image of the escalator, moving ever backward. This endless retreat seeks to account for the moment when rural bliss was first deformed by the hand of man, leading inexorably to decline from a long lost Edenic past. He cites a few lines from George Crabbe's 1783 poem, "The Village":

> No longer truth, though shown in verse, disdain
> But own the Village Life a life of pain.
> By such examples taught, I paint the Cot
> As Truth will paint it, and as Bards will not.

Williams describes Crabbe's bold move away from a tradition of pastoralism, which revered the country as untouched and Edenic, toward a new realism, a realism that is also pulp fiction, in which the truth of rural life—a life of toil and pain, of exploitation—becomes the basis for a new poetics of truth: a documentary rhetoric.[15] Williams brilliantly shows that although the rural is supposed to be a place modernity, and thus capitalism, left behind, the very ways culture imagines this space apart is precisely a product of the same developments supposedly alien to country life. The idea that rural people are outside modernity is itself a modern notion—one that provides an antidote to the problems of modern life: economic crises, urban decay, and so forth—generated through the images constructed by urbanites. "I'm goin' up the country . . . where the water tastes like wine," sang San Francisco band Canned Heat in 1967. Thus the country is both always idealized as the untouched zone and yet, within modern culture, is also painted as the site of truth, a truth found in the detailed documentary exposition of the labor and expropriation attendant upon making the country seem a space apart from capitalism. FDR and George W. Bush, both from East Coast patrician families, can claim to be farmers because they have access to a history of images of rural life drawn by those far removed from it. Dorothea Lange may have begun her documentary career walking the streets of San Francisco, shooting the disgruntled men she found waiting for work or protesting its exploitations, but the project that hired her to photograph poverty was the *Farm* Security Administration. What the government needed to persuade mostly urban middle-class Americans to support the New Deal were not images of a dangerous urban army of the poor; instead it reclaimed the vanishing land and its way of life as its core subject. While many relief programs targeted the urban poor, the documentary projects generated by and for the New Deal envisioned the United States as a series of rural regions inhabited by a folk population fast disappearing because of the forces of nature itself.

A desire to trace the prehistory of the dust bowl led Pare Lorentz to invest his 1936 documentary *The Plow That Broke the Plains* with a vision of natural forces at war with social and economic developments; his film was an act of preservation, even as it tracked the disappearance of topsoil blown off by incessant winds and excessive machinery. Lorentz left the investigation of faces to the still photographers. His two films—criticized by *Plow's* left-wing cinematographers Leo Hurwitz, Paul Strand, and Ralph Steiner for leaving out the human dimension and so the politics of land abuse and labor exploitation—exposed the larger ecological impact of wind, sun, and rain on the great central plains of the American continent. Shortsighted irrigation projects resulted in land damage, but profits, cities, and war—all human inventions—were destroying the land's capacity to renew itself. Lorentz's film, made through financing by the FSA and Resettlement Administration (RA), was meant to help various extension agents devise plans for alternative land use and convince local populations to implement them. Rural offices, however, bristled at the depiction of Texas as a barren zone and sought to have *Plow* suppressed.

A year later, Lorentz's vision of water covering over two thirds of the continent also submerged human faces into a saga of rain, floods, and erosion. In *The River* (1937), however, a solution worked by government agencies seemed likely to succeed. The great dams of the Tennessee Valley Authority (TVA) were among the most popular New Deal projects, employing thousands and bringing visible evidence of modernity—huge modernist structures of reinforced concrete—to the heart of rural America. Lorentz's majestic view of the American continent stressed its openness. The heartland was meant to remain empty; wind, sun, rain would never be vanquished. The scene of a demurely dressed woman, wearing a clean white apron and heels, bravely sweeping her porch steps as her baby sits amid the rising sand dunes forming around an abandoned plow called into question the hospitality of this continent a hundred years after European settlers pushed West. It is also a rare glimpse at the human figure stranded within this immense and barren landscape.

This image, like Lange's stark portrait, "Woman of the High Plains, Texas Panhandle, June 1938," offers a stoic, even heroic, refusal to succumb to natural forces. In these pictures, mothers still sweep and worry about their children even as the land around them threatens to swallow them up. In her attention to the "social scene of our time," Lange was limning the rhetoric of documentary visually. A few years later, in a catalogue put together by Ansel Adams for the 1940 San Francisco World's Fair, Lange verbally defined the genre:

> Documentary photography records the social scene of our time. It mirrors the present and documents for the future. Its focus is man in his relation to mankind. It records his customs at work, at war, at play, or his round of activities through twenty-four hours of the day, the cycle of the seasons, or the span of a life. . . . It is concerned with methods of work and the dependence of workmen on each other and on their employers. It is pre-eminently suited to build a record of change. Advancing technology raises standards of living, creates unem-

ployment, changes the face of cities and of the agricultural landscape. The evidence of these trends—the simultaneous existence of past, present, and portent of the future—is conspicuous in old and new forms, old and new customs, on every hand. . . . Documentary photography invites and needs participation by amateurs as well as by professionals. Only through the interested work of amateurs who choose themes and follow them can documentation by the camera of our age and our complex society be intimate, pervasive, and adequate.[16]

In her call for repetitive cycles chronicling changes over time—a day, a year, a life—and her assertion that amateurs as well as professionals record the simultaneous existence of past, present, and future, Lange was explicitly linking documentary photography to history. She saw in documentary the ability to link the residues of the past and of nature to the technologies of the present. In fact, it was through this technology—amateur photography, undertaken by those trained through reading *Life* magazine and seeing Hollywood films—that an image of America as a nation would emerge. Lange's 1940 manifesto also points to the ways in which the great FSA and *Life* photographers who produced "photo-textual books" during the Depression decade were responding to competing currents already traced by Hollywood.[17] Still and moving images, documentary and pulp genres, infected each other; they required each other in much the same way as rural imagery fed urban ideals. Those capturing the heartland were not its native sons or daughters. Images of rural poverty and collective labor—especially those staged to fulfill a national fantasy—eased the traumas of the Depression, insuring a troubled nation that neither poverty nor collectivity were threats to American political culture; rather they were signs of its permanence.

FINDING FARGO

Tensions embracing the dark and comic sides of the Depression, that is, anxieties brought up by urban ethnicity and rural poverty, continue to haunt popular culture as the discourse surrounding the Oklahoma City bombing shows. A modern urban center such as Oklahoma City can define itself as the heartland through the legacy of 1930s documentary rhetoric. Because of the ravages, grotesques,

FIGURE 31. Two-page layout from a cover story photo-essay on New Deal, Montana, in the first issue of *Life*, Margaret Bourke-White (November 1936). Note photo duplication.

and stoicism imaged by Lange, Bourke-White, and Evans, we believe it is somehow more disturbing for the countryside to face social, economic, and political upheavals. The heartland, repository of pastoral simplicity, site of documentary truth, not poetic invention, escapes the pulp fiction of urban life, even if cities with populations of more than a million can be found there.

After the Second World War, film noir reimagined the city—this time that quintessentially Western city, destination of the displaced tenant farmers from Oklahoma and Arkansas, sunny Los Angeles—as a dire, claustrophobic space where the individual will always be subsumed by the machinations of the larger immoral network of crime, guilt, and complicity.[18] These visions of terror erupting anywhere, coming after the revelations of the Holocaust and the destruction of European Jewry, were written and directed by the very same (often left-wing Jewish) artists who helped forge a countervision of proletarian resistance in the organization of violent ethnic gangsters, on the one hand, or the muscled shoulders standing in class-conscious solidarity, on the other. These left-wing visions of the machinery of urban solidarity never entered the popular imagination the way that those of rural privation had. However, as the Depression leaked into war preparation, and mobility seemed more purposeful—not dislocation, but mobilization—a new vision of a female urban space emerged. Dorothy Arzner's 1940 parody of Busby Berkeley's 1930s musicals, *Dance, Girl, Dance*, with a screenplay by literary radical Tess Slesinger, traces the darker side of chorus-line work. Sexual exploitation and objectification, competition not cooperation among the girls on the line, commodification and mechanization of a creative process, are both embraced and blown wide open in the ironic, darkly cynical tale of Maureen O'Hara's portrayal of ballet dancer Judy as burlesque "stooge" for Lucille Ball's "Tiger Lily White," a performer with "oomph." This noir musical rehearsed the divisions between documentary and pulp, rural and urban, popular and elite, and presaged the powerful bad girls of film noir.

By war's end, both the city and women's bodies had become sinister but intriguing again, filled with hidden vices and dangers lurking around each curve. The perils of an alien urban landscape and modern America had been temporarily allayed by images of rural poverty in 1930s documentaries, but they had never really gone away. James Agee's ventriloquized ruminations on Annie Mae Gudger's sexuality formed a pulp fiction out of the lives of these impoverished tenant women. Yet, almost immediately, even the more radical visions of those working for the FSA were tamed. Within a few years of Lange's "Migrant Mother" image of rural poverty and need, FSA photography head, Roy Stryker, was directing his photographers to find more wholesome images in the kitchens and clinics of Pie Town, New Mexico, and the new suburban Greenbelts that welcome the Joads at the end of Hollywood's *Grapes of Wrath*. Roy Stryker's job, now that the New Deal projects were in place, was not to convince middle-class Americans of the need and privation driving New Deal programs but instead to demonstrate their successful transformation of the face of rural poverty into a horn of plenty. One reason Agee and Evans's book, with pictures shot in 1936, was such a failure when it finally appeared in 1941 was that on the eve of America's entry into World War II, Stryker was directing photographer Jack Delano to gather "autumn pictures . . . cornfields, pumpkins . . . emphasize the idea of abundance—the 'horn of plenty'—and pour maple syrup over it."[19] The brief moment when rural poverty could be seen and spoken of in polite company was over; however, it was precisely its fact and its visibility that forged an American national identity with the rural heartland as a central icon of authenticity.[20]

The image of the blown-out, plowed-out family whose integrity was destroyed by weather, technology, and monetary policies was in stark contrast to both Hollywood's violent underworld and the working-class family whose burly rippling musculature would valiantly march forward into a new future free from hunger and exploitation promoted by the Communist Party USA. The images of wreckage and disaster won out within historical memory. Hugo Gellert's *New Masses* cartoons of muscled workers are just that, caricatures. The heroic face masks Hollywood's noir nightmare of anomie and alienation that quickly reappeared after the War. Properly modern American tragedies, like proper Americans, did not dwell in the corrupt mire of the modern cities made up of aliens whose ethnicity could be marked by Hollywood—as gangsters and B-girls—but remained unnoticed by the government documentaries. The subjects of 1930s documentaries were the last remnants of a rural order of dignity and pride and hard work, which, white or black, had its roots in the soil of the Midwest or the South. The endurance of the suffering tenants caught by Evans and Lange and the contorted figures of privation snatched by Bourke-White appear full repositories of truth despite the distorted, staged, rearranged, and posed elements of each image. Because each says "I am truthful," these visual accounts of an ever-receding past hold power over our present imaginations and memories. They do so through their content—their straightforward presentation of space, objects, people, and form—their black-and-white simplicity, purity of line, depth of field. These images serve as the backdrop for film noir, which relocated the probing camera's eye from the emptying land to the corrupt city, tracking the sons and daughters of those migrant mothers after they returned from war to settle into the supposedly comfortable bungalows lining the Los Angeles hills. Documentary's power still forms our vision, as the media continue to "expose and extol" both the political truths and pulp fictions of postmodern America by dividing the country from the city, even if it is called Fargo.

CHAPTER 5

MELODRAMA/MALE DRAMA: THE SENTIMENTAL CONTRACT OF AMERICAN LABOR FILMS

LABOR'S MELODRAMA

"Do not ask me to write of the strike and the terror. I am on a battlefield. . . . But I hunch over the typewriter and behind the smoke, the days whirl, confused as dreams," declared the young Tillie Lerner (Olsen) during the 1934 San Francisco general strike.[1] In this classic example of reportage, the division between observation and participation, between fact and fantasy, has broken down. "I am on a battlefield," not merely as a war correspondent but as one of the combatants. In Florence Reece's ballad trumpeting the news of the 1934 Kentucky coal strikes in bloody Harlan County, one must decide "Which Side Are You On?": "if you go to Harlan County / there is no neutral there, you'll either be a union man / or a thug for J. H. Blair."[2] The labor struggles of the 1930s had clearly defined battle lines, and everyone sympathetic to workers knew which side was right; yet the engaged writer, knowing she was on a battlefield, was left "behind the smoke . . . confused as dreams" by her double duty—to march and to type. Contemporary labor documentaries owe much to the literary genre of reportage, especially as practiced in the 1930s by committed journalists and worker correspondents. This form collapses distinctions between reader and participant by placing the observer/writer in the midst of the action as it happens; and because the two poles are clearly marked—you either are a union man or a thug—sentiment lodges on the side of labor. Florence Reece and the other balladeers could march *and* sing, but writers eventually left the line to tell the story. By leaving the line, the writer momentarily escaped the conflict, confusing her class allegiance; however, an either/or situation demands that both reporter and reader must choose sides within a dichotomous class structure. In reportage, documenters serve not only to witness, but to fight, like Frederick Douglass, who stresses that his indoctrination into the "hell of slavery" began when he recognized his role as "a witness and a participant" and ended only after he battled the overseer Covey, vowing never to be whipped again.

During the 1930s, many writers forged these sentimental contracts as they journeyed in search of "the trouble" befalling a nation suffering through extreme economic crisis.[3] In many ways, reportage mediated the feminized stance of the novelist—whether male or female, the writer was viewed by the Left as effete, bourgeois—and that of the hard-boiled reporter, as tough masculine worker, because these writers did not simply report from the sidelines; they put their bodies on the line. In modern times, radical intellectuals often have romanticized the industrial worker as the authentic vehicle of revolution. Moving into workers' homes to march with them became a standard activity of radical journalists following the strikes in coal, rubber, and steel during the 1930s. For instance, in 1934, a young Smith College graduate, Harriet Woodbridge, writing as Lauren Gilfillan, traveled to the coal fields of western Pennsylvania to report on the strikes there. She entered the struggle only to be reminded that she was an outsider. *I Went to Pit College* described her position as radical journalist within a mining community, riven by rival unions, political enmity, class conflict, and racial, ethnic, and religious divisions, which at least coalesced around a mutual suspicion of outsiders, especially those sporting linen dresses. Her book, widely reviewed and often denounced as sentimental tripe and a melodramatic portrayal of middle-class feminine thrill-seeking, was also praised for a willingness to bare herself as a voyeur and explore these class confusions, as it provided a vivid portrait of a community torn apart by labor strife.[4] Reportage, "in no way content simply to depict facts," risked sentimentality, according to Georg Lukács, because it "does indeed appeal to our feelings, both in its depiction of the facts and in the call to action."[5] Too much investment in one side of the battle, too much detail, a fetishistic "portrayal" of the victims of capitalism, however, got in the way of clear-sighted "scientific" analyses of the prevailing economic and political crisis. Because it opens the way for tears, reportage treads a fine political line, locating sentiment in the house of labor.

Sentimentality emerges in eighteenth-century England under curious and contradictory conditions. On the one hand, discussions about the proper use of tears were linked to a long history of antirational conservatism, starting with the embarrassingly sentimentalized male philosophers, such as Edmund Burke, resisting the Enlightenment revolutions in France. Claudia Johnson argues persuasively that "the welfare of the nation and the tearfulness of private citizens—actual as well as fictional—were understood in the 1790s to be urgently interconnected."[6] I would add that this was no less true of the 1990s. On the other hand, the rise of the bourgeois state required a break with the teary-eyed men who maintained a chivalric honor unnecessary under a new democratic regime. Men's tears are throwbacks to an era when the spectacle of men crying could be understood as part of the workings of an aristocratic order of "sentimentality [under which] the prestige of suffering belongs to men" (17). Within the culture of middle-class sensibilities, women became the vessels of feelings. The new forms of gendered subjectivity developing within bourgeois culture, feminist literary historians such as Nancy Armstrong, Cathy Davidson, and Jane Tompkins argue, require the "cultural work" of women's sentimentality to establish the modern subject, a being drenched in emotion and encased in privacy during the age of revolution and after. Sentiment became private because its public expression threatened social order. According to Raymond Williams, what Burke resisted was the incursion of the rational state into zones previously cordoned off as civil society. Emotions publicly displayed by citizens of a democracy led to the frightening spectacle of mobs and masses in the streets.[7] Bourgeois culture thus contained sentimentality within women's domain. Its leakage into "the methods of science" appropriate to journalism,[8] especially in the service of that most melodramatic public staging—the strike—threatened to undo political authority. That would seem a good thing if one's goals, like those of the literary radicals of the 1930s, were to overthrow a failed capitalism.

However, in the rhetoric of both the Left and modernism, bourgeois culture as a whole had taken on the sentimentalized characteristics of feminized, aristocratic decadence—an image repeated in IWW iconography, socialist cartoons, Thorsten Veblen's *Theory of the Leisure Class*, communist pamphlets, modernist manifestoes, and even in Teddy Roosevelt's speeches.[9] Only the heroic workers (or modernist poets, but that's another story) standing shoulder-to-shoulder in solidarity could break with sentimentality and usher in a new world. The working stiff, like the freelancing detective and the mobile femme fatale, offers a tough resistance to the decay of modern life. This picture of masculine triumph had its own sentimental logic that also dates from the eighteenth century. "The first great tribune of the industrial proletariat," William Cobbett, declared, according to Raymond Williams, collective action to be "a movement of the *people's* own," a concerted response to the "masters [who] combine against them," leaving them barely able to feed themselves and their families (*Culture and Society*, 3, 17). If a strike provides a stirring, emotionally-saturated, political tableau, its visual economy owing much to melodrama, where the forces of good and evil are decisively separate, that is because since the late eighteenth century, the working class has been cast in heroic and victimized poses.[10]

In twentieth-century America, the most powerful icons of this dual image of the working class have been found within the traditions of the documentary photography inaugurated by Lewis Hine. Hine's 1932 children's book, a photographic record called *Men at Work*, subtitled "Photographic Studies of Modern Men and Machines," offers a vision of labor poles apart from his earlier images of children dwarfed by massive looms. This volume carefully integrates the male body into the machinery of modern construction (many of the images are from Hine's on-location photographs of the Empire State Building rising from the streets of Manhattan as it was built). The scale of the masculine body establishes the size of the machine it works. Some of the "men of courage, skill, daring and imagination" are "heroes," says Hine paraphrasing Marx in his introduction, "the spirit of industry." Heroes because "cities do not build themselves; machines do not make machines. . . . [R]eal men make and direct them."[11] Hine shoots individual men intimately curled over and around their tools, but he also provides a vision of collective labor in shots showing how modern work requires cooperation among many men on the job.[12] This highly erotic, actually homoerotic, vision of men and machinery became a staple of documentary, culminating in Robert Flaherty's 1941 *Louisiana Story*, where the arrival of the enormous oil derrick moves the young boy to explore the world of machinery as he had once covered the natural landscape. The boy, embraced (literally) by this all-male world, ultimately integrates nature and machine and his body in the penultimate shot as he curls himself around the "christmas tree," the capped oil pipes, left standing in the bayou. Flaherty's film was hardly a left-wing celebration of machinery and labor; Standard Oil footed the bill for this "fantasy," as Flaherty referred to it.

Hine's 1932 photographs initiated a visual rhetoric of sentimentality that cloaked workers bodies and gigantic machinery in a celebration of the collective labors required to build America. In this, his images were visual updates of Melville's ecstatic whale-rendering scenes in *Moby-Dick*. This new sentimentality contrasted with Hine's earlier portraits of America's working victims suffering under capitalism's brutality. The recourse to sentiment among labor's documenters is tied to confusing gender codes, which have historically dictated who can and who cannot cry, and to conflicting class and national allegiances, which also involve delegating the proper expression of sentiment. Modern national allegiance requires tears—one need only watch any athletic segment or any commercial during NBC's broadcast of the 1996 or 2000 Olympics to get a shorthand lesson in the centrality of tears to national identity. We watch as athletes cry in victory or sob in defeat; we cry with them at home, our living rooms linked mysteriously through the flowing tears. Like nations, class formations, precisely because they require imaginative communities linked through ideas and sentiments, resemble these emotion-laden fantasies. Class codings can be made invisible with proper grooming and elocution, so says Henry Higgins to Elizabeth Doolittle in *My Fair Lady*, because unlike sexual or racial differences, they are not inscribed on the bodies' surfaces. For this reason, class is a slippery analytic category, even among feminists otherwise sensitive to nuanced gender, sexual, and racial differences. In the differing views of Burke and

Cobbett, workers combined, either sinisterly as a mass or rationally as a class, in response to the workings of the capitalist state, a state formed in the interests of one class, the bourgeoisie, in part by cordoning off sentiment. This is also why the rhetoric of sentimentality—so crucial to modern national and class formations—still circulates within labor documentaries, even those questioning the form of documentary itself.

ROGER & ME(N)

In differing ways, Michael Moore's *Roger & Me* (1989) and Barbara Kopple's *American Dream* (1990) tap this long-standing tradition of figuring class conflict through gendered discourses of sentimentality.[13] *Roger & Me*, ever ironic about documentary, General Motors, and government policies that favor corporate greed over human need, cannot escape its heritage. In the 1930s, Hugo Gellert, a cartoonist for the left-wing journal *New Masses*, illustrated a selection of writings from Karl Marx's *Capital* with his drawings of solidly muscled workers.[14] The butt of in-jokes within the Left, these heroic figments of radical imagination were fantasies of excessive virility.[15] A strong working class could overcome both the crisis of capitalism and the malaise the lost generation was suffering after the First World War. A heavy load to bear—making the revolution and saving American masculinity at once—this construction of the manly worker occluded a vision of the working-class woman, who, in Gellert's drawings, bulge with hefts of muscle and a muscled breast nourishing her buffed-out baby boy, the kind of "revolutionary girl" celebrated in proletarian poems by such forgotten poets as H. H. Lewis. By contrast the bourgeoisie was a feminized and decadent class: corpulent men stuffed into top hats and tails, like the banker on the Monopoly game, sucking the vitality from the labor of others; or desiccated spinsters whose dried up lives were doomed to disappear once the new working-class family took possession of its rightful place.

It was a ludicrous picture then, when at least a quarter of the work force was female. In the 1980s, it should have been trotted out only as parody; yet *Roger & Me* returns to these stock types with a straight face to cast its saga of deindustrialization. Almost all the scenes with women target the lavish lifestyles of the rich and infamous of Flint, Michigan, and feature chiffon-dressed women sound-

FIGURE 32. Hugo Gellert, "Primary Accumulation," from *Karl Marx 'Capital' in Lithographs* (1934).

FIGURE 33 Hugo Gellert, "The Working Day," from *Karl Marx 'Capital' in Lithographs* (1934).

ing like Marie Antoinette before the revolution. The one exception—the lonely rabbit breeder whose uncanny pragmatism (pets or meat) seems demented at best, vicious at worst—clearly survives outside the economy of contemporary American late capitalist relations. She is a holdover from another era and another place, perhaps the mountains of Kentucky from which many autoworkers migrated during and after the Second World War, like a character out of Harriet Arnow's 1954 novel, *The Dollmaker*, devastated by city life and industrial work discipline.[16] Moore is drawn to this odd woman; she reappears as the star of his short sequel, *Pets or Meat: The Return to Flint* (1993), which also aired on PBS stations.[17]

Sentimentality requires a hero, just as melodrama demands clearly defined sides. Moore is a contemporary (anti-)hero, a goofy guy who has shed his class origins just barely because his skills lie in intellectual labor—the production of words and images—not the backbreaking assembly work of his father's generation.[18] His film unveils "an anti-aesthetics of failure in contemporary documentary,"[19] an absence that looms large in this story of contemporary labor: no strikes; no "men at work." What *Roger & Me* finds instead is lack: the lack of union militancy; the lack of work, as thousands of autoworkers have been laid off; the lack of industry, as plants close and move their operations overseas. Flint, Michigan, stands as an emblem of militant union organizing; site of the 1936 sit-down strike, the most effective use of the strategy in American history, whose stirring images of men curled amid their tools and machinery asleep on the shop floor galvanized generations of organizers. Josephine Herbst had caught this scene, connecting it to the rise of "the worker-writer," when she closes her 1939 novel, *Rope of Gold*, with a striking autoworker penning his autobiography.[20] As a fantasy melding industry with aesthetics, like a bridge girder or a poured concrete dam, this quintessential modernist figure—an idle worker sprawled across the plant floor recording the details of the strike for the *Daily Worker*—has no place in a deindustrializing economy. Even the sitdown strike is ineffective against plant closures. The story has shifted elsewhere to the corporate and financial boardrooms where the flows of capital not productivity (which requires bodies) are key to profits.

Without the bodies of workers at their machines or the masses on the picket line, Moore's saga comes down to a lone quest for an elusive figure, General Motors CEO Roger Smith. Smith's continual absence is one more hole in the fabric of American industry; a boss can no longer be embodied either. The rotund cigar-smoking capitalist who lorded over a semifeudal "industrial valley" has also been displaced.[21] For example, in the new world order of virtual strikebreaking, to combat striking unions at Detroit's two largest newspapers, *The Detroit News* and *The Detroit Free Press* no longer needed to hire thugs. They set up home pages on the World Wide Web denouncing union tactics on the picket lines and praising those who cross the lines, including stories about the terrific food served to those who show up for work.[22] Moore fails to get close to the real boss—Roger Smith—so he goes for the cheap shot, the vacuous country club wives of Chevy's middle managers who declare Flint a wonderful city and wonder why everyone is complaining.

If the CEO cannot be located, neither can the worker; he is neither on the picket line nor on the assembly line. Charlie Chaplin's working-tramp represented the modern anti-hero of labor—dwarfed by the machine, encompassed by the masses. The counterpart to the Tramp's incorporation into the machine of capital is Chaplin's wonderful overhead crane shot, which offers a visual joke on working-class unity as the Tramp, after picking up a red flag that has fallen off the back of a carriage, unknowingly leads a demonstration of protesting workers only to find himself beaten and jailed by the police. Instead, Moore finds his postmodern worker-tramp in Ben Hamper, a contemporary Midwestern worker-writer, in the tradition of Jack Conroy, the "rivethead" whose column had previously appeared in Moore's alternative newspaper, *The Flint Voice*, now a novelist. Hamper explains, while aimlessly shooting hoops, that he was laid off with a medical disability because he had cracked up on the shop floor. He feels like a fraud compared to the women he met in the hospital—suicidal and depressed—whose mental illnesses were somehow more real, caused as they were by domestic, personal troubles. The public world of work is not supposed to cause mental breakdowns, but without the masses to provide a collective shelter for the worker, his psyche becomes as fragile as a housewife's.[23] Moore empathizes with his high-school buddy; they share history, each with a middle-aged, working-class inelegance that has no place, despite their new roles as intellectuals, circulating language and images.[24]

Moore's film, picked up and distributed by Time-Warner, sparked a major debate within corporate boardrooms and across business and industry pages;[25] his wry humor showed up GM as callous, the Flint Chamber of Commerce and Mayor's Office in the pockets of GM, and a citizenry suffering from delusions and privation so extreme that "recovery" appears unlikely.[26] Moreover, his decision to tamper with history, revising chronology to suit his narrative, caused a minor stir.[27] Moore's recourse to staged melodrama—placing Ronald Reagan in Flint in the midst of the shut down—gave ammunition to GM, which wanted to defuse the film's effects.[28] But Moore's manipulations came from a long tradition of documentary filmmaking. As he remarked: "With nonfiction, you have no idea when you go out to shoot what's going to happen, and you have to figure it all out once you're in the editing room."[29] Dziga Vertov's scissors cutting celluloid in *Man With a Movie Camera* had foregrounded the editing process as crucial to *Kino-Pravda*—a job requiring the hands of his female assistant editor, Yelizaveta Svilova. With absence—no jobs, no organization, no boss—as capital flows elsewhere and workers sit idle, its central feature, Moore's postmodern portrait of labor still rests on the prehistory of modern male worker's melodramas, embodied by the two forces—Roger, endlessly beyond the camera, and M(oor)e, endlessly performing for it.[30]

SPAM'S HOME

American Dream follows Kopple's magisterial view of worker solidarity in *Harlan County, USA* (1976) with a darker vision of the contradictions and complexities of contemporary union organizing in the heartland. Despite the ostensibly amiable atmosphere of Garrison Keillor's Lake Woebegone, Austin, Minnesota's, Hormel plant, and the efforts of meat packers at Local P-9 of the United Food and Commercial Workers (UFCW) to maintain union solidarity, *American Dream* presents a wretched scene. Anticipating the gruesomeness of *Fargo*, it lends bloody Harlan County a nostalgic glow. Kopple's complex gesture in *American Dream* traces the present conditions for union militancy in a typically Midwestern industry—hog processing—during this era of multinational corporate flight; its story of the multiple forces working at odds complicates the melodrama of union men vs. scabs staged in *Harlan County, USA*. The 1984–85 strike against the Hormel plant dramatized how the arena has been complicated with a proliferating cast whose allegiances and identities are not so easily coded as good or bad. This corrective seems in part a response to critiques of her earlier film as overly humanistic; perhaps deindustrialization forces another cinema as much as another politics.

American Dream begins with shots of the hog kill room, which Kopple was able to film with a hidden camera by posing as a New

York high-school student doing a report on the meat industry. The process of turning pigs into bacon is dangerous and disgusting work; the work site and work process, which are not central to the film's story, focusing as it does on the intricacies of local and international organizing, bargaining, and the strike and its aftermath, establishes the source of the action. If the establishing shot of the typing pool on the bottom floor of the Pacific All-Risk Insurance Company in *Double Indemnity* reminds us of the repetitive boredom of white-collar office work that contributes to film noir, the assembly line at Hormel presents pure horror and exploitation. In the brief encapsulated history the film provides, we hear Reagan's "off-the-cuff" remark about the economy: "I'm prepared to tell you it's a hell of a mess." Jesse Jackson then tells a packed crowd in 1986, "[W]hat Selma was to the civil rights movement, Austin is to the movement for workers' rights." The scene shifts two years earlier and follows two men past a playground where children swing and climb and slide to the front door of a large house where the wife of a Hormel executive lectures the men to be grateful they now receive $8.75 an hour: "When we were your age . . ." she begins, but the men cut her off: "Give us a fair shake, like you got." Although a town like Austin represses its class structure, visible evidence lies everywhere. In Austin, 22,000 people live in "a little world by ourselves," Hormel counsel Nyberg explains, echoing the boosterism found at the town's border: "Enjoy Austin, where the good life is here to stay." To some extent this civic hype rings true; as the Hormel promotional film Kopple inserts into hers outlines, the social contract the corporation struck with its workers decades ago guaranteed good wages, lifetime benefits, and profit sharing. But the ragged years of recession, corporate mergers, and wholesale assault on unions fostered by Reagan's administration have taken their toll. "Let us live in our house," pleads one woman stuffing envelops at the union hall, "our $32,000 house." The company that makes that quintessential American product, SPAM, staple of United States Army K-rations during World War II, now expresses "the mood of the industry," as CEO Knowlton declares; despite record 29.5 million dollar profits in 1984, Hormel workers receive a 23 percent wage cut.

Thus the stage is set for the nightmare to unfold; a dark romance Kopple scripts around the struggle of a "new family," as the striking P-9ers describe their changed relationships to each other and to their formerly paternalistic employer, to come to terms with the betrayal by the new "father," Jay Hormel, son of the corporation founder who instituted the "social consciousness" of the company. But the real battle in Kopple's eyes involves a conflict waged by out-siders, distant cousins arriving to contest the company's will: on the one hand, Ray Rodgers, New Yorker and vegetarian head of Corpo-rate Campaign whose successful national boycott of J. P. Stevens Co. finally resulted in union recognition in many southern textile plants; and, on the other, Lewie Andersen, hard-bitten vice-president of UFCW, former hog butcher and tough negotiator, who has finally accepted the UFCW's strategy of across-the-board contracts to bring up the wage floor in nonunion meat-packing plants. These giants battle on a grand scale for the hearts and minds of the P-9ers; their personalities are so charismatic that they seem to be determin-ing the action, sweeping the quieter, restrained Minnesotans along with them. Yet the determination of the strikers and their families is the real story: they keep on with the strike even after P-9 has been decertified by the UFCW; they keep gaining support from unions around the country even after the AFL-CIO, America's central union organization, discourages its affiliates from offering solidarity; they keep showing up at the picket lines even after the National Guard has been called out and some local members defy the strike. Playing out against the bleak snow-covered landscape is the new "American dream" of community and family and their fracture, with brother turned against brother, another civil war with the inevitable result.[31]

Kopple's fascination with grand melodramatic historical epics owes as much to D. W. Griffith as the fragile voice of Hazel Dick-ens's ballads in *Harlan County, U.S.A.*; but in Austin the heroes are less pure and villains less obvious, if more devious. Unlike the coal miners' strike in Kentucky, where "you either are a union man or a thug for D. H. Blair," the complexities of fighting on three fronts—against the corporation, against the state, and against the union's international—complicate the dichotomized narration of melo-drama. However, this multiplying set of powerful forces allied against the tiny P-9 local does not automatically call up greater sym-pathy for the strikers. Instead, those who gave up and crossed the picket line in the face of community censure invoke the rhetoric of sentimentality. Shedding tears is central to the labor documentary—

Lawrence Jones's martyred body and his mother's wailing marked the turning point for the United Mine Workers in *Harlan County, U.S.A.*—but in *American Dream* it is the scabs who mourn themselves as outcasts. The question is: Do we care about these crying men?

American Dream had its public debut in Minneapolis (following its premiere in Austin) as a fundraiser for the Pittston miners' strike. The stage was crowded with Kopple, Senator Paul Wellstone, author of the Replacement Worker Bill barring the hiring of permanent replacements for strikers, and striking miners from Pittstown, West Virginia, as well as the remaining striking P-9ers, still out of work yet offering donations to the strikers in West Virginia. The entire audience was moved to tears by the spectacle of solidarity, suggesting that Kopple's interpretation of the dream came from a textured vision of class in contemporary America as deeply contradictory and overdetermined. Many local union activists and P-9 supporters, however, condemned the film; they felt it to be a betrayal for failing to capture the culture that grew during the strike. Her conclusions question P-9's tactics, even blame them for losing the strike; but evidence to the contrary remained on the cutting room floor. (Actually unused footage for *American Dream* is housed in University of Wisconsin's archives.) The picture is complicated because the politics is complex, but also because the profound shift in the economy has dislodged the melodramatic form of this battlefield and its representation.

An inheritance from the CPUSA's 1930s Popular Front attempt to meld communists (overwhelmingly urban and immigrant and Jewish) into the People, the sentimental invocation of "family," "movement," "community," and "culture" can insidiously repress conflicts and differences within America's class and racial structure. In 1938, General Secretary of the CPUSA Earl Browder outlined *The People's Front* as a program whose "first consideration in promoting new forces is to find native Americans" to lead its organizations, because the Communist Party was "destined to carry on and complete the work begun by Tom Paine, George Washington, Thomas Jefferson, and Abraham Lincoln."[32] To an extent, *Harlan County, USA* participated in this "archaic aesthetic," as Jesse Lemisch calls it,[33] and Kopple received a series of critiques for her "conventional" portrayal of social events from a position of "knowledge" available to the outsider.[34] The postmodern condition of labor in the 1980s demanded another sort of story; Kopple responds by exaggerating the rhetoric of sentimentality until its claims collapse. Kopple manipulates the codes of sentimentality to the point that our tears seem to merge the viewer with the scabs and against the strikers.

This direction comes in part because the situation in Austin, unlike that in Harlan County, is multiply fractured. Kopple may just be doing her job as a documentary filmmaker by presenting a comprehensive picture of strikers, scabs, and international representatives; or she may be paying a debt to the many locals and internationals that contributed funding for the film; or she may be attempting to enter the action, much as she did in Harlan County, at the picket line, by witnessing the sense of emptiness and hostility of those who break ranks. In Kentucky, her presence at the daily "sunrise revivals" became a factor in the escalating violence during the strike. At times it appeared that Kopple's crew egged on the scabs and company goons; at others, the camera clearly helped avert violence. In Austin, when she shows the scabbing P-9ers (the P-10ers, as they were derisively called) crying as they decide to cross their union's picket line, Kopple would seem to be siding with their unpopular decision. Yet the scene is filled with bathos, its emotional timbre highly suspect as the men cry on cue about how hard it is when you can't feed your family. Their tears are supposed to elicit our sympathy; but clearly their actions do not. Which side are we, the viewers, supposed to be on?

Unlike me, most critics of the film—such as Peter Rachleff, who wrote *Hard-Pressed in the Heartland* in part to counter Kopple's Academy Award–winning portrait of the Hormel strike—consider Kopple a sell-out because she provides a forum for these men, who from the first worked hand-in-hand with the UFCW leadership to undermine the strike and now run the trusteeship union that replaced P-9.[35] Rachleff refers to the local treasurer, John Williams, as her "star" because he gets so much screen time to anguish over his actions.[36] Maintaining a nostalgia for working-class authenticity and community characteristic of America's Left since the Popular Front, Rachleff fails to register the squeamishly maudlin and trite picture being painted. Kopple is relying on the left-wing conventions of picturing the scab as feminized (a scab, like a thug, is not a union *man*) that would seem to reinforce Rachleff's position, but the men's tears are powerful visual cues calling forth audience sympathies. So the picture is confusing, but this seems to be precisely the point: in the era of deindustrialization, it is not so easy to distinguish the union man from the scab.

While the strikers are presented as full of conviction—perhaps a bit naïve in their faith in Ray Rodgers—they are still proud and angry folks, even if their militance includes media-savvy campaigns. The scabs snivel about their lost manhood and the betrayal they feel: they hate to cross a line; the union has driven them to it. Lewie Andersen may steal the screen with his hard-nosed cynicism about P-9, but the UFCW comes off as retrograde and suspect, especially after UFCW President Wynn storms into a meeting shouting that he will make the P-9 local sign the contract: "[A]ll it takes is a few good men, oh and some women too," he nods to "the little lady there with the camera." Perhaps because Kopple's style is so consistently illusionistic—she appears to offer a pure vision of the struggle in Harlan County and a balanced version of the strike in Austin—the excesses in *American Dream* don't read as critique; but I think they should—not necessarily of the P-10ers but of the aesthetics and politics lodged in the sentimental itself as much as in the paradox of union politics in deindustrializing America.

Although correcting Kopple's film served as one impetus for both of the book-length accounts of the Hormel strike, neither does more than mention Kopple's presence in Austin.[37] Her authority is implicitly challenged by the reports of these partisan insiders who were active in the support systems—either Corporate Campaign (Hardy Green) or Twin Cities Support for P-9 (Peter Rachleff); Kopple remained an outsider. Falling for the charismatic Lewie Andersen, she failed to see the transformative effects the strike had on the lives of the union members and their families as she had in *Harlan County*. This transformation from alienated labor to a "movement culture" requires the creation of the alternative "prefigurative" institutions through which working people can galvanize into a collective agent for social and economic change.[38] To understand this process, outsiders need to get inside the homes, churches, and meeting halls of the strikers, but Kopple's up-close-and-personal moments more often come between her and the P-10ers or Andersen. Rachleff provides a prehistory of P-9 through analyses of its earlier incarnation in a consumer and producer union, which had achieved wall-to-wall unionization in Austin during the 1930s, establishing the base for the militancy and solidarity of the 1984–85 strike, the first against Hormel in fifty-two years. The two books also explain the changes in the meat-packing industry as a whole since the 1970s and in the contracts at Hormel that led Hormel to slash wages by 23 percent after promising to maintain them. What had been a locally owned, paternalistic company in a homogenous town in southern Minnesota became a lean and mean corporation with national and international subsidiaries linked to other major corporations during the era of mergers and buy-outs. Kopple fails to give this kind of background from the point of view of Austin; instead of letting the strikers speak, as she had in Harlan, where old-timers recounted the bloody days of the 1930s strikes for her through memories, songs, and photographs, she leaves it to Andersen to fill in the background.

Rachleff accuses Kopple of turning the P-9ers into "victims" rather than seeing them as victimized by the collusion of business unionism, state and local police, and corporate conglomerates, all working in tandem to destroy a renegade local that had taken on enormous symbolic significance in the antiunion climate of Reagan's America. Yet the only ones to appear as victims, in the classic melodramatic sense, are the "P-10ers" who sob before the camera after deciding to cross their union's picket line: "A person takes a lot of pride in being a breadwinner," says Ron Bergstrom. Since the eighteenth century, sentimentality, argues Robert Markley, has served as a "theatrics of virtue" for the display of feminized emotions; within the sentimental, the "passive victim" is always female, and it is up to the sensitive male to sympathize with her.[39] This is a class politics of bourgeois affects, thus hardly the virile profile of labor militancy so crucial to left-wing romance; the P-10ers vamp as hero(in)es. Kopple positions her camera with the men who do cross the line and, with them, gets barraged with insults from neighbors, friends, even brothers, such as R. G. Bergstrom, who is a firm supporter of the strike. He lives outside Austin on a 4 3/4-acre farm with his wife and three kids and explains that he goes to the picket line to watch his brother cross it as much as to perform strike duty. R. G.'s brother, Ron Bergstrom, by contrast, has accepted the logic of Hormel and 1980s corporate concessions for workers: "If you want a job," he tells Kopple, "you're going to have to take it." Ron Bergstrom becomes one of the original seven local members to return to work after twenty weeks on strike. In a telling scene later on, these seven watch themselves crossing the picket line and being jeered on the television news that evening: "The minute we crossed that line," remarks one, "we left them, left that organization."

POLITICAL TEARS

Because the union itself, Hormel's policies, and the subsequent reconstructions of the events have turned on the familial make-up of the town, its work force, and its organizations, the act of scabbing is more than a betrayal of a lifetime of working-class upbringing and consciousness; it is also a divorce, a disownment, a severance of all family ties. These men have placed themselves outside the gates of the city when they reenter the factory gates. Their overly melodramatic responses to their own acts fail to exculpate them however: they may have been forced by circumstances to return, yet the circumstances are outdated, based on an ideal of the male breadwinner providing fully for his family. In both working-class and middle-class American homes, the family wage has failed to provide adequately since the 1970s. These men are victims as much of a passé vision of masculinity as of an outmoded form of unionism that is apparently ineffective against vicious corporations, although they do all right for themselves. Lewie Andersen has predicted from the start that the P-9 strike will fail, and it appears—though not so clearly in the film as in the written accounts of the strike—that the UFCW has actually worked to ensure failure, in part by courting these few dissident critics of the Corporate Campaign. In a reversal of fortune reminiscent of melodrama, these men assume leadership of the local after it is put into trusteeship.

If the P-10ers are pathetic, even bathetic, the P-9ers occasionally appear misguided. Lacking strategy, lacking a program, they are a bit too smitten with the New Age self-esteem assertiveness-training mentality that Ray Rodgers trumpets with quotations from Bruce Springsteen. Yet when one of the women leaves the "war department" (the office in the union hall for strike committee meetings) after a meeting with Lewie Andersen, she explains, "I want a union for the 1980s." The strikers are trying to explain to Andersen that something more than wages is at stake in this strike. In part, they have bought Ray Rodgers's theory that traditional organizing tactics are ineffective under current corporate structures with easy flows of capital allowing quick relocation. Unions must use intensive media campaigns to dishonor companies by targeting investors and stockholders. More important, however, is the alteration of the community's social fabric. P-9 President Jim Guyette and many others describe how the union hall became a "fun place to be" where people "did what they liked to do," fixing cars, carpentry, cooking, in an informal bartering economy set up during the strike. Vying for the power inherent in its sentimental invocation, they claim that "a whole new family" was formed through their union activism. This is especially true of the women's support network, which both Hardy and Rachleff contend accounts for the widespread "movement culture" P-9 was able to create. That Austin is an extremely homogenous and insular small town with a paternalistic company that stably employed generations contributed to the ease with which a "new family" could be formed within and through the union, but it also explains the sense of betrayal the Hormel workers felt at the concessions demanded of them by both the company and the UFCW, which set the stage for rupturing Local P-9. But this (women's) story does not grab Kopple as it did in Harlan County; she's watching the men cry this time.

This feel of intimacy is a modern feature characterizing both oral history and documentary. Kopple had moved in with the miners' families in Harlan County. Her attendance at meetings and on the picket lines and road blocks happened because of her connections with the strikers, even though she came from the outside. The presence of her camera became central to some of the action that happened. When Kopple is asked by the coal company thug for her press pass after she comes up to him with camera and tape recorder to ascertain his opinion of the strike, she turns the question on him, demanding to see his identification. They come to a testy truce, after each refuses to produce these documents of identity. The camera watches as he turns his pick-up truck around and leaves, averting violence. When a miner's wife pulls a revolver from her bodice, she directly addresses the camera, daring her viewers to judge how violence escalates. The media contribute to its eruption, heightening the rhetoric and action of the strikers, even as it may rein in its actual expression. The camera's presence sometimes provokes confrontation and violence, as when the armed thugs single out the camera as if it were a body to be beaten. Like the infamous scene in *The Battle of Chile*, in which cameraman Leonardo Henricksen filmed his own murder at the hands of Pinochet's army, this scene suggests that despite a legacy of bloody confrontations, the filmmaker's presence may be provoking violence. However, Lawrence Jones's death occurs off-screen, leaving us to wonder whether he might still be alive if the crew had ventured out that morning. Instead, Kopple films the emotion of the funeral, lingering on Jones's mother's anguished cries, tracking her collapsing body as it is carried from the church. The raw feeling spilling out inappropriately for public consumption accentuates the keenly divided world of victims—strikers—and tyrants—mine owners and their goons.

Watching *Harlan County, USA* still moves me to tears, despite my recognition of the discourses of sentimentality at work; the carved worn-down faces of the old timers and the incredible youth and poverty of the others, the violence and fear, the haunting ballads pull at the heart strings just as any tearjerker out of Hollywood might. Yet the tough talking women, the humorous encounter between the miner picketing the Wall Street offices of Brookside's parent corporation and the New York City cop comparing benefits, wages, and working conditions, the old miners—black and white—suffering from black lung joking that, although when they entered the mines each day they were different colors, when they left they were all "soul brothers" temper the pathos with humor. It gives *Harlan County, USA* the feel of solidarity. The escalating crisis and its violence are offset by the heady sense of power gained through collective actions. The sheer brutality of the labor miners perform pales compared to the degree to which companies will go to keep workers from improving their lives. In the United States, in the mid-1970s, citizens who worked full time in a major industry still lived without plumbing, without heat, in rickety shacks. Mines are not metaphors for hell; they are hell. Despite her obvious differences as a young, single New York Jew with a camera, she entered the privacy of the miners' lives. Unlike Lauren Gilfillan's more ambivalent attempt in 1934, Kopple's move had opened a hidden world of exploitation to public view and garnered tremendous support for the mineworkers. A strike still looked noble in 1976, especially when it was clear which side one was on.

American Dream, unlike *Harlan County*, slips the veil of sentimentality over the wrong faces. When Peter Rachleff refers to the

P-10ers as the "stars" of Kopple's film, is it because they get too much screen time? Or is it because they get to explain their decision more fully than those who remain on the line? Or because in their explanation, they resort to emotional outbursts of tears, rather than the anger expressed by R. G. Bergstrom at his brother's betrayal, and so appear conventionally sympathetic? Kopple's grim tone, set early in the film and accentuated by the bleak, blanc noir, Minnesota winterscapes of Austin, the tacky interiors of meeting rooms and negotiating suites in hotels, the gruesome images from inside the Hormel plant, offer none of the elevating and alleviating humor, hope, warmth, or sarcasm that occasionally lightened *Harlan County, USA*. The miners' pineboard shacks nestled in the hollows of West Virginia conveyed the picturesque, aestheticizing poverty in a way that James Agee deplored, even as he lyricized the perfect symmetry of the tenants' housing he found in Hale County, Alabama, in *Let Us Now Praise Famous Men*.[40] Nothing of the sort exists in Austin, a tidy middle American town of postwar tract housing. The spirit of possibility following the democratization of the United Mine Workers is also missing from *American Dream*. It seems the dream of solidarity is over too—another casualty of Reaganomics. If Moore undermined the heroic male worker through satire, Kopple finished off his image as the one who will lead us from the brutality of capitalism through united movements of militant solidarity. The American dream of the 1930s Left, that the male working class holds the keys to revolution, rests on modernist economic relations and their melodramatic stagings. It served as the background for the dilemmas of the noir hero caught in a cruel and overdetermined world ruled by rank corruption and uncontrollable desire. The film noirs of the 1940s and 1950s appeared as cynical antidotes to both the melodramatic romance of the 1930s working stiff and the nostalgic portrait of the 1930s migrant mother. But the power of genre is such that labor's sentimental contract persists. Kopple undercuts the rhetoric of the labor documentary by thoroughly inscribing the sentimental. Obsessively observing the contract to the letter, she uses men's tears against their modern origins to tell a postmodern tale still unfolding around us.

CHAPTER 6

NOT "JUST THE FACTS, MA'AM": SOCIAL WORKERS AS PRIVATE EYES

INVESTIGATING RACKETS

The urban underworld of noir always includes a woman with a past who pulls the man into the orbit of crime. We know these images: Barbara Stanwyck's anklet and cat glasses in *Double Indemnity* snare Fred McMurray; Rita Hayworth's black sheath and gloves in *Gilda* destroy Glenn Ford; Ava Gardner's flowing black hair and diamond necklace choke Burt Lancaster in *The Killers*. But how did these troubling women get there? How did they land in a world of gang kingpins and petty thieves, hapless working stiffs looking for a break and cynical detectives seeking the facts? In the classic noir narrative of male criminality and male investigation, this question is never posed. It is simply a given, a verity, like the palm trees lining Hollywood Boulevard, themselves hardly native, but so tall they seem to have grown from time immemorial. In a draft of *The Outsider*, Cross Damon learns that Jenny, the Chicago prostitute he helps, is headed for California, dreaming of a career in the movies. Her background as pregnant runaway who undergoes an abortion, then becomes rape victim, and finally a prostitute suggests she is headed West to disaster, not discovery. This chapter delves into a few possible sources for the story of Jenny and her fatal sisters, sources found in the files of the female counterpart to the private eye, another appendage of the state (even Philip Marlowe works sometimes as investigator for the DA's office), the social worker. Often an attaché of the court and sometimes child-protective investigator for the District Attorney, the social worker operates as the state's prying eye.

The 1930s and 1940s detectives were independent operators. They may have started with a partner, as do Philip Marlowe in *The Maltese Falcon* or Jeff Bailey in *Out of the Past*. But, conveniently, the partners always die, leaving the private eye free of the institutional structures of the bureaucratic workplace; he has no bosses, coworkers, or employees. However, his investigations into the homes of rich and poor alike are enabled by his quasilegal connections both to crime and the courts (but always in competition with the police). The femme fatale also moves alone among this dangerous world of men. Her upward mobility made possible because of her sexual debasement or her willingness to debase men sexually. Like the detective, she's stepped outside of the domestic frame, though she may inevitably become part of another frame-up snaring the detective. As an enigma, she works against the male detective's desire to get to the bottom of the case, to zero in on "just the facts." The detective, no matter how cynical he appears, is committed to the facts. He uncovers corruption because he is unattached, free to circulate. No such status is available for the female truth-seeker. In the noir world, she is by definition corrupt if she is on her own. An unknown and unknowable, she is false, a double-crosser, so even if she is after the goods, they will elude her. However, during the 1930s, a large number of women began to investigate, looking for truths. They worked for the state and its agencies as the profession of social work became central to ameliorating the effects of the Depression. Middle-class women's access to poor women's homes occurred through a supervisory effort to protect children's welfare during a decade of unprecedented attention to poverty's effect on children. Like the dick, the social worker has multiple allegiances; but unlike him, she is not free to work as a private eye—her eyes are resolutely public. Representing at once morals and the state, she condemns faulty mothering, violent fathers, greedy degenerate girls, and delinquent boys, even as she works to help them. Still, she shares with the nihilist detective a belief that there is no way out of the "racket": the system that produces poor women produces her too.

In 1930s crime films or hard-boiled novels, gangsters called *Little Caesar, Public Enemy,* or *Scarface,* on the one hand, and detectives named Sam Spade or Philip Marlowe (both played by Humphrey Bogart), on the other, circulate within seedy urban spaces. These genres of crime invariably feature male activities—accession through the criminal ladder in urban ghettoes to "top of the world" before inevitable death, or lonely battles with the corrupt world of police and petty crooks in not-so-sunny California that take place in masculine spaces—cars, gambling halls, jails, dusty offices—by small men who ultimately get snared by seductive, two-timing women. It's certain that these deadly women will appear from *Out of the Past.* But one rarely learns how they became so brutal. Horace McCoy's chilling 1935 novel, *They Shoot Horses, Don't They?,* offers clues about their origins in a parallel, feminized, world of deadly competition. A retrospective tale, narrated by a condemned murderer, it explains how Robert Syverten came to shoot his marathon dance partner Gloria Bailey. As Syverten awaits his death sentence, his first-person monologue details how he met Gloria (another aspiring Hollywood bit player), decided to join in her pursuit of the dance marathon prize, and finally acquiesced to her desired suicide by shooting her in the head, just as he had witnessed his grandfather put a lame horse out of its misery as a boy back in the rural Midwest. Gloria, cynical and taciturn, increasingly despairs as the two dance their way through days and nights of derby racing, Lindy hopping, and polishing the big apple, under the scrutiny of a loyal audience until the Mothers' League and the cops disrupt the action. His deadly private act, and the state's public murder, provide a vehicle for Gloria's story to unfold. But the court records do not reveal her narrative. Because she falls outside of conventional femininity, the state and its guardians of morality have no access to her experience. Only her killer knows what has driven her to beg him to pull the trigger.

"You—goddam—whore!" shrieks Mrs. Higby, president of the Mothers' League for Good Morals, after Gloria Bailey, on the dance floor for more than a month, challenges her authority to dictate what constitutes proper behavior for poor women. "You ought to be in a reform school!" continues the frustrated Mrs. Higby. Seven hundred sixty-three hours into the dance marathon, the leaders of the Mothers' League arrive at the Santa Monica pier dancehall to condemn the "low and degrading" contest.[1] The women announce their intention to pressure the city to end the marathon unless the promoters disqualify a visibly pregnant woman and renege on an advertised promise to marry a couple on the dance floor; the women invoke "our duty to keep our city clean"(130). The battle-ax— derived from Carrie Nation's efforts to control male drinking through social housekeeping—is a stock image of nineteenth-century domestic melodrama, a staple of silent film, including the original scenario for D. W. Griffith's classic *Intolerance* and his two-reeler, *The Mother and the Law*.[2] In it, a young woman dressed in rags defiantly resists the guardians of state morality trying to rescue her child from poverty and abuse by declaring her an unfit mother. By the late 1930s, popular culture was full of parodies of these types—think of Claire Trevor (as the prostitute Dallas) and Thomas Mitchell (as drunkard Doc Boone) being hounded out of town by the wizened members of the Ladies' Law and Order League in John Ford's *Stagecoach*, among many examples.

But unlike Dallas, who silently leaves Tombstone on the stage, Gloria unleashes her anger at Mrs. Higby: "Your Morals League and your goddam women's clubs filled with meddlesome old bitches who haven't had a lay in twenty years. Why don't you old dames go out and buy a lay once in a while?" Gloria has seen her share of moral mothers: "While you two noble characters are here doing your duty by some people you don't know, your daughters are probably in some guy's apartment, their clothes off, getting drunk. . . . You drive 'em away from home with your goddam lectures on purity and decency, and you're too busy meddling around to teach 'em the facts of life." Gloria lands the last word of this argument. She speaks from experience as marathon dancer, Hollywood extra, and reform school runaway: "I was in one once. . . . [T]here was a dame just like you in charge. She was a lesbian" (131–34). Gloria Bailey, depressed and exhausted, speaks for all the lone bad girls who, having fled violent, abusive homes, end up on the street corners of Cincinnati or the breadlines in St. Paul—or in Hollywood looking for a big break.[3] This heated exchange crystallizes essential elements about the modern interdependence of poor women's sexuality and middle-class women's professionalization. Because class is structural, each social position can only be understood in relationship to the other. Through designating the female body as mother or whore or lesbian within spaces cordoned off from, yet contained within, the state, these structures become legible within personal stories.[4] The Mothers' League investigates and polices the marathon as a scene of a crime—after all, an accused murderer was arrested on the dance floor—that is especially troublesome for women.

"I feel that this investigation may help in some manner. / I do hope it may. / I am now making a very general statement as a beginning." Thus concludes Muriel Rukeyser's "Statement: Philippa Allen," a section of her long poem, "Book of the Dead," in *U.S. 1*.[5] Philippa Allen, a social worker who offered key testimony to the congressional hearings on silicosis, a lung disease contracted by the 2,000 workers on the Gauley Tunnel in West Virginia, is cited by Rukeyser as among "the many investigators and writers who made this poem possible" (146). Recognizing the special expertise and patience of Philippa Allen, whose casework sent her hitchhiking back and forth across Gauley Bridge tracking the effects of disease on the families—white and black—living in towns named Alloy, Vanetta, and Gamoca, Rukeyser insisted, "Poetry could extend the document" (149). In this, Rukeyser was herself extending the genres from reportage and fiction to poetry that used social workers' cases as the basis for literature—a practice Henry Street Settlement House leader Helen Hall had used in her collaboration with writer Clinch Calkins, who had turned case histories from the settlement house into literary narratives in order to detail the horrors of unemployment for a broader audience, providing fodder for sensational and political fiction.[6]

Caroline Slade, described in the jacket blurb of her fourth novel as "a reformed social worker" whose fiction was derived from her cases as an attaché of a children's court and an investigator for a district attorney, was the first executive secretary of the Saratoga (N.Y.) County Board of Child Welfare before lobbying in Albany, New York, for state protective legislation for women and children. The five novels she wrote during the 1940s feature intriguing portraits of the failure of one aspect or another of the social welfare system. These thinly disguised case studies elaborate the stories of child prostitution that Slade recounted almost verbatim in her scandalous first novel, *Sterile Sun* (1936).[7] Her 1940s novels serve as diatribes against the failures of Aid to Dependent Children (ADC) and other relief programs to address the poverty and violence endemic to unemployed Depression-era workers by focusing on the intimate family arrangements that very often result in child prostitution. These five novels (*The Triumph of Willie Pond*, *Job's House*, *Margaret*, *Mrs. Party's House*, *Lilly Crackell*) contrast a politically astute social worker, who fights the courts and welfare bureaucrats by arguing that they should take a more systemic view of delinquency, with a savvy delinquent girl who ends up in the social worker's caseload after she is caught in "the business." Social workers in Slade's novels, no matter how empathetic, such as Mrs. Sleight and Miss Southard—dressed in real silk stockings and tailored suits—cannot help but condemn the vermin-infested cramped households they enter in their efforts to aid poor mothers and children. They are emblems of respectability, representatives of the state. Yet, as professional women, they too are suspect. As Gloria says, they are "lesbians." While they fault the slack housekeeping of their charges as moral defect, their sexuality is questioned by the families they investigate and by the authorities to which they report.

In the middle of Philippa Allen's testimony, a congressman interrupts: "You found the people of West Virginia very happy to pick you up on the highway, did you not?" Allen, like the many young girls who end up in reform schools, is picked up on open road. Her age, her class, and her profession protect her body; people "are delightfully obliging," all asking, "What can be done?" (15). Allen's authority as a representative of the state may help them, so they protect her. Like doctors and journalists, her mobility and expertise as a "reality definer" mean she can speak on their behalf and get their story out.[8] Stories of crime and detection, including corporate "rackets," as Congressman Marcantonio calls them, often feature first-person narration (*U.S.1*, 57). Thoroughly modern in their literary influences and in their juridical ones as well, first-person accounts, whether testimony or confession, counter the official paperwork in police files and social workers' case records. They are immediate, getting at what the bland machinery of the state cannot convey through its carbon copies. Yet both the detective and the social worker (and the scholar, if you follow the trail far enough) do not merely record data. Their files are filled with judgments about the characters, gleaned from the appearance, speech, dress, and so forth of those under investigation; these judgments, of guilt or innocence, deserving or undeserving poverty, determine state action.

Miss Allen may come in for congressional approbation for getting picked up on the highway, but she never felt in danger as a pick up. Girls hitching alone, however, are usually not so well protected. Fleeing a family so poor it has farmed her out as a servant to a better-off couple, fourteen-year-old Sue, one protagonist of Slade's *Sterile Sun*, hits the road. She takes the money she has earned having sex with her employer's husband and an old man who was the couple's gardener and runs away to survive on her own. Picked up on the highway by a traveling salesman, Sue keeps running away from fleabag hotels and fancy whorehouses until she ends up in "the business" alone on skid row. No one will listen to poor girls' stories, or rather no one will believe them. If they are on the road thumbing or walking the streets, they must be looking for it. After all, they are just "goddam whores" so deserve what they get. The kindness of strangers leads this girl to an opium den (white slavery is an incessant theme in Slade's novels). She escapes to a skid row hotel, where she dies from a botched self-induced abortion because she doesn't seek help from the two older prostitutes who befriend her.

Sue's story is told in three parts: a run-on flood of her girlish words, which is picked up by her two friends in Allie's tough tale and Winkie's sad delusions. Each woman explains how she came to the seedy upstate New York town—maybe Albany or Troy—as a young teen, entered "the business," got into trouble with the law, and then, in the case of hard-bitten Allie and sentimental Winkie, watched Sue die. Like Robert Syverten's story in *They Shoot Horses, Don't They?*, *Sterile Sun* too is a recounting from the grave, shading into roman noir. It became a textbook in social work classrooms because it vacates the bland and moralistic voice of the case report by giving voice directly to the girls. Caseworkers' reports, typically no more than a few paragraphs, judge these delinquent girls by using the language of social science fact-finding. Even so, some measure of "voice" comes through. For instance, feminist historian Linda Gordon provides details of one case: Susan, an incest victim of her father and her mother's boarder/lover and brothers, who, along with her younger sisters, was removed from her home, while all the male members were never charged with a crime and allowed to remain living at home. In her case history, Susan's story, a mixture of self-contempt and defiance, reads like the fictional Sue's. "I was always a whore," Susan concludes. Her social worker's prose and the actions she takes to remove Susan concur.[9]

STREAM-OF-CONSCIENCE

Sterile Sun eliminates investigative interpretation and offers the girls' cogent analysis of the sexual economy of poverty directly. Sue begins her story: "I am a prostitute the Judge said to me young lady if you keep on going the way you're going now you will be nothing but a common prostitute so I kept on and I am only us girls don't call it that we call it doing business. I do business on the street now and we all get good and mad if anyone calls us like whores and prostitutes" (15–16). Allie's narrative begins, "Sure, I'm a goddamn sonofabitch whore, I get what money I have selling myself to men" (95). Winkie starts her story, "This is a wicked business for a girl to be in, I bet I get out of it just as quick as I got enough money in the bank. When I think about how I am a dirty whore I get cold all over me, my heart gets to going fast I get choked up, I got to get out of this business and live decent and respectable" (121). In essence, each of these girls elaborates Susan's declaration into a profoundly social theory of justice, religion, work, and the state. Self-pity and self-loathing are tempered with pride; without the moralistic intercession of the caseworker's commentary, the girls' insights become political.[10] Gordon points out that during the Depression, child protection workers and social welfare agencies came to believe that "the children of the poor were by definition neglected"(152). However, this increasing awareness of poverty as a primary cause of child neglect and abuse did not necessarily result in a greater sensitivity to gender and sexual inequalities in girls' and women's lives. These daughters (and sometimes mothers) know things neither the Mothers' League nor social workers can imagine. Thus Slade's novels are essentially instructional manuals in the political economy of "sexual delinquency."[11]

For example, Slade's 1946 novel, *Margaret,* hailed on its cover as "a novel of profound significance to every mother," fills in the girls' stories Slade ventriloquized without analysis or commentary in *Sterile Sun* and only sketchily outlined in her second and best-known novel, *The Triumph of Willie Pond.*[12] Invariably, deficient mothers are the problem: one might be too lax, a slovenly woman who loves her children too much and cannot refrain from bearing them endlessly; another is too restrictive, a withdrawn woman suffering her husband's beatings and failing to protect her daughters from male violence. In either case, the precocious daughter, such as Mary Pond, knows (and knows she knows) more than her mother: "I don't like you talking that way, Mary. If you know things you ought to pertend you didn't. A girl your age," complains her mother.[13] Mary quickly discovers she can make money when the rest of the family cannot and becomes embroiled in a prostitution ring organized by an older girl. One of the things all the wayward daughters know—they go to school and have access to a world of objects (like the toothbrush Ruby wins in class, in Martha Gellhorn's *Trouble I've Seen*)—is that their families are lacking: the food is dreadful, the clothes ragged, their mothers affectless, naïvely allowing the official women of the state to enter and pass judgment on their lives.[14] These poorer younger cousins of Daisy Miller and Lily Bart, both insufficiently mothered American daughters brought low by society's censure, are subjected to society's professionalized embodiment, the social worker, who, as high society does, exercises pervasive control over these wayward daughters.

In the social-worker novel, adolescent girls discern the social order more keenly than others: "They don't own us, do they?" demands Mary Pond. "Coming in here all the time! . . . They just walk right in . . . coming in our house. Bossing us around"(29). The mothers are dependent: "But they give us relief. We couldn't get by without the Welfare." The daughters see instead that "they get paid for it! They all've got swell clothes and cars . . . and wear real silk stockings"(30). Still these modern representatives of the modern state—who often appear as enemies of the poor women they aid—challenge the far more censorious moral judgments of the courts and police by intervening (invisibly) for the girls. Nevertheless the daughters are deemed incorrigible, or the household deemed unable to nurture them. Social workers, with names like Mrs. Sleight or Miss Southard, oversee their detention in reform school. It is for their own good, of course, even though the girls' attachments to their mothers—a crucial (antimodern) aspect of immigrant working-class families—is profound. In her study, Gordon cites a 1927–28 Boston Children's Aid Association Annual Report that acknowledges the agency's failure to save a delinquent girl from her mother: "Born out of wedlock, her first ten years spent with an immoral mother who lived in a wretched tenement in a poor district

... thirteen-year-old Jane who came to us from one of our courts as a delinquent child ... proved to be untruthful, restless, never happy. She had great affection for her mother and was determined to be with her although she knew the kind of life she was living. Several times she ran away to her, and to the vicious old neighborhood which she seemed to love. . . . We believe the chief factors in our failure were the bad home background, strong affection for a mother she knew to be immoral" (135–36). In the rationalist view of social welfare, knowledge (and morals) should trump affection. That it doesn't is Slade's central point.

Slade knew firsthand the dilemma facing social workers. In her various capacities, she observed the devastation of poverty and the failures of state solutions to child neglect. She witnessed the double standard that let wealthy male pedophiles off while jailing their young poor prey. She was among the earliest left-wing critics of Aid to Dependent Children (ADC).[15] She gave up social work for novel writing out of frustration with the welfare system. She hoped to effect changes through broadening her appeal to a reading public primed by 1930s literary radicalism.[16] Still her novels resort to every stereotype circulating within popular culture to portray both young female delinquency and social reformers' officiousness. Why? In part, she is a turgid and plodding writer who cannot creatively maneuver around the conventions of the genre. Moreover, these are cautionary tales and as such fall deeply within the melodramatic imagination. They are designed, as Ruth Blodgett writing for the *Book-of-the-Month Club News* noted, to instill in readers "a burning responsibility to insist such dreadful living conditions must not continue in our post-war world."[17] There is more to it. Slade's lesson, particularly in *Margaret*, is a modern, Foucaldian one: unless the courts and social workers intervene early to protect children from brutal beatings, overwork, and poverty, their environment will inevitably turn them into incorrigible delinquents; children must learn to internalize proper behavior. Mrs. Sleight discovers the depths of depraved delinquency when she meets Margaret, who has been pimping for a ring of pedophiles. Grown weary of sex with their ringleader, Pinky, Margaret lures her upstairs-neighbor friend Sophie to the men's apartment; twelve-year-old Sophie slips into madness when she is raped and beaten by Skinny, the fat sadist who bankrolls the ring. As the social worker overseeing Sophie's family,

Mrs. Sleight is assigned to Margaret's case. But she has met her match; thus she argues with the judge that preemptive moves to protect children are essential to avoid their degradation by adults. He argues firmly for the rule of law that limits court intervention until after a crime has been committed. Poverty is not criminal in capitalist America; however, poor girls' solution to it—sex for money—is. It is only after the fact that something can be done about child molestation, and then only to the girls who are now criminals; the rich men are never found much less charged.

This pedagogical aspect of Slade's 1940s novels may have been a reaction to reviews of her 1936 book, *Sterile Sun*, many of which rebuked her for offering no solutions. Comparing her novel to Gellhorn's series of four bleak novellas gleaned from her work for the Federal Emergency Relief Administration, *The Survey* decried the "bitterness of her hatred of society" and Slade's failure to "lift the banner of faith that would lead on to social action."[18] Yet social action—a favorite of radicals, liberals, and New Dealers—is precisely what Slade engaged in as a fiction writer. Faith in society was not going to solve these girls' problems. Slade's years as a social worker had taught her that already. These girls' Depression stories are about survival and desire (for sweets or stockings); deprivation sets the stage for "sexual delinquency." The first time these eleven-, twelve-, fourteen-year-old girls have sex, it is with men older than their fathers. Always it is excruciatingly painful; each bleeds profusely, screams, passes out, withdraws, and (with the exception of Sophie, who regresses to mute fear, and her defiant sister Mary, who squeals on Margaret) keeps quiet, then returns because the scared, furious, or guilty man pays her well—fifty cents, a dollar, even a fiver.

In these novels, the girls are not only matter-of-fact about the exchange of sex for money, they are remarkably savvy about the welfare and legal systems. Even as the older ones pimp for the younger girls, they share whatever knowledge they have gleaned from experience and rumor whenever they get together—in the makeshift whore houses where they work or the jail cells and reformatories where they end up in custody. The girls learn to tell sympathetic social workers how sorry they are and remind their case workers how much they miss their dead mothers. These scams, along with the enlightened treatment the girls receive—coaching in proper hygiene and housekeeping, learning "useful" skills, like waiting tables (though the *Daily Worker* reports this line of work as little better than slavery) instead of the water hoses and ice baths used in the past to cure girls of their sexual depravity—turn the social workers into fools, easily duped and mocked by these worldly wise girls. Yet social workers were not entirely naïve. The important journal of social commentary, *Midmonthly Survey*, ran a regular column—later collected into a series of pamphlets—entitled "Ask Miss Bailey," offering caseworkers practical advice on problematic clients: the ones who refused a CCC (Civilian Conservation Corps) job, bought a car instead of food, went to the movies too often, indulged a sweet tooth, or, more sinisterly, had daughters who earned extra money from unknown sources to buy themselves silk stockings. Miss Bailey's approach was soundly ridiculed within the pages of *Social Work Today*, the left-wing journal of the radical social work movement. She might be well meaning when she allows relief families "the fifteen-cent motion picture, the permanent wave and the family dog," but she is hopelessly ineffectual, blaming bourgeois mores rather than capitalism itself, for caseworkers' difficulties with clients. The editors note, "the gain in social insight afforded the relief worker is highly questionable."[19]

The author of the Miss Bailey columns and Slade's reviewer in *The Survey*, Gertrude Springer, claims, "there wasn't a thing the matter with the Ponds but poverty."[20] Unlike Slade, she believes that relief work can make a difference: "social workers never come out very well in Mrs. Slade's books," however, "they are less the villains of this piece [*Lilly Crackell*] than the victims of the same social stupidity that blighted Lilly," she concedes.[21] Slade offered a more nuanced view of the social worker—one in line with left-wing critiques of poverty. *The Triumph of Willie Pond*, praised by James T. Farrell and Diana Trilling, received a rave review from *Social Work Today*: "to say every single social worker in the United States ought to read it is to do it injustice;" it should be read not out of "professional *obligation*" but as "one of the high points of his [sic] reading experience. Willie Pond is your client. You know him right away."[22] Yet Slade was still working within the social-worker story—the tale of how better-educated, better-dressed women fronting for a repressive state apparatus intrude upon the lives and homes of the poor, condemning the defective mothering that fails to maintain proper order.

Vanguard Press, publisher of Farrell's somewhat risqué novels, printed disclaimers about the content of Slade's books. In a terse preface, Vanguard Press warned readers that it was issuing *Sterile Sun* "in a special edition, the sale of which is limited to physicians, psychiatrists, sociologists, social workers, educators and other persons having a professional interest in the psychology of adolescence." Ruth Blodgett worried that "some doubtless will read this [Margaret's] story out of the same morbid curiosity with which they read of sex crimes in the tabloids."[23] Seeking to distance Slade's fiction from the tabloids, Vanguard publisher Jim Henle enlisted the Reverend John Howard Melish to write an introduction to *Sterile Sun* justifying its publication for "professionals." The book "should not be placed on the shelves of a public library for young people with a pornographic urge to read," he exhorts (11). The pornographic urge to read among young people, like their delinquency, is in part caused by adults procuring children and enticing them with gin, candy, money, even books. But it is also part of their modern psychosexual make-up. With the Depression and War over, "the social evil . . . juvenile delinquency," notes Blodgett, "is one of our increasing concerns."

In fact, Reverend Melish goes so far as to compare *Sterile Sun* to Joyce's *Ulysses*, a book he, as an expert, "hate[s]." Nevertheless, he assures readers that hateful as its subject may be, *Sterile Sun*, like *Ulysses*, is serious art. The comparison may seem bizarre—an obscure tale resembling the Number One novel, a pulpy exposé comparable to high modernism? Yet *Sterile Sun* owes much to *Ulysses*.[24] In a short note written to the *New Masses* in 1929, novelist Josephine Herbst explained that female literary radicals, rather than rejecting modernist stream-of-consciousness for socialist realism, were seeking to write like "Marcel Proust, and maybe Balzac."[25] These literary radicals extended modernist narrative experiments to American workers and the poor. Slade, like Joyce, gives voices to loose women, a stream-of-conscience novel, a case report as stream-of-consciousness. Like the illegal copies of *Ulysses* that Herbst and her husband, John Herrmann, carried back from Europe, *Sterile Sun* is a rarity.[26]

All of Slade's novels include a scene in which the errant girl rages against the invasions—and the moral censure accompanying them—of the social worker into their private lives. Miss Bailey's relief workers notes these outbursts as well: " 'She's a stubborn, ungrateful, little piece who ought to have a good spanking,' snapped the home worker. . . . A too-tight coat and black-cotton stockings were, it seemed, at the bottom of fourteen-year-old Carrie's rebellion. . . . 'They're perfectly good stockings, and she ought to be grateful she has any kind of coat at all. Instead she fights me every inch of the way. Says I'm just a dumb old maid. She's getting the family turned against me,' " complained one.[27] Interrogations are routine in casework, but they often reveal more about the lack of the social worker's knowledge than information about child abuse. The children are working under a code of honor to each other (or fear of each other) that social workers, unlike detectives, cannot fathom. As middle-class women, no matter how extensive their education, they are limited in their mobility and access to the depths of social depravity. But they may also be realists, unlike the cynically idealist private eye, understanding the limits of their power to change the situations they confront. In *Sterile Sun*, Sue describes her social worker as "a old maid I could guess that because I see how much she didn't know about things she kept saying to me dear and dear child and then she tried to make me tell what I done she said to me dear child have you had intercourse—no of course that—no I mean have you slept with a man or a boy—well I mean not only slept but you know—that is—she acted so funny I had to try and not laugh right in her face but I told her no ma'am I never did because I promised Mr. Smith I never would tell and I never did" (16–17). The detective always knows when he's being lied to; he has ways to get to the bottom of the story. The social worker, although she too may know she's being lied to, can do little about it. She is dealing with a child who is labeled a criminal but is really a victim.

For instance, Carmen Sternwood, the younger daughter of General Sternwood, Marlowe's employer in Raymond Chandler's *The Big Sleep*, is drugged and photographed naked by the pornographic bookseller Arthur Gwynn Geiger. She too is a child of insufficient mothering. Sternwood is a widower who had his children late in life. Carmen's wealth protects her from predatory men who offer poor girls fifty cents for sex, but it makes her an easy mark for blackmail. Her gambling debts and drug habit further deplete her desiccated father, who spends his days dozing in his orchid hothouse. Marlowe oversees Carmen in ways that social workers can never protect their young cases. Carmen has the sheen of money. Marlowe has the power of a badge (and a gun); he is both within and above the state. A bachelor is not the same as an old maid, a widower not the same as a single mother (and obviously money talks). The PI is employed secretly to rescue an errant daughter, even if she is a murderer, and bring her home. But the state sends the social worker to officially investigate the home life of a delinquent girl already in its charge because her home cannot shelter her.[28] When her mother is found, she is found wanting. In these situations, the state is a meddling force with overarching powers to steal one's children away. Social workers become enforcers in a state-sanctioned protection racket, especially when they perform their mid-monthly surveys. One of the first questions Miss Bailey answers, "Are Relief Workers Police-women?" is resolutely negative: "With the woman 'living in sin' with the lodger. The worker's concern with the lodger is only his economic status in the family." Yet, quoting a supervisor, Miss Bailey opines, "I don't know whether we are policemen or not. . . . We try not to be, though I suspect that the public would support us in a high moralistic stand."[29]

Poverty, particularly among single mothers and their children, is always cause for suspicion. Ruby, the relief girl Gellhorn found, was lured into prostitution with promises of money for roller skates, candy, the canned peaches her mother cherishes, and even a tube of toothpaste. Eventually removed from her home, she is placed under court supervision. Eleven years old, she cannot gauge the time away from her mother when she arrives weeks later to inform Ruby that she cannot take her home: "They say I'm not fit to keep you. They say I should have known what you were doing, and if I didn't then I'm not a good mother" ("Ruby," 172). Mrs. Mayer leaves Ruby literally in the clutches of the warden Miss Mayfield, walking off in the wrong direction from home, now a lone woman on the street. In Ann Petry's *The Street* (1946), Lutie Johnson's son, Bub, is paid by her crazed building superintendent to steal mail. She also loses her child to state custody. After Bub is placed in the children's shelter when he is found home alone, Lutie immediately assumes her son will "graduate from reform school into DannemoraSingSing."[30] Bub has absorbed his mother's worries over money; left alone while she works days in an office and nights as a singer, he too is insufficiently mothered. When she ventures to the shelter to see

Bub, Lutie is struck by the huddled-over bodies of black and white women—foreigners mostly—waiting to see their kids. Lutie's poverty, not race, transforms her and all these "waiting women" into "animals" (409). Lutie eventually abandons Bub to this brick institution after she murders the pimp she has approached for money to pay a lawyer. Reasoning "the Court wouldn't parole him in her care either, because she was no longer a fit person to bring him up," she buys a one-way ticket to Chicago, leaving Bub to survive alone (433).

Lutie's terrible logic, that it is better to abandon her son to the institutions of the state than to try to fight for him, is based on her experience as a foster mother and a black woman. Harlem nightclub singer, single mother—Lutie's life appears a cliché: she's black, she's bad, her son criminal. Thus, in rebellion, Lutie refuses to allow Bub to know himself through this narrative: the son of what racist social convention deemed she was—a violent, slutty mother. Racism adds another dimension to the poor mother's dilemma.[31] For instance, the mother in Marita Bonner's 1935 story, "The Whipping," inadvertently kills her son Bennie after spending three nights in jail for slugging her relief worker, who promises "an investigator" will check on her story—"no food, no coal, the water frozen, the pipes burst."[32] Lizabeth cannot run away from the women's reformatory, where she has been placed after hitting Bennie. Her unsuccessful attempts to find relief for her son and mother send her into a rage, and hunger blurs her judgment. She takes it out on her son: "Bad character! Keep her! the court decided"(77). The streets of Chicago or Harlem, or seedy upstate towns, invariably result in violence. Poverty kills in many forms: black, single mothers find themselves unable to get relief; white families, those deserving poor who do get relief, are demeaned by inspection and supervision. In these narratives, the welfare and court system is at once overzealous in monitoring its white clients and utterly apathetic to black women's needs. In all cases, once the women or children encounter authority, the family is doomed. The ever-practical Miss Bailey assures us that a relief worker's job is to provide food, clothing, and shelter, not to club slovenly housekeepers into cleaning up their smelly, bug-infested houses or punish those who don't.[33] These fictions from the 1930s and 1940s suggest the facts are otherwise.[34]

WHAT FILM NOIR KNOWS . . . ABOUT WELFARE

Half a century later, in 1996, when President Clinton promised to "end welfare as we know it," he indulged in his now legendary parsing of the English language. He was not going to end welfare *tout court*, just welfare as we know it. But no one questioned whether we as a nation actually did know it, either experientially or theoretically. Certainly, speculation ran to what the new configuration would look like, but little attention was paid to its history as detailed by Caroline Slade and Miss Bailey, not to mention Marita Bonner or Ann Petry. What is the welfare we know? Is it the Social Security Act of 1935, the 1944 GI Bill of Rights, the Interstate Highway Act of 1956, all of which have been enormously successful in alleviating poverty through pensions, education, health insurance, and subsidies for construction and jobs, and most of which have benefited white male workers and their families? No. Welfare is a program that enables welfare queens to drive Cadillacs, as Ronald Reagan once asserted. It is a devious tool pathologizing the black family, as Daniel Patrick Moynihan once implied, the root cause of the "culture of poverty," which could not be alleviated even when Lyndon Johnson declared a "war on poverty."[35] In short, under the reign of Cadillac queens, lodged in the pathological family and culture, welfare, as we know, is about greedy, slothful women and their delinquent, possibly illegitimate, children, no matter how much Miss Bailey had argued otherwise.

Welfare as we know it is feminized, localized in decaying urban housing projects or in shabby trailer parks, hardly visible in the expansive American university system, the ten-lane highways crisscrossing the continent, or the tree-lined suburbs ringing our cities that are the legacy of postwar social investments. These strategic investments were made to help the millions of returning World War II veterans reenter civilian life—a process understood to be fraught with the enormous "problems of homecoming" that required the same massive federal intervention to stave off the potential chaos, violence, and dangers facing the men, their families, and the nation as had the Depression.[36] The 1940s problem of homecoming, like that of 1930s unemployment, was debated endlessly among "experts" and in the pages of such diverse publications as *Reader's Digest* and *The New Yorker*. Like the concern for girls' delinquency during the 1920s and 1930s, it too became the subtext of much post-war popular culture. Addressing the problem of homecoming became a way to remasculinize, in Susan Jeffords's term, welfare.

For instance, like many film noirs of the mid-1940s, *The Blue Dahlia* focuses on the strains three returning World War II veterans face as they reenter civilian life. Set in Los Angeles, the film contrasts the bright exteriors of sunny Southern California with the gloomy reality of shell shock, unemployment, war wounds, and psychic estrangement GIs faced on homecoming: Buzz (William Bendix) suffers whenever he hears "monkey music." The hot jazz screaming from radios, jukeboxes, and nightclubs makes the steel plate in his head vibrate, leading him to violence and amnesia. After Johnny (Alan Ladd) confronts his two-timing party-girl wife who has taken up with a Hollywood club owner, he's accused of her murder. The men react violently to the incursion of black America, or its "monkey" music, into the all-white bars and homes of suburbia, and to the parallel excursion of married women into the workforce and onto the dance floors that occurred while they were away at war. Through their own detective work, Buzz, Johnny, and their buddy, George, are eventually cleared of the crime (and Johnny gets a new girl [Veronica Lake]) setting up the possibility of a smooth future. But the scenario of adultery, murder, amnesia, and bar brawls conveyed a distinctive uneasiness about these "heroes."[37]

The plight of the returning GI had been seen as a "problem" years before the War ended. Scores of local newspapers featured articles headlined, "Vets Seen as Big Problem." The pages of social work journals and social psychology studies within the Research Branch, Information and Education Division of the United States Army, and other federal agencies fretted about the massive influx of young men into an America now booming with war production.[38] These GIs had left a far different America—one reeling from a decade of depression, which forced the first unified federal welfare programs to secure Social Security and unemployment insurance, as well as provide "relief " for poor, unemployed urban families and displaced rural farmers. During the 1930s, welfare was understood as a response to a crisis—as a defense against social disarray, anarchy, and fascism, and as relief from privation. By the time the United States entered the Second World War, welfare was officially trumpeted as national defense.

War meant an improved economy, but social welfare advocates, especially those on the Left, warned against the possible dependence on a heated up war economy as a substitute for a system to combat perennial unemployment. They viewed the WPA, which had been cut back throughout the 1930s by probusiness forces in Congress, as the only solution to maintain full peacetime employment. Discussions about welfare during the depression years of the 1930s stressed images of relief and recovery. The crisis was understood as temporary, and only federal intervention could provide the necessary aid to those in need. Roosevelt's New Deal goal was "freedom from want." The language of aid, relief, and recovery made the welfare recipient seem a foreigner in her own land—a refugee, a disaster victim—and the sheer magnitude of the crisis required military-style intervention. As the crisis in Europe and Asia made war inevitable, and U.S. involvement seemed only a matter of time, the discourse on welfare shifted considerably. Welfare became an aspect of national defense and security. The forces of fascism would best be staved off through social security, unemployment insurance, and, most important, full employment, especially for youth whose delinquency was increasingly seen as incipient fascist behavior. The communist-oriented journal *Social Work Today* praised the report in the *Annals of the American Association of Political and Social Sciences* special issue, "Prospects for Youth," which linked child welfare to democracy. It favorably quoted Aubry Williams's comment that "government responsibility for youth has as its primary basis the fundamental democratic principle of equal opportunity for all."[39] At least among left-wing social workers and political scientists, government welfare programs were indispensable for assuring a democratic nation. Only guaranteed work could eliminate the disparities in income that spelled the end of freedom. In this era of the Hitler-Stalin Pact, left-wing social workers also characterized welfare as "the first line of national defense" against Roosevelt's stepped up war production and its incipient militarized economy.[40] Gwen Barclay called for "Welfare, Not Warfare," and Henry Doliner proposed full employment "In Answer to War Hysteria."[41] However, when the Communist Party had shifted its line about the war, after Germany's invasion of the USSR, a new department had been added to the journal: "Social Work and Defense," with headlines declaring "Social Work: 'A Defense Industry.' "[42]

Once the United States entered the war, this left-wing discourse became more widespread. Not only communists insisted that welfare was necessary to the defense of democracy, the armed forces did too. Welfare served the national defense by insuring a supply of well-nourished and healthy young men, by aiding in the mobilization of all citizens into war work, whether as soldiers or civilians, by providing childcare to working mothers, housing to relocated defense industry workers, and education and recreation for young people who were the nation's future soldiers and workers. Through its association with defense, welfare would "give soldiers something to fight for as well as with."[43] The shift from defense to war, according to the November 1940 Executive Order authorizing the Office of Defense Health and Welfare Service, meant the "obligation to provide the basic social services in wartime rests with the Government." Federal responsibility for "Family Security" was part of the "Defense Activities" of the Federal Security Agency. Welfare demanded national mobilization, and mobilization required national welfare: first to defend the nation, then to win the war. As a social worker in Slade's 1943 novel, remarks: "Roosevelt said a while ago that undernourishment was one factor in the cause of illiteracy, and when he discovered that over four hundred thousand men have been refused by our Army for being illiterate, poor feeding comes out into the light and becomes a national issue."[44]

In addition, with the rise of ADC during the 1930s and 1940s, the threat of delinquency—black and Chicano urban men hanging on street corners in zoot suits and sexual promiscuity by white women out walking the streets to defense jobs—emerged as a national concern for welfare workers and civic leaders. War and the Depression, it was felt, had unhinged American morality and the cachet of a uniform—whether of a "cult" member's zoot suit[45] or of the Armed Forces' draftees and enlisted men—meant young women were swooning: "juvenile delinquency is on the up-and-up and Children's courts can't stop it. You can't help what war does—poor people getting a lot of money to spend and women working out instead of at home," remarked one of Slade's fictional social workers.[46] The focus on delinquency, especially new sexual mores among urban youth, appeared as a return to nineteenth-century social welfare concerns. Yet, as Eliot Ness reported to the National Conference of Social Workers, the 1941 Social Protection Program to "reduce venereal disease hazards to those in the armed forces . . . and to rehabilitate women and girls . . . exposed to prostitution and promiscuity" was part of the Federal Security Agency.[47] *Lilly Crackell* tracked the changing concerns of social welfare caseworkers, family and juvenile courts, charity agencies, and federal and state welfare programs, following the life of a wayward girl as she matures through successive pregnancies into the mother of four sons bound for war. The novel's end finds a group of social workers paradoxically worrying that with the booming war economy they will be the ones who end up unemployed. They worry too about "what the men will be like after they've seen so much blood and killing."[48]

DEFENDING A NATION

As social workers were reading Slade's withering dissection of welfare's history, they were already dealing with the next "national issue," returning veterans like George, Buzz, and Johnny. Like Hollywood, social welfare discourse avoided reference to the massive death and destruction of the war. At most, veterans might suffer "postcombat jitters" or "battle dreams."[49] The real "Big Problem" with veterans was that they would flood the job market sparking postwar recession. Again, a welfare program conceived as yet another essential aspect of security and freedom, the 1944 Servicemen's Readjustment Act (GI Bill of Rights) launched the most extensive health, education, housing, and jobs program in U.S. history; it was aimed at reintegrating men trained in armed combat into a world with little semblance to the one they had left. Social work journals, echoing national agencies, outlined the concerns as follows: guys returning who had not worked before the war, guys returning to new families and wives they barely knew, guys expected to return to their homes as dutiful sons. They'd seen Paris, and much, much worse. Local newspapers were exhorted to stop running headlines stressing the problems vets posed to the newly recovered, newly relieved economy and start broadcasting the federal resources available to them. To further secure the peace and insure that the vets troubled by the Blue Dahlia would become solid citizens, not aging juvenile delinquents, the Servicemen's Readjustment Act expanded the 1934 Federal Housing Authority program guaranteeing mortgage insurance and offered stipends for higher

FIGURE 34. Esther Bubley, "A sign." Washington Courthouse, Ohio, September 1943.

education and job training. Along with the Interstate Highway Act (1956), these social welfare programs for building a postwar middle class (by 1946, for the first time in U.S. history, more than 50 percent of Americans lived in their own homes) masked massive welfare expenditures to the upwardly mobile new residents of suburbia as cold-war defense spending. Throughout the mid-twentieth century, welfare expenditures were considered crucial to national security. In the 1930s, they maintained democracy and freedom (not to mention capitalism) through relief, especially through Aid to Dependent Children (precursor to today's Aid to Families with Dependent Children [AFDC]). Then during World War II, they helped defend the nation. Finally, during the cold war, they functioned to secure the peace. In short, welfare was not just a women's issue as welfare rights activists in the 1960s asserted.

Relief, freedom, security, defense: the large-scale fulfillment of human needs was obviously a task for the federal government, one intimately connected to the economic and military goals of American stability and democracy. In the wake of postwar neo-domesticity, what became understood as welfare returned to earlier constructions of mother's aid, even when President Johnson launched the War on Poverty, again invoking the military metaphor to achieve the goal FDR's Vice-President Henry A. Wallace outlined in 1942: "freedom from want." The language of welfare returned to dependence as AFDC with its suggestion of weakness, both personal and political, dominated welfare debates. The feminization of welfare insured its demise as "a national issue" to be addressed positively and shifted its visibility from heroic efforts to preserve democracy to shameful handouts to the undeserving. Since the 1960s, as the picture of poverty appeared increasingly nonwhite and the cities emptied of well-paying jobs, leaving the only laissez-faire capitalist enterprise—drug dealing—in their place, welfare became localized within deteriorating neighborhoods. By the 1980s, what had once been touted as national defense became personal dependence. The shift resurrects ideas of deviancy and delinquency, not as temporary social and economic results of altered family structures during depression and war, but as the inevitable result of the perennial culture of dependence fostered by "the chains of welfare," as Representative Bill Archer called it.[50] In a classic Orwellian move, freedom (from want) now became a prison.

Welfare as we know it means AFDC the incarnation of 1930s relief programs, among them ADC, itself a federally instituted program building on early twentieth-century "mothers' pensions," which repeated late nineteenth-century charity work by the "friendly visitor."[51] Early twentieth-century social welfare workers responded to "sex delinquency" among girls by inspecting the households of their poor mothers. In 1972, welfare rights activist Johnnie Tillmon proclaimed "welfare is a women's issue," forcing feminism to address poverty, but also indicting a policy that cordons poor mothers off as a "cancer," the "undeserving poor." Responding to Moynihan's characterization of the "black matriarchy," she noted, "AFDC is like a supersexist marriage. You trade in *a* man for *the* man."[52] The 1990s attacks on welfare again castigated poor women, immigrants, and racial minorities, whose opportunities to partake of the economic boom are severely limited by lack of affordable housing, transportation, childcare, and education—the same issues plaguing the nation's security and defense in the 1930s and 1940s. It is as if the entire nation suffers Buzz's amnesia as we forget the mid-century history of welfare. When these same problems threatened white men's ability to serve as breadwinners or as soldiers, they became "national issues," not of dependency, but of freedom and security. The crises Buzz and other GIs faced surfaced in film noirs through the exposure of the rotten world faced with existential resignation by the lone hero. Welfare mothers never were so exalted in their degradation. Instead, they were marginalized within the social-worker novels and case reports as unfit, incapable of dealing either with their corrupted daughters or their curious social workers.

ON THE CASE

Caroline Slade was a woman obsessed, you might say. Like Raymond Chandler or Erle Stanley Gardner or their detectives who return again and again to the scene of the crime, Slade couldn't stop worrying her story of pregnant teens, child prostitutes, inept mothers, acidic welfare workers, and the sad, strange spaces they inhabit— filthy apartments, stuffy courtrooms, fumigated reformatories. Her 1948 novel, *Mrs. Party's House*, tells the life story of a "madame." It begins with a psychiatric social worker's naïve comments about how "society keeps you in the business," to which Mrs. Party replies to the contrary that she has found her "call" (3). *Mrs. Party's House* offers a history of government, legal, journalistic, welfare, and economic investments in prostitution. Mrs. Party is party to the system that periodically mobilizes against her whores: first the officials come to call as patrons, then they sit in judgment from the bench.[53] *Lilly Crackell*, Slade's sequel to *Willie Pond*, traces the many generations of Crackells, labeled "bad" by city elders, who become the clients of the newly established Board of Child Welfare's "executive secretary, typist, case worker, bookkeeper, cleaning woman, and general factotum," Miss Ethel Stalling (161). Following the story of Lilly, impregnated by a rich boy at age fourteen, through the births of her five "bastards," the novel is about Miss Stalling's attempts to rationalize child welfare—and so move it away from its moralistic refusal to aid "unwed mothers"—to provide emergency relief for all children. The novel begins in the aftermath of the First World War and ends with the Japanese bombing of Pearl Harbor. As poverty, malnourishment, and illiteracy become issues of national defense, the focus of child welfare shifts from policing the "wayward girls and immoral women" to nourishing the boys who will fight overseas.[54]

It is only when the class dimensions of the state come into full relief (so to speak), that is, appear detached from female sexuality, that Ethel Stallings allows herself to ask questions of a larger systemic nature. Yet she shies away from the inevitable conclusions. She's not a communist; still "she was forced to ask herself: 'Why should some people be so destitute?' And then: 'Why should there be so many poor in a land capable of supporting many more than are already living upon it?' And then: 'Why should there be any poor?' And at last: 'Why should there be a large group of people living upon the poor?' " (586). The last questions answers itself: " 'The truth is, I live upon the lives of hungry, cold, poverty-stricken people; their misfortunes make possible my good job. . . . Why, my own income rests upon the backs of the poor!" Miss Stallings's realization that she is "one of the poor" horrifies her because she knows what poverty looks like, having made her living closely monitoring it. " 'Social workers and people on relief should be hand in hand, demanding—' " she muses (587). Miss Stallings cannot go on with her analysis, because, like Mrs. Party, the establishment whore, she has always submitted to the powers controlling her job—judges, wealthy board members, supervisors—who might fire her at any time.

Philippa Allen believed her investigations made while hitching across Gauley Bridge would "help in some manner" to alleviate the suffering caused by silicosis. Unlike Miss Bailey, she viewed social work as a cause in the struggle against capitalist exploitation; yet she believed in its premises—investigate and report. Her optimism that a sympathetic ear found in high places (Congress, court) would effect change, however, mirrors Miss Bailey's homespun belief in the merits of relief work. It helps. Another Miss Bailey, Gloria, perhaps her client once, dancing endlessly, failed to find relief. For her, there was no escaping capitalism's daily derby race to weed out the weak; nothing could help her; she had already been "reformed." In the obsessive way that Marlowe returns to Geiger's shady house, each time finding new evidence and culprits, Slade returns again and again to the scene of her crime—the "two hundred years or more of tight reins and poor laws and power over giving out relief," and how "we've set this relief business apart . . . never considered it in relation to the whole" (*Lilly*, 601). She finds no relief but much to reform, though it is not necessarily delinquent girls. These awkward, ungainly novels *do* consider this relief business "in relation to the whole"—from the monologues of prostitutes, to the case reports of bad girls and good girls gone astray, to the musings of officious social workers and their radical critics—offering tantalizing clues to unravel the larger racket of capitalism that was the subject of so many film noirs.

I too have been tracking down clues, pillaging files of New York State Family Service offices in search of Caroline Slade née Beach, born 1886 in Minneapolis, died 1975 in Saratoga Springs. I have unearthed her novels from dusty library stacks (last checked out in 1954) or in dank used bookstores, the pages yellow, brittle; her prose old fashioned, but her tales amazingly current. I have searched the New York archives. I have listened to a distant relative recount her genealogy.[55] Sergeant Friday of television's *Dragnet* demanded, "the facts, ma'am, just the facts," but he did so with a deadpan flourish. The private eye, like the novelist and the professor, knows that reconstructing the crime requires elaborating—through observation, investigation, narration—the secrets of private lives. My mother remembers the dread her mother felt before a relief worker's visit. Like Carolyn Steedman, who watched her mother humiliated by a house visitor and vowed never to endure this herself, my mother got a college degree and, briefly, a job as a caseworker.[56] These stories of poor women's encounters with the state and its face—an educated woman: social worker (Slade, my mother) or teacher (Steedman, myself)—shadow me too. It is not just the facts that need investigating, as film noir knows, but the investigators themselves.

PART 3

NOIR

HOUSEHOLD OBJECTS

CHAPTER 7

BARBARA STANWYCK'S ANKLET

FETISH, ICON, SYMBOL?

"That's life. Whichever way you turn, fate sticks out a foot to trip you," moans Tom Neal into his half-full coffee mug as he begins his grisly tale in *Detour*. In the noir world, where lowly objects assume large proportions, that foot is bound to be shod. This chapter considers the plight, or more properly, the power of objects. To redeem the object, I argue that, compared to the subject, it has gotten an unjustifiably bad rap. Film noir achieves its identifying texture from an array of formulaic images, plots, locations, visual styles, and objects—cigarette lighters, car windshields, doorways, Venetian blinds, and, the focus of this chapter, shoes. Investigating shoes as essential elements of noir's cultural work salvages these lost objects, making it clear that the abject state of objecthood holds compelling authority within psychic and social formations. There can be no subjects without objects.

Why, from Karl Marx and Vincent Van Gogh in the nineteenth century through Martin Heidegger, Charlie Chaplin, and Walker Evans in the twentieth, have men tracked aesthetic value, social standing, and the meaning of labor through the boots of workers; while women, following Sigmund Freud's consideration of the shoe as fetish object, have understood shoes to signal freedom and constraint—at once powerful symbols of mobility and icons of and for desire? I speak of two modes of desire: for the commodity itself, objects of use—products, "equipment," as Heidegger called them—no matter how apparently excessive; and within its representation in paintings, photographs, films, novels, and advertisements. These, as Jacques Derrida goes to great lengths to point out, are not the same thing; yet because of the oddity of this particular object, an object in need of another for it to be put to proper use, desire doubles back on itself, collapsing differences between materiality and representation because the "shoes are always open to the unconscious of the other."[1]

The shoe as emblem of death and icon of sex collapses within the tawdry mise-en-scène of film noir. When femme fatale Phyllis Dietrichson (Barbara Stanwyck) descends the stairway to meet insurance salesman Walter Neff (Fred McMurray) in Billy Wilder's 1944 film *Double Indemnity*, the camera lovingly focuses on her gleaming white legs, feet sheathed in puffy high-heeled mules; above one drapes a gold anklet. Moments later, seated crosslegged before Neff, Phyllis waves her foot ostentatiously in his face, distracting him enough that he mentions the "nice anklet you've got there." She removes her foot and straightens up primly; but the scene evokes the power of the woman's foot to control a man. The anklet, no matter how thin its gold chain appears, is always one-half of the shackles that snare him. Cinderella got her prince because only she among all his subjects could fit into the tiny glass slipper styled for her by her fairy godmother. The anklet, that piece of jewelry adorning one leg, at the bottom of the body rather than the top, calling the eyes to travel down the length of the body and fix on one foot, foregrounds the fetishistic quality of women's footwear, especially, as in the case of Cinderella as well, the isolated, single bare foot and its adornment. Cinderella got her prince; Stanwyck's golden snare leaves Neff a man silently walking home alone after murdering her husband. He hears no sounds, not even his footsteps: "It was the walk of a dead man," he recalls. Derrida points out the important differences between a pair of shoes and a single one: the pair, useful, regular and normal, a heterosexual couple; the lone shoe, perverse, bisexual, destabilizing.[2]

The iconic pan from the floor up to the star's face tells us everything we need to know of her character.[3] So that, for instance, when the camera, with Cornel Wilde, first gazes at Ida Lupino draping one shoeless bare leg over the boss's desk before traveling up to a close-up of her face in the 1948 film noir *Road House*, we know that despite whatever nasty banter ensues, they will eventually become lovers. Wilde moves across the room toward the desk dividing them watching Lupino smoke and play solitaire and picks up her shoe—a platform sandal, designed to replicate Stanwyck's anklet and open-toed mule, displaying "toe cleavage" and a bound ankle.[4] She snatches it from him and hides it behind her back as one would any intimate article found lying about in plain sight. Ida Lupino's shoe is out there in a public display so raw she might as well have been naked before his and our eyes. Worse, her naked display is not only of her sex, but of his as well. The single shoe "combines in a system the two types of object defined by Freud: elongated, solid or firm on one surface, hollow or concave on the other." Shoes, for Freud, like "a whole number of dream-symbols are bisexual and can relate to the male or female genitals, according to the context."[5] Hollywood's Hays production code forbade nudity and other overt representations of sex, sending directors and cinematographers to search out legible covert symbols. Like Walter Neff, they knew where to look. After all, as Wendy Lesser points out, a far different Stanwyck had already tripped up a man a few years before snagging Fred McMurray. In Preston Sturges's wonderful 1941 screwball comedy *The Lady Eve*, Stanwyck surveys the ocean liner dining room through her compact mirror—which makes a tiny movie screen—and comments, like a knowing critic, on the various types of women eyeing the oblivious herpetologist Henry Fonda, who's been "up the Amazon" researching snakes. As he passes before her, she sticks her foot out to trip him into her lap, snagging him.[6]

For women in the movies, especially postwar B-movies, shoes, most likely high-heeled pumps, clatter methodically along the hard concrete sidewalks. They sing a chorus combining vulnerability— she cannot run too fast in them—and menace—her relentless approach or retreat signal her ever-presence. They tap the cobblestones like armor, like weapons. In Jacques Tourneur's 1942 *Cat People*, Serbian designer Irene (Simone Simon) pursues her American rival, the wholesome "new kind of other woman" Alice, through a Central Park tunnel at night. The camera pans from one set of black pumps to another. As the clicking magnifies and echoes within the space and the sounds merge, Alice is overtaken with a terror that lifts only when she is startled by an oncoming bus that she boards even though it takes her back the wrong way. *Phantom Lady*'s Kansas (Ella Raines) threatens bartender (Andrew Tombes Jr.) by following him after sitting immobile night after night in his bar. Her slender trench-coated figure waits for him under the streetlight, and again we see only her black pumps swiftly pursuing him through the night, their rhythm matching the man step for step. By all logic, high-heeled women should not constitute a threat: but they do. Critic Farah Jasmine Griffin recalls hearing that her Aunt Eartha fought back when her second husband tried to hit her, striking him on "the head with one of her tan stilettos. . . . [She] never understood high heels to be an impediment to women's safety."[7] The opening shot of the British noir film *Yield to the Night* follows Mary as she paces across a square and into an alleyway; clicking heels foreshadow the gun shots she will unload into her lover's girlfriend that land her in prison, where she gets religion and repents. The opening sequence of *Caged* (1950) shows Marie (Eleanor Parker) seated in the paddy wagon among an assortment of jaded prostitutes; her demure and plain flats set her apart from them. However, by the time she is released on parole, she has been transformed. She signals her "new" life outside, on the streets, by entering a car full of men and crossing her legs so that her high heels are visible and her knee available for fondling. The black high-heeled pump was an essential element of postwar working women's attire. She doesn't find God; instead she seeks cold cash, this being a very American noir.

These examples from classic film noirs (or their 1960s British variation) contrast with Van Gogh's invocation of work boots as signs of poverty; they speak of women's aggressive mobility in postwar urban spaces. The physical movement and sexual predation available to women emerge visually from their shapely legs and aurally from the sound of their heels beating the pavement. They walk the streets—streetwalkers—turning public spaces relentlessly into scenes of crime and themselves into objects of desire. As streetwalkers, their shoes are also useful; they work/walk the pavement nightly. However, the icon of the high-heeled pump rarely registers as working apparel. It is a marker of sexual violation and allure, not labor. Yet an economy of desire is always first an economy, a point exaggerated to absurdity in Samuel Fuller's 1964 noir spoof *The Naked Kiss*, in which prostitute Kelly (Constance Towers) beats her pimp by pummeling him with her rigid black patent leather purse while standing over him in stilettos to retrieve the money he owes her. She then disappears into small-town America to enter her new life as a nurse for disabled children, only to discover that she cannot escape corruption: in Grantville, cops pimp for the brothel across the river, and the leading citizen and philanthropist is a pedophile. To protect the young women and girls of Grantville, Kelly beats the local madame with her stiff black leather purse and kills the pervert with his black Bakelite telephone receiver (both repeating her shoes, one in its material, the other in its form), only to end up in jail when her pimp presses charges for assault—the shoe was prologue.

In his discussion of "Fetishism," Freud puts it quite simply: "I announce that the fetish is a substitute for the penis. . . . To put it more plainly: the fetish," he continues, "is a substitute for the woman's (the mother's) penis that the little boy once believed in and—for reasons familiar to us—does not want to give up."[8] The fetish, as the simultaneous sign of disavowal (of woman's castration) and attachment (to the fantasy of the female phallus), is often connected to this contradiction through its partial nature. Thus the single foot or the single shoe—seen first from below as the child looks up at the vagina—suits at once "both the disavowal and the affirmation of the castration."[9] As a synecdoche, the fetish is at once too much and not enough, anticipatory and remainder. "The fetish, like a 'screen memory', represents this phase [a submerged and forgotten phase of sexual development] and is thus a remnant and precipitate of it."[10] "What is substituted for the sexual object," says Freud in "Three Essays on Sexuality," "is some part of the body (such as the foot or hair) which is in general very inappropriate for sexual purposes, or some inanimate object which bears an assignable relation to the person whom it replaces and preferably to that person's sexuality (e.g., a piece of clothing or underlinen). Such substitutes are with some justice likened to the fetishes in which savages believe that their gods are embodied."[11] Thus the shoe, which, like the foot that holds power "as an age-old sexual symbol which occurs even in mythology," is a "corresponding symbol of the *female* genitals."[12] Age-old and savage, the fetish is antimodern.

Possession and disavowal overvalue the fetish as a relic of an image of plenty destroyed, never quite admitted, and so reinvested with god-like power. Freud's description of the fetish locates the trauma of castration within the "little boy" and presents the fetish object as *his* substitute. Gilles Deleuze remarks that as "the last object he saw as a child before becoming aware of the missing penis (a shoe, for example). . . [t]he fetish is . . . not a symbol at all, but as it were a frozen, arrested, two-dimensional image, a photograph to which one returns repeatedly to exorcise the dangerous consequences of movement, the harmful discoveries that result from exploration."[13] Deleuze distinguishes between the object and its representation. The fetish is a photograph, frozen and arrested; yet the photograph, as Roland Barthes mournfully insists in *Camera Lucida*, is a melancholic object, par excellence.

Can women fetishize shoes? Or is it instead shoes that stir desire, turning the woman herself into fetish? As phallic mother substitute, the fetish, like the phallic mother, presents the girl an ambivalent homosexual identification with the female phallus as a woman's genitalia. It circulates, but just barely. The shoe, as Freud admits in "On Dreams," especially the high heel, is both phallus and its lack. As such, it fulfills Victor Turner's definition of a ritual symbol. These incorporate contradictory social practices: "symbols are social facts, 'collective representations,' " he says in *The Forest of Symbols*, that are "multireferential," at once "sensory" and "ideological," whose "empirical properties" include "(1) condensation; (2) unification of disparate meanings in a single symbolic form; (3) polarization of meaning."[14] Rather than being immobile—frozen, as Deleuze calls the fetish—shoes as "social facts" are in constant flux. The shoe and the pair of shoes have almost nothing in common, no matter how redundant (but of course not, they're different) the two are. Hence freedom and death, sex and labor, accessory and necessity, object and symbol: magic, a mysterious thing. "Yes yes, we're magicians," assures Vladimir as he and Estragon struggle to get Estragon's boots on in *Waiting for Godot*.[15]

As lowly objects, abject objects, shoes remain as reminders, remainders of death. The lone shoe lying in the middle of a street following the shooting of German SDS leader Rudi Dutschke is a melancholy memento; its photograph part of the collective archive of 1968 and the German Autumn that followed.[16] The piles of shoes lining the railroad tracks of Auschwitz that appear in Alain Resnais's

Night and Fog, like the recent catalogue of photographs of articles of clothing, mostly shoes—remains of the men slaughtered and buried at Srebenica during the Bosnian War—are monuments of horror, reminders of the destruction of twentieth-century genocides. Articles meant to take the wear and tear of daily use, shoes remain in tact after other personal effects, and with them, their owners, have disintegrated, disappeared. "The Still Life as a Personal Object," from which Meyer Schapiro argues with Martin Heidegger over a pair of shoes, are the very shoes, as Derrida notes, left behind in the flight from the soil still clinging to one's work boots for an urban exile. *Nature Morte*, indeed, death follows their footsteps.[17] Shoes, as symbolic objects themselves, travel across three fundamental planes of human experience: work, sex, death.

"A MAGICAL OBJECT"

"The fetishism of commodities has its origin . . . in the peculiar social character of the labour that produces them," Marx wrote. "It is value, rather, that converts every product into a social hieroglyphic."[18] His example of this oxymoronic process of collective indecipherability goes as follows: "When I state that coats or *boots* stand in a relation to linen, because it is the universal incarnation of abstract human labour, the absurdity of the statement is self-evident. Nevertheless, when producers of coats and *boots* compare those articles with linen, or, what is the same thing, with gold or silver, as the universal equivalent, they express the relation between their own private labour and the collective labour of society in the same form." It is this "fantastic form," this "mist-enveloped region," this "mysterious thing" that fetishizes the commodity, separating it from its use-value as a product of human labor into an abstract value of exchange equivalent to all others and masking the "social character of the labour that produces them."[19] Walter Benjamin notes that Karl Korsch pushed Marx's insight into the fetishism of commodities to account generally for "human self-alienation . . . [b]y revealing *all* economic categories to be mere fragments of one great fetish."[20] As a religious practice, "fetishism seem[s] to appear only among peoples who have already attained to a certain degree of civilization."[21] In those "mist enveloped regions of the religious world" where "the productions of the human brain

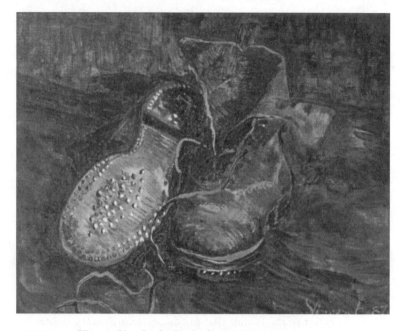

FIGURE 35. Vincent Van Gogh, *Les Soulieres* (1886).

appear as independent beings endowed with life, and entering into relation with one another and the human race" fetishism emerges as a transition after totemism (72).

Relying on the same primitivist ideas animating Freud's work on the fetish, Marx also views its power as suspiciously ancient.[22] It depends, according to Marx's story of *Robinson Crusoe*, on circulation, that is, on alienation and the division of labor, and on consumption, the appropriation and incorporation of objects as values. Thus commodities carry within them, and thus within capitalism, the residue of the past. In a characteristic gesture, Benjamin, quoting Theodor Wiesengrund Adorno, describes the fetishized commodity as a "phantasmagoria," creating "a consumer item in which there is no longer anything that is supposed to remind us how it came into being. It becomes a magical object, insofar as the labor stored up in it comes to seem supernatural and sacred at the very moment when it can no longer be recognized as labor."[23] Again, anxiety about the non-Western, primitive, irrational basis of fetishism—"we're magicians"—the commodity and its consumer, like the fetish and its worshipper, are suspiciously feminized, or at least as emasculated as Gogo and Didi.

Unpacking his library, Benjamin notes the peculiar fascination with ownership that certain items produce for consumers within bourgeois culture. These items, like books or shoes, are those that can form a "collection," and collections produce "collectors" for whom "ownership is the most intimate relationship that one can have to objects."[24] Collections, like genres, operate on the principle of repetition with a difference, as every item resembles its other yet must be distinct at the same time. In his dissection of bourgeois living room objects, in "Paris, Capital of the Nineteenth Century," Benjamin discerned the origins of detective fiction as a genre that required objects, collected idiosyncratically by their owners, to provide clues, traces of evidence. The generic formula depended on the generic nature of the objects surveyed—every parlor has a chair, but what kind? Is it upholstered and draped by antimacassars or wooden, etc.? Susan Stewart calls this "the total aestheticization of use value."[25] For Stewart, this aspect of collecting acts to annihilate history; however, a shoe collection must always retain its historicity—that is the trap of fashion, it's of a moment, au courant. The collector acts like a criminal in his relentless pursuit of the missing items, rare editions, and so forth. "Every passion borders on the chaotic, but the collector's passion borders on the chaos of memories" such that "the life of the collector [is] a dialectical tension between the poles of disorder and order" (60). Within a commodity fetishistic culture, then, ownership becomes both a sickness and its cure. Furthermore, collectors oscillate between stasis—one needs some place to put the objects collected—and movement. Travel is essential to collecting: Benjamin remarks that he made his "most memorable purchases on trips, as a transient. Property and possession belong to the tactical sphere. Collectors are people with a tactical instinct; their experience teaches them that when they capture a strange city, the smallest antique shop can be a fortress, the most remote stationery store a key position" (63). In short, the collector is always one who walks; she needs a good pair of shoes.

Calling Benjamin our greatest theorist of the object, critic Douglas Mao argues that the "feeling of regard for the physical object as object—as not-self, as not-subject, as most helpless and will-less of entities, but also as fragment of Being, as solidity, as otherness in its most resilient opacity—seems a peculiarly twentieth-century malady or revelation . . . one of the minor trademarks" of modernism.[26] For Mao, the object and desire for it cannot resemble the fetish and fetishism as charted by either Marx or Freud, despite Benjamin's obvious reliance on their sources. Suggesting that "solid objects" were under siege as the concrete and particular gave way to vast abstract systematizing of science, Mao sees a melancholy rescue of the object in the Anglo-American high modernist writers, such as Virginia Woolf. Orlando's feat of Restoration consumption in redecorating the ancestral home is matched when, as a modernist poet, she drives to the department store in pursuit of various household necessities, including "boy's boots, bath salts, sardines," only to be foiled by the plethora of stuff spilling across the aisles she glances as the elevator lifts her from floor to floor of loaded counters. Orlando, however, rather than dispute seems to confirm, even in her choice of words, Marx: "In the eighteenth century, we knew how everything was done; but here I rise though the air; I listen to voices in America; I see men flying—but how it's done, I can't even begin to wonder. So my belief in magic returns."[27] All this magic; yet she fails to return with any of her shopping list items—so many products, incommensurate things. Woolf implies that for the modern woman commodities are interchangeable and inconsequential; but Woolf's modern woman is educated, a woman of privilege, striding purposefully through time and space, even if her mansion has become a museum.

OTHER SMALL OBJECTS

In *The Gold Rush* (1925), Charlie Chaplin's Tramp cooks and serves himself his boiled boot to fend off starvation in the Klondike. His careful dissection of the boot, picking each hobnail out as a finely-trained waiter might debone a trout, and precise twirling of the laces into a mound of spaghetti calls forth the animal quality of shoes— made of leather, absorbing the odors of the feet (one aspect that makes them so likely to become a fetish according to Freud)—and thus close to edible; yet their proximity to the filthy ground, their sweaty smells make them unappealing, disgusting. Chaplin had his boots constructed from licorice—sometimes called shoe-leather— and thus ate them with relish. In the section of *The Arcades Project* on the Saint-Simonians, Walter Benjamin quotes from a "revealing" Leon Halevy poem, "La Chaussure":

> This people, whose head and hand you fear,
> Must march, must march—no halting!
> It's when you stop their steps
> They notice the holes in their shoes.[28]

They notice the holes in their shoes only when they have time to contemplate their poverty, that is, when they no longer even have work and thus become a curious kind of excess, the detritus of capitalism. This impoverished proletariat, presocialist and anarchic, like the Tramp, as Roland Barthes calls him, is "still hungry . . . expressing the humiliated condition of the worker."[29] Work boots full of holes have no use. They no longer can be considered "equipment," in Heidegger's sense, and, like their unemployed wearers, signify a miserable supplement to their lack. Those gone to extremes—forced to eat their own shoes, self-devouring and empty—are useless as either producers or consumers within capitalism.

> Of shoes: ordinary work shoes may be called 'typical'; only if you remember that old Sunday shoes, tennis sneakers, high tennis shoes, sandals, moccasins, bare feet, and even boots, are not at all rarely used: it should be known, too, that there are many kinds of further, personal treatment of shoes. Mainly, this: Many men, by no means all, like to cut holes through the uppers for foot-spread and for ventilation: and in this they differ a good deal between utility and art. You seldom see purely utilitarian slashes: even the bluntest of these are liable to be patterned a little more than mere use requires: on the other hand, some shoes have been worked on with a wonderful amount of patience and studiousness toward a kind of beauty, taking the memory of an ordinary sandal for a model, and greatly elaborating and improving it. I have seen shoes so beautifully worked in this way that their durability was greatly reduced.[30]

James Agee's treatise on the clothing of the tenant farmers of Hale County, Alabama, like his "counter-spy" Walker Evans's

FIGURE 36. Walker Evans, "Boots." Hale County, Ala. (1936).

photographs of George Gudger's Sunday shoes drying before the "altar" of the decorated fireplace, or his work boots airing in the sun, refute Agee's call to avoid considering their book as art. Still they cannot help themselves: Agee compares the blues of the farmer's overalls and workshirts to "the blues of Cezanne" (267); Evans quotes Van Gogh's peasant boots. Each emphasizes the beauty of objects so thoroughly tied to use-value, yet conveying the most private longings for aesthetics. Agee writes:

> There is great pleasure in a sockless and sweated foot in the fit-ted leathers of a shoe made of most simple roundnesses and squarings and flats, of dark brown raw thick leathers nailed, and sewn coarsely to one another in courses and patterns of doubled and tripled seams, and such throughout that like many other small objects they have great massiveness and repose and are, as the houses and overalls are, and the feet and legs of the women, who go barefooted so much, fine pieces of architecture. . . . They are worn out like animals to a certain

ancient stage and chance of money at which a man buys a new pair; then, just as old sunday shoes do, they become the inheritance of a wife. (270)

These clay-encrusted objects placed symmetrically before the fireplace are emblems of labor, of poverty, and they are symbols of the essential uniqueness and dignity the reporters find in the lives of America's forgotten. "Clay is worked into the substance of the uppers and a loose dust of clay lies over them. . . . The shoes are worn for work" (270). Shoes carry within them the traces of the struggle to survive. Carved up, they are heavy with the grind of fieldwork; they are vessels of pain. Yet, like a wife, they are open, they exist to receive: a sweaty foot in fitted leather.

According to Swedenborg, shoes signify a "lowly nature," at once "humble and despicable." Men's shoes, claims Gertrude Jobes, served as "ancient means of binding a contract," because the removal of the shoe meant "loss of legal rights," which corresponds

FIGURE 37. Dorothea Lange, "The commodities on the counter represent two week's allotment for four people. Photograph made in FSA distributing station for emergency grants of food and clothing to destitute agricultural workers." Bakersfield, Calif., Nov. 1938.

to religious interdictions against wearing shoes in sacred places as they possess "contagion from the secular."[31] Yet Jean Servier "observes that 'to walk shod is to take possession of the ground.' "[32] These images of land and its ownership entrust the shoe with powers at once menial and imperial. The workingman's shoe carries the earth in its ancient creases and thus remembers labor and its equipment. In their iconic usage, the work shoe becomes attached to lowly peasant labor in the fields; whether Heidegger registers Van Gogh's boots as belonging to the farmer's wife (or, as Schapiro insists, as "clearly" the painter's own), we know they must be read as figuring some form of abject masculinity. As Agee points out, women's work shoes began as men's, only becoming their wives' (or daughters' or mothers'-in-law) possessions after they were near disintegration. This becomes clear in two of Evans's photographs where women are shown wearing shoes—the family portrait of the Woodses in which Miss Molly wears a battered pair of boots and the picture of Margaret Ricketts washing dishes in an old pair of men's shoes. The destination of worn boots means that they are not firmly latched to masculinity—or that the masculinity to which they are attached is hardly secure; it is the province of "humble" men tied to the earth; their movement is toward dissolution—the eventual wearing away of the leather soles, but not before they have been transferred onto women's feet—sunk even lower. Heidegger relied on Van Gogh's paintings of peasant shoes as a secondary, rather than immediate, way to consider the movement from equipment (as a pure useful thing) to its apprehension in the truth of an artwork. Tellingly, Heidegger reads Van Gogh's shoes as belonging to the farmer's wife—hand-me-downs, already-used, second-hand equipment, leftovers.

According to Joseph Kockelman's rendering, those shoes evoke for Heidegger a loneliness and rugged tenacity of earth and the "wordless joy of having once more withstood want" through the endless repetition of wearying field work.[33] This "heavy pathos of the primordial and earthy" denied what for art historian Meyer Schapiro was the central point of Van Gogh's paintings—that the still life objects were the *artist's* personal belongings—his self representation.[34] Work shoes symbolized the labor of the artist. Heidegger frequently referred to shoes and shoemakers as exemplary of being in a world in which materials and labor create meaning.[35] In

FIGURE 38. Hugo Gellert, "Money, or the Circulation of Commodities," from *Karl Marx 'Capital' in Lithographs*, 1934.

short, workingmen's boots—as useful products—and shoemakers—producers of use-values par excellence—aestheticize, even romanticize, human drudgery as survival. Hence Van Gogh's multiple returns to this readily available subject. In one of the remarkable moments in Art Spiegelman's *Maus*, Vladek describes how he survived liquidation by claiming to know how to repair boots, thus securing himself a source of income by fixing a guard's broken sole. Without any skills, except hustling and a good memory, Vladek lands a position in the shoe shop and earns enough to bribe various capos into transferring his wife Anja into a barracks near him in Birkenau. Ever practical, not only does he describe the story to Artie, he draws a picture for his son, showing how to repair a boot.[36]

What all this thingness of equipment and beauty of utility and earthy broken shoes and so forth have in common is a remarkably consistent image of the peasants' shoes and the toiling shoemaker as central icons of heroic survival, of noble yet lowly subsistence, of a beauty and truth to be found in the very scraped bottoms of the filthy boots that trudge the heavy furrows to bring forth the meager means of human subsistence, to establish the ground for mid-twentieth-century philosophical musings on death, art, time, work, and being. Left-wing cartoonist Hugo Gellert also quoted Van Gogh's shoes for his illustration of Karl Marx's explanation of the "circulation of commodities" in his illustrated edition of *Capital* because shoes connect the laborer to the earth, and to toil and deprivation. They show the shoemaker as a craftsman who transforms raw materials—leather, itself an organic material—into a useful item. Like evocations of the land and rural life, as antidotes to industrialism (or even as evocations of productive work in general), these images of solidity, earthiness, and use are sentimental; left-wing iconography of labor, on the one hand, fascist icons of soil, on the other, would redeem a bereft manhood. Men's work boots reek of hard labor; and while Agee and Evans revered this, Preston Sturges was mocking it in his satire of proletarian social realism, *Sullivan's Travels*. Joel McRae ends up on a chain gang after his shoes, in which his servant has hidden his ID, are stolen by a tramp in a flophouse.

But enough with the heavy trod of hobnails and creaky mud-encrusted leather! Yes, men's boots and shoes evidence the nobility of soil and the grind of stoop labor. Shoes, even men's work shoes, also have other uses; they signal other kinds of labor. In the 1950s, Nikita Khrushchev banged on the United Nations table with his hefty black Oxford, declaring "We will bury you!" His denunciation of American capitalism—made in New York City, capital of capital, was a reminder of his peasant origins; yet the shoes were resolutely corporate in their anonymity. Van Gogh and Agee and Evans evoked the individuality of the work shoe, molded by years of wear to the foot; but the black leather Oxford was meant, like the Organization Man who wore it, to fit in and disappear. The opening shots of Alfred Hitchcock's *Strangers on a Train* (1951) track the rushing commuters' shoes crisscrossing up and down the aisle until they come to rest when Bruno (Robert Walker) and Guy (Farley Granger) bump into each other, two men outside the corporate economy (as wealthy gay man and tennis player, respectively) who wear more distinctive footwear. In Robert Aldrich's *Kiss Me Deadly*, another 1950s thriller that explicitly refers to the Soviet nuclear threat, Mike Hammer (Ralph Meeker) is able to discern the killers who have gotten hold of the "great whatsit" by recognizing their two-toned wingtips, a distinctive sign of precarious masculinity.[37]

6″ WITH ANKLE STRAP

Women's shoes, especially those meant for dress-up, are so much more useful; even Mrs. Gudger put on "[b]lack lowheeled slippers with strapped insteps and single buttons" on Saturday, market day at Cookstown.[38] The work they do is invisible as work; yet they too point to sites of labor. For Agee, shoes are cunts—the worn leather molded to the sweated bare foot, and none more surely convey terror and desire than the spiked high heel—*vagina dentata*. Mrs. Gudger's demure flats hint, with their straps and buttons, at the sexual intimacy connected to the removal of shoes. A *New York Times* article pictured a Tristan Webber sandal, with four-inch tapered heel featuring spikes protruding from the instep strap, the heel, and the ankle strap; over the image was the caption: "Shoe or weapon?"[39] Pierre Silber's advertisement for a $35 six-inch spike, available in sizes 6–14, offers a woman's shoe destined for a transgendered foot walking across skin, not pavement.[40] The stiff black pump of 1940s film noirs operated as a bullet case, sheathing the woman's foot and hardening it against the concrete pavement she traversed in her search for desire and power.

The woman's shoe as weapon begins Fuller's campy film noir *The Naked Kiss*, but it is also a pivotal scene in Herbert Biberman's 1953 left-wing labor film, *Salt of the Earth*. In this saga about a New Mexico miners' strike and the increasing activism of the miners' wives, Esperanza (Rosaura Revueltas), wife of macho strike leader Ramon, breaks free from her husband and children to join the women who have taken over the picket line after a Taft-Hartley injunction prohibits the men from marching. Handing her newborn infant to a stunned Ramon when the sheriff's deputies draw their guns at the women, Esperanza "stops for a second, slips off her right shoe [as deputy] Vance knocks the other woman down, pulls his revolver from his holster. Esperanza whacks him over the wrist with her shoe, knocking the weapon out of his hand."[41] Esperanza joins the women's group and forcefully helps lead the strike, leaving Ramon to take over the domestic chores. This labor melodrama, made during the height of McCarthyism by blacklisted actors, screenwriters, and directors, condenses many left-wing feminist and labor ideals in this one scene, which taps into latent fears of female autonomy. After this episode, Esperanza, still wearing her demure flats, is rarely home as housewife; she carts her kids to the picket line or else leaves them with Ramon to feed.

Shoes facilitate women's social mobility. In *Salt of the Earth*, a simple flat bests a gun, averting violence; but a hooker's spiked heel can almost kill a man, as Constance Towers demonstrates. So we arrive at the third "meaning" of the shoe—as symbols of travel, especially the journey to freedom, and/or death—an abstraction that cannot be seen despite its objectification.[42] Dorothy skips her way along the yellow brick road protected by the ruby slippers, which will eventually transport her home when she clicks their heels. The shoes transfer their power from one body to another, as they are themselves transferred from the Wicked Witch's shriveled feet onto Dorothy's, precipitating the journey and the ensuing struggle to possess them. The ruby slippers are very powerful, as Glenda surmises; yet their power is clearly gendered: no man seems interested in them.

This lavish 1939 MGM musical signaling the end of the Depression anticipated the ubiquitous sound of the femme fatale's heels. These postwar emblems of women's newly acquired sexual freedom, in turn, became powerful indexes for female fantasies of escape during the 1950s. Twice in Sandra Cisneros prose poem *The House on Mango Street* (1983), the narrator, Esperanza, astutely notes her sexual vulnerability as a girl on the verge of adolescence, a child of Mexican immigrants living on the edges of urban poverty. Both of these moments occur through her recognition of her unsettled footing within her world. This footing, literalized in the form of shoes, oscillates between a clunky 1950s girlhood, epitomized by bulbous saddle shoes, those sturdy markers of practicality bought by Depression-era mothers to last a whole school year, worn to the fancy party for which Esperanza is dressed in a new frock. Her ceremonial coming out—a dance with her uncle—is thus forever marred by the twin signs of poverty and gawkiness. No party shoes accessorize this dress. Esperanza has glimpsed the power of impractical shoes when she and her friends try on a few discarded pairs of dyed high heels and wobble around the block eliciting catcalls from the men and boys hanging on the street corners. Thrilled and terrified by their newly acquired swaying hips, the girls toss the heels as soon as they discover that men now see them as sexually desirable. With these two scenes, two crucial aspects of modern female footware are represented: that class position is instantly recognizable by looking at the soles of all folk, and that women's desires are tied to their (in)ability to move within them. Ultimately, Esperanza dreams of leaving the confines of Mango Street, changing her name to Ze Ze the X and possessing a house of her own emptied of all furnishings save blank paper and a pair of shoes neatly stored by her bedside.[43]

Women's decorative shoes, especially high heels, like Cinderella's glass slippers and Esperanza's yellow heels, reveal female sexuality. They become weapons and as such also convey those attracted/attached to them toward danger, even death. Women appear vulnerable in these wobbly unstable objects, but they elevate themselves to greater heights, commandeering space through the constant clattering of their heels on the hard surfaces of city streets and work places (whether office buildings or bedrooms). As objects of desire for both men (who, unlike the aristocracy of sixteenth century, now only watch them) and women (who can both watch and wear them), these icons also slide across genders. They lead inevitably to death. Not the inexorable, slow death of decay, but rather a sudden, violent death.[44] "These boots are made for walking," sang Nancy Sinatra in her thigh-high white boots, "and one of these days they're gonna walk all over you." Through work or sex, shoes journey to death; but the path they take, at least partially, runs through freedom. Pursuit is dangerous, but it's better than bondage. The broken feet of aristocratic Chinese women curtailed their movement, forcing them to take small mincing and painful steps unless carried. Shoes move us across space; desire for mobility leads us to death. When Marlene Dietrich kicks off her heels to follow Gary Cooper across the sands of *Morocco*, is it desire or death that propels her? She'll never make it barefoot, yet she grabs the camp followers' recalcitrant goat and walks on out of the screen. In the Hans Christian Andersen fairy tale, the Little Mermaid, pursuing her desire for her beloved prince, succumbs to a witch's brew that allows her to silently walk on legs as sharp as knives piercing her body, only to be left mute and alone. In "The Red Shoes," a young girl's desire for shiny red shoes, inappropriately worn to church and funerals, leads to her being controlled by her independent red shoes. Try as she might to take off the perpetually moving shoes, they remained fast on her feet, dancing her frenetically past the coffin of the old woman who had cared for her. Only when an executioner chops off her feet, leaving her crippled, can she stop dancing and repent her vanity. Broken in spirit, like the Little Mermaid, she dies blessed, another terrifying story of female lust set in motion, then crippled, by footwear.

Carolyn Steedman recalls a recurring dream she had as a child of a woman in a New Look coat entering a doorway, her severe black pumps clicking along the bleak, postwar London sidewalk just out of young Carolyn's reach. Steedman's mediation on "the politics of envy" dictating the terms of her mother's brutal life's landscape depended upon a thorough understanding of the connection between female mobility and clothing. Buy a good pair of pumps, a New Look coat, a smart suit, and a working-class woman, skillfully shedding her accent, could transform her destiny.[45] Leaving her ratty Lancashire mill town for the precarious possibilities open in London during the Depression, Steedman's mother used her sexuality to secure another future for herself and her two daughters. Fundamental to her mobility—spatial and class—was her ability to wear the proper articles of clothing appropriate to her desires. The trajectory from Lancashire to London depended on learning how to move in the smart pumps of postwar women's autonomy. Like the many femme fatales in film noir who traverse the dark city streets of San Francisco, New York, and Los Angeles in search of power, pleasure, and money, Steedman's postwar London mother knew how to dress for success.[46]

Success for the young middle-class girl growing up in this postwar world was mapped out, as Charlotte Nekola remarks in her memoir, *Dream House*, by "the progression from childhood to full womanhood . . . Mary Janes to flats to pumps with a small tasteful heel, and finally to the realm of pure sex and authority, 'spike' heels." Remembering an incident when she moved her "convertible" strap on her Sunday dress-up Mary Janes so that her girlish shoe would magically appear as a mature flat, Nekola describes how this gesture "instantly transformed [her], now a sinful Cinderella with some new shoes of big-girl life."[47] However, when she showed her mother her magnificent maturity, she was enraged by her disapproval. Like the old woman who tries to steer Karen from the red shoes, Nekola's mother insists Charlotte keep the strap tightly fixed around her instep, maintaining the freedom of her "native girlhood" as long as possible (49). Cisneros's Esperanza and her girlfriends had quickly retreated from "Cinderella" to their native girlhood after their triumphant "tee-tottering" in the "lemon shoes and the red shoes and the shoes that used to be white but are now pale blue" cast-offs of the family of little feet because the threat of their sexual allure—men were suddenly whistling, offering each a dollar for a kiss—would inevitably lead to dangers—sex, pregnancy, marriage (40). Or worse: Barbara Stanwyck's anklet and heels, her cigarette and whiskey, her cat glasses and gun would indeed turn you into a femme fatale—murderous, deadly, and doomed to die in a hail of bullets.

Growing up in the 1950s, many young girls studied these films, found on late-night television, as documentaries of lives our parents might have lived, if not for the fortunes of free education from City College and the GI Bill enabling the installation of the nuclear family in the suburb. Office of War Information photographer Esther Bubley had recorded actual noir women who rode midnight buses and trains across the country in search of war work, residing in rooming houses along the way. Her bus trip throughout the Midwest and the South undertaken in 1943 took her to bus stations where she photographed single women sleeping on benches waiting for the 5 A.M. to Memphis, their black pumps dangling from their swollen feet. These intimate images of migrant women, solitary and vulnerable, hint at a fleeting return to innocence forever gone with war mobilization.

Bubley's single working women in transit during World War II presaged the "evil women [who] were women of psychological difficulties . . . who lived entirely in scenes of blood, murder, suicide, and physical and psychiatric violence of all kinds. Barbara Stanwyck's career . . . [was] built on the portrayal of this type of gangster woman." These women's crime films were so popular, noted one of American popular culture's critic C. L. R. James's female informants, who was "a sensitive and well-read observer," because, according to her, "they are the only performances that seem to be *real*."[48] Quoting documentary photography and dramatizing the pleasures, powers, and terrors of women's new-found mobility, made visually and aurally explicit in the erotic high-heeled slippers and anklet of Phyllis Dietrichson in *Double Indemnity*, the relentless clatter of

Kansas's black pumps in *Phantom Lady*, and Kelly's vicious spiked heels in *The Naked Kiss*, film noir turns women into magicians. If commodities could speak the secrets therein, they might tell us just what a woman wants—Shoes! Wedgies, platforms, sandals, thongs, mules, flats, pumps, loafers, heels, slingbacks, sneakers, and don't even start on the boots.

CHAPTER 8

MEDIUM UNCOOL: AVANT-GARDE FILM AND UNCANNY FEMINISM

"THE MOVIES ARE A REVOLUTION" (TAYLOR MEAD)

In his examination of the uncanny, Freud teases out the definition of the sensation accruing when "everything . . . ought to have remained hidden and secret, . . . yet comes to light."[1] The uncanny, that which is most familiar suddenly estranged, manifests itself in a curious dance between repression and recurrence. In chapter 7, I investigated the gendered residue clinging to the worn shoes repeating themselves iconically throughout modern culture. In this chapter, I offer a microhistory of the interconnections—both literal, in the form of personal relations, and theoretical, in the form of shared ideas—between early radical feminism in the United States and 1960s avant-garde film culture. Each bears an uncanny relation to American popular culture and its pulpy politics by examining what "ought to have been concealed but which has nevertheless come to light" through the intense personal self scrutiny that was a hallmark of both the avant-garde and feminism (148). Microhistories of local events, movements, and cultures form a central component of the new scholarship on women. Seeking a method that avoids globalizing assumptions drawn from relatively limited data, microhistories assert the authority of the local to explain how theory becomes activated and experienced. This is not simply an academic claim that "Small is Beautiful" or an exhortation to "Think Globally, Act Locally" but rather an attempt to understand how superstructural processes of cultural production and political organizing create what Raymond Williams calls "lived experience" through "structures of feeling."[2] Western Marxism since Antonio Gramsci locates culture as a site for struggle, in part, because of the unprecedented capital tied to it. Thus organizing countercultures is a hallmark of late capitalism because "an immense and inflationary issuing of superstructural credit; a universal abandonment of the referential gold standard; an extraordinary printing up of ever more devalued signifiers" unleashed "social energies" that built new movements, including radical feminism and the avant-garde.[3]

My argument is that the movement for women's liberation in the United States, which exploded within the New Left and captured the attention of the mainstream media in 1968, owed much of its rhetoric and practice to postwar avant-garde film, which, in turn, was indebted—albeit oppositionally—to America's pulp modernism. These two movements would appear to have nothing in common with the pulp fiction, government documentary, and Hollywood B-movies I have been discussing throughout this book. However, even in this cultural and political realm seemingly cut off from popular pulp, the same process by which cultural form anticipates political action is at work. Revealing the seamy underside of postwar America occurred across a wide spectrum of film cultures. The very repetitive nature of this exposure hints at feminism's uncanny investment in rescripting domestic melodrama, especially when staged during wartime, by bringing its noir elements "to light."

Because it is an uncanny one, this story of American feminism, film, and the long 1968 requires the kind of doubled and crisscrossed narrative technique of film noir.[4] Jay Boyer declares "you will never read the novel you might like to" about the 1960s because "there is no way to say it."[5] The 1960s defy verbal representation—or rather narrative—because words fail; image and sound—helicopter blades chopping the air over Vietnam and urban America, rock 'n' roll, nightly body counts from the battles at home and in the jungles of Southeast Asia—are what remain. Todd Gitlin offers a more verbose but essentially similar point: "the years 1967, 1968, 1969, and 1970 were a cyclone in a wind tunnel. . . . When history comes off the leash, when reality appears illusory and illusions take on lives of their own, the novelist loses the platform on which imagination builds its plausible appearances. . . . Reality was reckless, and so there is the temptation to dismiss it—say with the cliché of compilation, snippets of pure spectacle, in the style of a ticker tape or a clunky documentary:"[6] He goes on to reel off the following list:

> draft card burnings . . . the Pentagon . . . Stop the Draft Week . . . the Tet offensive . . . the McCarthy campaign . . . Johnson decides not to run for another term . . . Martin Luther King killed . . . Columbia buildings occupied . . . Paris . . . Prague . . . trips to Hanoi . . . Robert Kennedy killed . . . Democratic Convention riots . . . hundreds of students massacred in Mexico City . . . Miss America protest . . . Nixon elected . . . deserters, flights to Canada and Sweden, mutinies, "fragging" in Vietnam . . . Eldridge Cleaver underground . . . San Francisco State, Berkeley, Stanford, Harvard, etc., etc., besieged . . . People's Park . . . police shootouts with Black Panthers . . . student, freak, black, homosexual riots . . . SDS splits . . . Woodstock . . . women's consciousness-raising . . . the Chicago Conspiracy trial . . . Charles Manson . . . Altamont . . . My Lai . . . Weatherman bombs . . . Cambodia . . . Kent State . . . Jackson State . . . a fatal bombing in Madison . . . trials, bombings, fires, agents provocateurs, and the grand abstractions, "resistance," "liberation," "revolution," "repression"—to name only some of what was swirling."[7]

Of this long litany, two entries interest me: Miss America and women's consciousness-raising with "clunky documentary," his visual metaphor describing the whole rapturous horrible vortex, providing the means to suture the images. Like a clunky documentary edited together from a stockpile of found footage, I compile images from multiple sources of feminist film culture in 1968.

First Reel:
1967 *Bonnie and Clyde* (Faye Dunaway)
1968 *Rosemary's Baby* (Mia Farrow), *Barbarella* (Jane Fonda), *Funny Girl* (Barbra Streisand), *Vixen*, *Night of the Living Dead*

1969 *Butch Cassidy and the Sundance Kid, They Shoot Horses, Don't They?* (Jane Fonda), *Easy Rider, Midnight Cowboy, Once Upon a Time in the West* (Claudia Cardinale), *Medium Cool*

Like the long eighteenth century, which stretches for British cultural historians from 1660 to 1832—Restoration to the Reform Act—1968 is not so much a year as an era.[8] Gitlin runs 1967, 1968, 1969, and 1970 together in his tale of the white male New Left. The long 1968 for United States feminism and film stretches from 1965 to 1972, from Gunvor Nelson's and Dorothy Wiley's *Schmeerguntz* to the founding of Women Make Movies. However, one can always push the inaugurating moment back further and further.[9] Samuel Fuller's *Naked Kiss* was released in 1964, a year after *Griswold v. Connecticut*, the Supreme Court case opening the way for widespread distribution of contraception, including the newly available birth control pills. It, along with Grace Metalious's pulpy yet political novel *Peyton Place* (1963), unveiled the simmering desire and rage beneath the prim hedges clipped by small-town American women. Going back a few more years, Shirley Clarke's 1960 film of Jack Gelber's off-Broadway play, *The Connection*, was banned on grounds of obscenity by the motion picture division of the New York State Board of Regents. As I have been arguing, Clarke's exposé of an urban underworld owes its debt to Hollywood B-movies, which in an uncanny turn, like its antithesis the American avant-garde, could trace their lineage to Maya Deren's 1943 experimental noir exploration of the domestic uncanny, *Meshes of the Afternoon*.

By 1975, when Chantal Akermann released her beautiful and unsettling probe of noir domesticity, *Jeanne Dielmann, 23 Quai du Commerce, 1080 Bruxelles*, the whole picture of feminist work in film had changed: Laura Mulvey's influential article, "Visual Pleasure and Narrative Cinema," signalled the shift. It contributed to what became the emergence of feminist film theory as a discipline by substituting a rigorous semiotics for a simplistic sociological approach to women and film. ("Visual Pleasure and Narrative Cinema" being in some sense Laura Mulvey's answer to Molly Haskell's *From Reverence to Rape* (1974), this British Marxist-feminist Lacanian analysis of the system of desire paralleled the deft theorizing of female subjectivity in *Psychoanalysis and Feminism*, Juliet Mitchell's rib at

American feminists' anti-Freudian bent, exemplified by Phyllis Chesler's *Women and Madness*.) Women Make Movies supplemented New Day Films and Third World Newsreel as sources of women's documentaries and expanded to include independent films challenging Canyon Cinema and Filmmakers' Co-op by only distributing women's films. Thus by the mid-1970s, feminist film practice was firmly institutionalized, spanning filmmaking collectives, narrative, documentary, and experimental films, distribution companies, film festivals, journals, and women's studies courses, which tracked "images of women" in Hollywood and European art cinemas or sought to recover lost women's visions by unearthing the feminist subversion of Ida Lupino or Dorothy Arzner.

Three tendencies can be traced in United States film practices of the long 1968: New Hollywood, a commercial response to the end of the studios and the rise of television (filmmaking as industrial production); new documentary, tracking issues within New Left politics (filmmaking as collective activity); the Underground, celebrating the counterculture (filmmaking as individual art/craft, personal vision). Paralleling this, feminist cultural politics move against female stereotypes—e.g., Miss America (and in so doing get into view through the news media), document the politics and history of women and women's struggle—e.g., Newsreel's *The Woman's Film* (and in so doing challenge the news media), and experiment with visions of femininity—e.g., the personal films of Marie Mencken, Carolee Schneemann, Gunvor Nelson, and others (and in so doing detail domesticity—its bliss and horror—the daily life of a woman artist, often an artist's wife outside of the media). Like the projectionist in Robert Coover's "Phantom of the Movie Palace," who splices films, projecting two and three at a time, canting the projector at crazy angles to gather all of film's history into one monument, I need at least three screens for this exhibit on feminist film practice: one confronts popular culture, especially its pulpy aspects, a concern for radical women since at least the 1930s, but taking on greater urgency in the 1960s; another documents an alternative female culture, a concern for women artists since the 1920s, but assuming new political guises in the 1960s; a third builds an apparatus, both scholarly and institutional (journals, courses, distribution companies, festivals, etc.), for its dissemination. Sometimes the images fuse in lap dissolves, sometimes they run separately at competing venues.

Second Reel:

1964 Obscenity cases ban *Scorpio Rising* and *Flaming Creatures* (connected to the "clean-up" of New York for the World's Fair)

1965 NEA and state arts boards funded; 428 university film courses offered in the United States

1967 AFI established; *Cineaste* founded

1967 Marshall McLuhan's *Mechanical Bride* reprinted

1968 *Un Chien Andalou* (1929) first screened in the United States

1968 Hannah Arendt biography of Walter Benjamin published in *The New Yorker*

"THE PUBLICITY OF THE PRIVATE"
(ROLAND BARTHES)

Roland Barthes describes photography's impact as effecting a vast inversion of two reigning terms within modern culture—private/public—by relentlessly bringing the daily and personal into public view, on the one hand, and pushing the historic and political into daily life, on the other. "[T]he age of Photography corresponds precisely to the explosion of the private into the public, or rather into the creation of a new social value, which is the publicity of the private: the private is consumed as such, publicly."[10] An uncanny refashioning of the snapshot, the news photo, the official portrait, the wedding picture, each a specific genre with a discrete function, meant they began to merge. Faces and bodies become at once strange and familiar. Barthes is talking about still photography, with its fetishistic quality of a memento mori, at once sacred and disposable in its common place around the homes of the modern working and middle classes. But moving images, especially in the television age of the 1960s, the age of home movies, assume aspects of this eeriness, as if the images coming from the blue light of the television or flickering across a living room screen in eight millimeter conveyed "spirits and ghosts."[11]

Stan Brakhage's "amateur" films—home movies of his family life scratched over by hand—Jack Smith's "Baudelarian" films of friends camping in his apartment, and Jonas Mekas's diary films all bring into public view highly erotic, private fantasies of seeing.

Despite fairly wide distribution (in 1965 Mekas estimated that in New York, more than forty venues screened non-Hollywood films), these early films of the New American Cinema, routinely became the object of state censorship. They pushed into view a personal cinema—accomplished with minimal funds, cheap equipment, no crew, and committed to celebrating the particular, idiosyncratic visions of its maker—"a way shaped . . . by an ever-increasing knowledge of historical aesthetics AND, as is of primary importance, a being true to my senses in all my experiencing of the present," declares Brakhage. In the summer of 1961, twenty-five New York film artists, known as The Group, published their "First Statement of the New American Cinema Group," declaring "official cinema all over the world . . . morally corrupt, esthetically obsolete, thematically superficial, tempermentally boring . . . we know what needs to be destroyed," they continued, "and what we stand for . . . . our rebellion against the old, official, corrupt and pretensious is primarily an ethical one. We are concerned with Man . . . with what is happening to Man."[12] Published in Jonas Mekas's journal, The Group signaled that, just as *Cahiers du Cinema* was the organ of the Nouvelle Vague, *Film Culture* gave voice to the New American Cinema.

Film Culture itself is like a family album—hand-typed letters and taped conversations—in which the personal and private lives of "troublemakers and beatniks" form the public documents of a new age (Aquarius begins in 1962) and art. Shirley Clarke (along with Mekas and the others in The Group) figured "there must be 40 or 50 others like me in the country, with a desire for self-expression and no urge to move to Hollywood and make soap opera."[13] One such filmmaker, Stan Brakhage, was living and making films in the Colorado Rockies. In a letter to his daughter's principal, after Myrrena's body odor had become a topic of concern to the Rollinsville Elementary School, Brakhage cites his own "life's work, as a film artist, [which] particularly qualifies me to search out and create thru the finest qualities of human vision" in his refusal to be shamed into bathing Myrrena, if she is not so inclined.[14] This letter appears with a selection of Brakhage's correspondence in *Film Culture*. By decade's end, in his "Defense of the 'Amateur' Filmmaker," Brakhage summarizes the move from private to public as New American Cinema became institutionalized: "I have

FIGURE 39. Kenneth Anger, *Scorpio Rising* (1963). Museum of Modern Art Film Stills Archive.

been making films for over 15 years now. . . . Mostly I have worked without title in NO collaboration with others—I have worked alone and at home, on films of seemingly NO commercial value . . . 'at home' with a medium I love, making films I care for as surely as I as a father care for my children. As these 'home movies' have come to be valued, have grown into public life, I as the maker of them have come to be called a 'professional,' an 'artist' and an 'amateur.' "15

Preceeding Brakhage's correspondence in this issue of *Film Culture* is an interview with Kenneth Anger about *Kustom Kar Kommando* and the first screening of *Scorpio Rising* after Anger had won its censorship case. "What *Scorpio* represents is me cluing in to popular American culture after having been away for eight years . . . living in France." His luscious, idiosyncratic observations of American male homoerotic subcultures obsessed with cars and motor bikes became a documentary: "I don't see the difference between a symbol and a thing: its the same."[16] Anger, who grew up in Hollywood and would use his early experience in his wild excursion into *Hollywood Babylon,* found the sugary lyrics of early 1960s pop songs menacingly strange; blue velvet was scarier than black leather. For Anger, the icons of working-class American male popular culture—cars, motorbikes, leather jackets—all of which suggested a deeply homoerotic attachment to certain objects were intimately tied to popular music's ironic send-up of heterosexual romance. Anger understood what Adorno never quite got, or more aptly never quite got over: America is the modern uncanny often found in pulp.

Anger's "cluing in to popular American culture," like Brakhage's "being true to [his] senses" formed the central tenets of 1960s arts and politics—expose the weirdness of normality and express the dailiness of wild originality. One can find versions of these declarations everywhere, as in Carolee Schneemann's "Notebooks" for "Round House," her Happening created for the July 1967 International Congress on Dialectics of Liberation. Her notes range among thoughts on quantum physics, the Vietnam War, casual meetings with friends, ideas for the piece: "Happening as basic psycho-social guerilla life-fare," she quips. Then, "expose exposure demystification yes get rid of old deadly mysteries women *our genital and our pronoun* new mysteries waiting for us get it all out tell and show"

> the waitress. . . . .?
> the airline. . . . . ?
> the heiress. . . . .?
> the hostage. . . . . ?
> the steward. . . . . ?
> HOST*ESS* STEWARD*ESS.* . . . .![17]

As in her early 1967 five-screen film/performance, "Snows," which she described as "a work based on Vietnam atrocity images," Schneemann's nude body was central to the politics of her art.[18] In 1960s America, according to Schneemann, both Vietnam and

Woman are known through airing "atrocity images" and the struggle against the devastation of each entailed reclaiming those images. In her next piece, "Naked Action Lecture," Schneemann discusses the "Istory" of her work while dressing and undressing. It asked the questions: "Can an artist be an art istorian? Can an art istorian be a naked woman? Does a woman have intellectual authority? Can she have public authority while naked and speaking? Was the content of the lecture less appreciable when she was naked? What multiple levels of uneasiness, pleasure, curiosity, erotic fascination, acceptance or rejection were activated in an audience?"[19] For the woman "amateur," cluing in to popular culture and being true to her senses required a public display of her body, the nude female body—always object of art, retrieved into subjectivity—"to bridge the conventionally public/private areas of experience."[20] By collapsing subject and object—art work and art historian—into one, Schneemann foregrounded her body as a battleground. Other women artists focussed instead on the role the image apparatus itself played in both constructing and violating privacy.

Third Reel:
1966 Charlotte Moorman arrested in New York for performing "TV Bra" with Nam June Paik
1966 *Chelsea Girls* cannot be screened at the Cannes Film Festival because it requires two projectors
1967 "New Documents" at Museum of Modern Art
1967 *Portrait of Jason*

These last two 1967 events—Jason camping at the New York Film Festival and the Jewish Giant hanging in the Museum of Modern Art (MOMA)—are crucial installments of my tale of feminism, film, and 1968. Each brought the mundane quality of daily life into weird relief by forcing spectators to look carefully at what was usually ignored, avoided, and repressed. As the only female founding member of The Group, Shirley Clarke made her reputation through the avant-garde narrative films *A Cool World* and *The Connection*, which explored African-American and drug cultures. When she created the self-mocking cinema vérité film *Portrait of Jason*, she declared the result "a portrait of a guy who is both a genius and a bore."[21] Like Diane Arbus's photographs, it forced viewers to confront their

FIGURE 40. Shirley Clarke, *Portrait of Jason* (1967). Museum of Modern Art Film Stills Archive.

investments in voyeurism because each accorded the objects of her camera's gaze some element of subjectivity. Each woman—wealthy intellectual New York Jewish Bohemian—defiantly took her camera into the urban underworld of men and forged a new kind of intimate documentary: Arbus as a street photographer; Clarke in her "fictional documents" of various black male underground cultures. Unlike Schneemann, who was in part responding to Brakhage's lyrical cinepoetics of his family's bodies by insisting that hers be looked at, these New York women artists choose not to display their own bodies. Instead they foregrounded other culturally marginalized, even disreputable, noir subjects.

Although she rarely got releases, Arbus claimed she developed deep relationships with her subjects—they told her their "secrets" as she clicked away. Unlike Walker Evans, who was "counter-spy" to James Agee's "spy" in *Let Us Now Praise Famous Men*, Arbus relished in the subtle intrigues of street photography. "I can figure myself into any situation. I choose photography projects that are somehow Mata Harish. I'll not risk my life but I'll risk my reputation or my virtue." Arbus's black-edged photographs of "freaks"— Jewish giants at home in the Bronx, identical twins, transvestites, nudists, prowar demonstrators with bad acne—fascinated and repelled the MOMA's audience to its major photography show: New Documents. Esther Bubley had also carried her camera through the streets shooting everyday events with a certain freedom accorded her as a woman: "It has helped particularly with people in the street, the women and children who seem to accept me sooner," she told an interviewer in 1957.[22] Arbus spent hours hanging around the gallery with her thirty images eavesdropping on the remarks of those disgusted by her depictions of outlaws and outsiders. As she said of her work style: "[I]f I stand in front of something, instead of arranging it. I arrange myself."[23] Her arrangement included the gallery space where she could spy on the voyeurs she had created through her own relentless voyeurism.

Clarke's relationship with Jason undercuts her position as filmmaker; but instead of arranging herself, she arranged her camera. Shot on an Auricon camera that needed to be reloaded every ten minutes, Clarke set the camera in one position and filmed Jason Holliday talking for twelve straight hours. Clarke observed "never had anyone [been allowed] to speak for themselves for more than a few minutes at a time" in traditional cinema; thus she gave Jason license to talk and talk, sometimes responding to the prods of her off-screen voice. Ultimately, Clarke does not succeed in unmasking Jason. Instead, he unmasks the very assumptions of cinema vérité; it becomes obvious that his stories about black gay transvestite life are being *performed* for the camera. Most likely they are lies. "For the first time I was able to give up my intense control and allow Jason and the camera to react to each other."[24] Arbus, however, despite her demurral, always maintained control, at least of her shoots, often lying to her subjects to get the pose she wanted. Andy Warhol superstar Viva and feminist Ti-Grace Atkinson both claimed to have been violated by Arbus after she photographed them sprawled naked like ODed junkies for spreads in *New York* and *The London Sunday Times*, respectively.[25] Yet Atkinson had been righteously celebratory of Valerie Solanas's *S.C.U.M. Manifesto* and of her actual shooting of filmmaker Warhol—that celebrity thief deluxe.[26] In their differing excesses, Arbus and Clarke set the stage for feminist ambivalence toward media, exposure, and a politics of celebrity that would mark post-1968 events.

Fourth Reel:

1968 Valerie Solanas, author of the *S.C.U.M. Manifesto*, shoots Andy Warhol

1970 Marie Mencken dies

1971 Diane Arbus commits suicide; a madhouse erupts for possession of her Westbeth studio

Moving private life, fantasy, and obsession into public view and in so doing challenging economic and political structures—through censorship battles, through distribution and exhibition collectives—is the uncanny story of the New American Cinema of the 1960s. Yet, at the same time, the explosion of new filmic forms and images serves paradoxically to reinforce postwar corporate America. As Susan Sontag, riffing on Walter Benjamin and Guy Debord, astutely notes: "A capitalist society requires a culture based on images. . . . Cameras define reality in the two ways essential to the workings of an advanced industrial society: as a spectacle (for masses) and as an object of surveillance (for rulers). The production of images also furnishes a ruling ideology. *Social change is replaced by a change in images.*"[27] Sontag was an early champion of the New American Cinema, penning an important analysis of *Flaming Creatures* in 1963; however, by the mid-1970s, she had soured a bit on the radical possibilities of film and photography. In many ways (and Sontag is exemplary, as we'll see later), The Group, its art and its organization, provided a model for radical feminism. Through new forms of political organizing, which included the production of new images—consciousness raising, guerilla theater, all-women's actions and speakouts—women's liberation forged a new movement for social and political change; however, the stumbling block to feminist revolution remained ever in the realm of culture and consciousness (or ideology, or psychology, depending upon to whom one talked). Because, in a capitalist society, social change is replaced by a change in images, altering images—a struggle to find new ways of representing woman to herself, to women collectively, and to men— became central to every aspect of radical action.

"THE PERSONAL IS POLITICAL" (CAROL HANISCH)

In her 1970 "Critique of the Miss America Protest," Carol Hanisch recalls how the action, which launched contemporary radical feminism—the Women's Liberation Movement—into the public eye,

> came out of our group method of analyzing women's oppression by recalling our own experiences. We were watching *Schmearguntz* [sic], a feminist movie, one night at our meeting. The movie had flashes of the Miss America contest in it. I found myself sitting there remembering how I had felt at home with my family watching the pageant as a child, as an adolescent, and a college student. I knew it had evoked powerful feelings. When I proposed the idea to our group, we decided to go around the room with each woman telling how she felt about the pageant. . . . From our communal thinking came the concrete plans for the action.[28]

Hanisch understood the process of consciousness-raising, gleaned from Chinese cadre criticism/self-criticism and speaking bitterness sessions as "a political action," not a therapeutic one. As Kathie Sarachild later noted, "the importance of listening to a woman's feelings was collectively to analyze the situation of women. . . . The idea was not to change the woman. . . . [I]t's male supremacy we want to change."[29] It was out of talk that theory, then action, proceeded to build mass female solidarity.

Hanisch and Sarachild, proponents of the "prowoman line" within radical feminism, sought to support women in their limited choices, even those considered oppressive. Historian Alice Echols contrasts these radical feminists concerned with organizing women as women to those "politicos," who advocated organizing separate women's contingents to antiwar demonstrations. Just as *Schmeerguntz* catalyzed the Miss America action, these too often took their inspi-

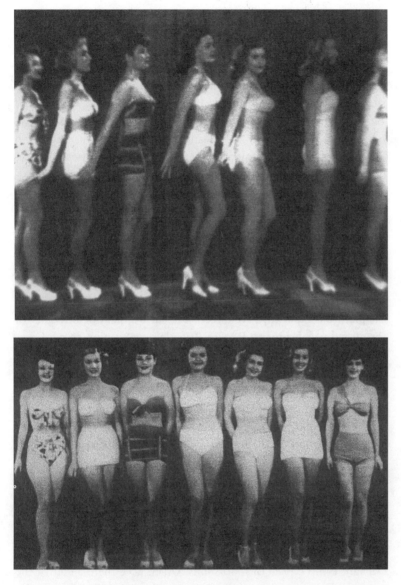

FIGURES 41 and 42. Gunvor Nelson and Dorothy Wiley, *Schmeerguntz* (1965).
Frame enlargements property of Gunvor Nelson and Dorothy Wiley.

ration from the movies. For instance, "at Florika's suggestion, a number of New York Radical Women members participated in an April 1968 anti-war demonstration as a contingent from NYRW. They dressed like Vietnamese women, handed out leaflets about women's liberation to women only, and ran through the crowd ululating like the Algerian women in Gillo Pontecorvo's 1966 film *The Battle of Algiers*."[30] Echols relates these two incidents to distinguish between the actions of feminists and politicos. However, these two films—one lyrically documenting two women's uncanny experiences of women's daily life in postwar United States; the other fictionalizing a document about Algerian anticolonialist struggle, featuring militant women setting bombs and amassing in the streets—chart the range of feminist political action in 1968. Public feminist action made tangible "the Society of the Spectacle," in which seeing obscure films, talking about them, demonstrating, and then seeing the political actions eventually broadcast on network TV become steps in mass political organization. All that's needed to complete the picture is New York Newsreel's first all-woman documentary of the all-women Jeannette Rankin Brigade's 1968 action at the Capitol. From critiques of popular culture to celebrations of revolution to documents of women's mobilization, radical feminism and alternative film trailed one another, and each sought to explode the uncanny world of complacent domesticity in the face of the noirish nightmare of violence, assault, and war.

Tellingly, none of these films was part of the dominant film culture of the American 1960s—Hollywood's unraveling studio system and European art cinemas. Arguably, these two film practices, being more pervasive, should have been instrumental in forming a feminist film culture. However, feminist responses to Hollywood and its Other, European art cinema, were not central to the critiques of mass culture mounted by feminists. Despite the edgy rebellion or outright camp typical of 1960s films, which gave them an air of the counter culture, they were not viewed as radical breaks with postwar American pulp even when they came from Europe.[31] Thus they came in for attack for their unreal depictions of women (Jeanne Moreau as the male-identified Catherine in Truffaut's *Jules et Jim* was universally denounced) and for their exploitation of the star system. Yet, poems by lyn lifshin reimagining Marilyn Monroe or Karen Lindsey mourning Jayne Mansfield spoke to the ambivalence feminists felt toward the culture industry's use of female bodies. "Elegy for Jayne Mansfield, July 1967" reads:

> she was a
> sunday news centerfold
> bosoms thrust toward subway-
> rush men leaning on the
> legs of pretty secretaries
> always a bleeding
> divorcé or a beaten child,
> she had a pink voice, and lived in a pink house.
> no hints of a self
> cringing away from sticky headlines
> or an art groping beyond
> barebreasted titters.
>
> we used to have fun laughing at her.
> when she lost her head, the joke turned sick.[32]

The joke turned sick; Jayne Mansfield, Marilyn Monroe, and Miss America tested the limits of radical feminist analyses of culture and its industry.[33] How to come to terms with women who used the system of male supremacy to make it? Hanisch ultimately condemned the Miss America action, with its free-for-all theatrics, admitting slogans such as "Up Against the Wall Miss America" alienated women and blamed those participating in sexist institutions—including marriage—for their self-contributions to an enforced victimization. A "prowoman" line would celebrate women's many subversive responses to her oppression. Thus even Jayne Mansfield needed to be reassessed, perhaps rehabilitated, or, more accurately, the feminist response to Jayne Mansfield needed revising. Solidarity among women required recognition of the underground submerged stream of women's culture within a sexist world, including its most ludicrous and debased extremes.

Ever attentive to the zeitgeist, new stars in updated, hip genre films commercialized dissent, further complicating the relationships among popular culture, public life, and private desire. A smile stretches across the ashen face of platinum-blonde, spit-curled Faye Dunaway as she strokes Warren Beatty's pistol in the opening sequence of *Bonnie and Clyde*. The graphic violence of Arthur Penn's 1967 film came to be seen as a touchstone for the New Left, especially media speculations about it. Bonnie's beret, echoing Che's, was the dress code of the Black Panthers, eventually hitting the fashion pages. *Bonnie and Clyde* retrofitted America's past, showing how the body counts racking up on the nightly news were not aberrations but a key aspect of U.S. history. In one scene, Bonnie sits engrossed in a motion picture theater watching the Busby Berkeley musical *Golddiggers of 1933* for fashion tips. Bosley Crowther of the *New York Times* lambasted the "slap-stick" of *Bonnie and Clyde*, its romance of guns and gangs. His dismissal was mild compared to Page Cook's denunciation in *Films in Review*: "One final word," he appended to his review of the opening night of the Montreal Film Festival, "there is *evil* in the *tone* of the writing, acting, and direction of this film, the calculated effect of which is to incite in the young the delusions that armed robbery and murder are mere 'happenings.' " The period dress and antique cars never for a moment masked the contemporary feel of the images *Bonnie and Clyde* purveyed, as Richard Schickel noted in his *Life* magazine review: "Bonnie and Clyde are the products of the rootlessness of ill-taught youth growing up absurd in a period of historical transition. The parallel between the middle 1930s and the middle 1960s is never too far from the minds of the movie's creators."[34] As Hollywood's studio system increasingly fell apart, independent productions mainstreamed radical critiques of America. *Bonnie and Clyde*'s resurrection of the 1930s, the era of America's Old Left, aestheticized violence by politicizing style according to these mainstream critics.[35] However, young radicals flocked to the film, boosting its flagging attendance after Warner Brothers re-released it in the wake of 1968 assassinations, civil unrest, and Democratic convention police riot.[36]

Film as just such a system of contradictory thought and experience—not merely as a source of negative and positive images—was crucial to at least one feminist theorist. Shulamith Firestone's 1970 manifesto, *The Dialectic of Sex*, found in film the precursor to her ideal postrevolutionary "anti-culture": "the young art of film, based on a true synthesis of the Aesthetic and Technological Modes (As Empiricism itself had been) carried on the vital realistic tradition. . . . [I]t broke down the very division between the artificial and the real, between culture and life itself," she exclaimed ecstatically.[37] Much like Maya Deren, who practiced both critique and art-making, Firestone, an art student at the Chicago Institute of Art during the mid-1960s (where Stan Brakhage would later teach) and "star" of *Shulie*, a cinema vérité documentary about her, saw film as a philosophic system.[38] In this, she paraphrased the conclusion to The Group's "First Statement": "[W]e are not only for the new cinema, we are also for the New Man. . . . [W]e are for art, but not at the expense of life. We don't want false, polished, slick films—we prefer them rough, unpolished, but alive; we don't want rosy films—we want them the color of blood."[39] However, few feminist theorists took up Firestone's line on cinema as prefigurative. Instead, more often they, like Sherry Sonnett Trumbo, asked, "where is the movie that shows us what alternatives and possibilities are open to us as women?" Trumbo noted, "For women, there are very few relevant models offered by movies or the rest of culture that will help ease the fear and pain of liberation."[40] If "A Woman's Place Is in the Oven" rather than behind the camera, how was a feminist film vision to be expressed? In these minor nods toward film criticism, so-called second wave feminists were rehashing debates among Popular Front feminists. Muriel Rukeyser's poem "Movie" skewered the nascent fascism in Hollywood fantasies of female stars: "Spotlight her face her face has no light in it / . . . We focus on the screen: look they tell us / you are a nation of similar whores remember the Maine / remember you have a democracy of champagne— / And slowly the female face kisses the young man, / over his face the twelve-foot female head / the yard-long mouth enlarges and yawns / The End."[41] Like Trumbo, Joy Davidman, film critic for the *New Masses* during the 1940s, challenged the commercial culture and female objectification endemic to Hollywood and America, yet she relished the possibilities mass culture offered radical organizing.

"THE REVOLUTION WILL NOT BE TELEVISED"
(GIL SCOTT-HERON)

If "movies and the rest of culture" offered little of use to feminists, notwithstanding Firestone's attempt to argue otherwise, movies, even alternative cinema, and the rest of culture were still central to maintaining women's oppression. In the "Fourth World Manifesto," Barbara Burris, writing on behalf of her collective, declares:

"A Female culture exists." The emphasis on finding and nurturing that submerged female culture became the genesis of what Alice Echols calls "cultural feminism" because "male culture, which is the dominant culture in every nation, i.e., is synonymous with the national culture, cannot accept a female view of things as expressed by female writers, artists and philosophers."[42] Burris based her conclusions on a dissection of the Algerian revolution's betrayal of National Liberation Front (NLF) women, evidenced in part by Pontecorvo's film *The Battle of Algiers*. She offered a thorough-going critique of Frantz Fanon's emphasis on postcolonial male identity formation through anti-imperialist struggle. Her ideas resonated among black feminists, many of whom had been active in the Black Arts Movement. For instance, Francee Covington writing in Toni Cade's influential 1970 anthology, *The Black Woman*, also uses *The Battle of Algiers* as a source for analyzing the revolutionary potential of U.S. radical movements—anti-imperialist, black nationalist, or feminist.[43] Because, as Sontag would argue in "The Third World of Women," "all women live in an 'imperialist' situation in which men are the colonialists and women are the natives, . . . the same basic relations of inferiority and superiority, of powerlessness and power, of cultural underdevelopment and cultural privilege, prevail between men and women in all countries."[44] Thus a film, such as *The Battle of Algiers*, that offered a blueprint for anticolonial struggle, moved from the realm of representation to that of strategic manual. It is a virtual given among all these women that the film is a documentary, because, if film, in general, "broke down the very division between the artificial and the real, between culture and life itself," then this one did so in a powerfully self-conscious way. The impact of the film turned many feminists to documentary to secure the truth of women's lives within a liberated women's cinema.

The collective of documentary filmmakers known as Newsreel updated for a new era of political activism a tradition of destabilizing documentary narratives, stretching from Dziga Vertov's *Man with a Movie Camera* in postrevolutionary Soviet Russia through *Salt of the Earth*, Herbert Biberman's fictional defiance of the blacklist in McCarthyite America. Newsreel's films opened with their trademark film projector and machine-gun staccato, resurrecting the 1930s Film and Photo League's assertion that "the camera is a weapon." In December 1967, the collective announced its birth in the *Village Voice*: "Films made by Newsreel are not to be seen once

FIGURE 43. Gillo Pontecorvo, *The Battle of Algiers* (1968). Museum of Modern Art Film Stills Archive

and forgotten. Once a print goes out, it becomes a tool to be used by others in their own work. . . . We intend to cover demonstrations; to interview figures like LeRoi Jones and [Jim] Garrison; we want to show what is at stake in a housing eviction or in consumer abuses in Harlem; we should provide information on how to deal with the police or on the geography of Chicago."[45] The logic behind Newsreel's perceived need was, in part, "documented" by Haskell Wexler's extraordinary 1969 movie, *Medium Cool*, which follows a television news cameraman as he shoots scenes of Chicago life leading up to the 1968 Democratic convention. *Medium Cool* earned an X-rating (no one under 18 admitted) under the Motion Picture Association of America's newly instituted rating system. A clear move to censor a political film, branding it "pornography," the MPAA appeared to be doing to commercial cinema what the cops had done to underground film a few years earlier and what the television networks were doing to the Vietnam War and domestic resistance almost daily. According to Newsreel: "The news that we feel is significant—any event that suggests the changes and redefinitions

213

taking place in America today, or that underlines the necessity for such changes—has been consistently undermined and suppressed by the media" (*Movie Journal*, 305).

For all its radical form and content—intercutting actual black-and-white documentary footage into the color narrative, improvisational acting, hand-held camera, highly self-reflexive commentary on filmmaking, etc.—*Medium Cool* still featured a man shooting footage of men shooting guns (camera as weapon) and of women at home who may or may not want to be looked at (camera as voyeur). In one scene, Robert Forster has gone to a Southside Chicago apartment to interview a cab driver who found a wallet containing $10,000, turned it in, and then got arrested. As he exits, he is challenged by a black actress who demands he put her on television because "the tube is life," as someone remarks. Delivering images, perhaps the cameraman is obstetrician, but he is nevertheless cut off from real life. The hot everyday life of summer 1968 is antidote to that cool medium, the tube, and it is embodied in the earth mother: a young Vietnam War widow serving canned tomato soup to her teenage son. She challenges Forster to take responsibility for the pictures he takes that end up on her television, invading her life, making her home uncanny, a war zone. But, in Wexler's quotation of Jean-Luc Godard's *Contempt*, she ends up dead in a car smash-up as the two vainly search for her missing boy during the chaos of the convention. The final credits mimic the opening sequence: a passing car slows as someone snaps of photo of the dead couple. The question remained, especially for women, how to "serve the needs of people who want to get hold of news that is relevant to their own activity and thought"? How to film in medium uncool?

The women active in New York Newsreel offered one answer: demand that the white men who were already filmmakers—in effect, the ringleaders of the collective—cede their power by spreading their knowledge to those working in the crew. Rather than lecture the cameraman about his complicity in the violence of the shot, women demanded access to the cameras themselves. They wanted to shoot back. Newsreel collective's female members felt that by making films about black male radicalism, like *Black Panther Party*, the white male filmmakers were either homing in on another's vital revolutionary culture (a form of imperialism), or in making films of *The Columbia Strike* were celebrating their own struggles as if they con-

FIGURE 44. Haskell Wexler, *Medium Cool* (1969). Museum of Modern Art
Film Stills Archive

stituted the revolution (another form of imperialism). In one of their
first actions, in January 1968, Lynn Phillips and an all-women crew
from Newsreel's original thirty members filmed the Jeannette
Rankin Brigade, an all-women antiwar organization named for the
first woman elected to Congress who voted against U.S. intervention in both world wars, in its attempt to petition Congress to end
the war.[46] However, a year later, Christine Choy was filming the
Newsreel footage of the Attica prison uprising as a complete novice
after Robert Kramer and other founders, including Phillips, had left
New York Newsreel.[47] Explaining her early departure, Phillips con-
cluded, "Preciousness and pandering are the Scylla and Charybdis of
left culture. Newsreel, to avoid the pandering of 1930s nice-guy sentimentality, lapsed into a muscular kind of French intellectualism;
and for all our trashy surface and rough posturing, I think we got as
precious as well, Waiting for Godot, or Godard, Waiting for Godard.
. . . Besides the women's movement had grown a great deal by then,
and there was too much in the feminist critique of the left leadership
that was too true and too slow to change."[48]

The slippage between "real life" revolution or struggle—say in Algeria or in Chicago—and filmic ones—say *The Battle of Algiers* or *Medium Cool*—what Phillips called "Waiting for Godard," is precisely what sutured Miss America to revolutionary ululations. That *The Battle of Algiers* recreates the feel of documentary—using techniques *Medium Cool* also mimicked—points to the conventions of truth-telling so important to 1960s political investments in cinema. As Shirley Clarke declared in 1962: "Right now I'm revolting against the conventions of movies. Who says a film has to cost a million dollars and be safe and innocuous enough to satisfy every 12-year-old in America?"[49] Jonas Mekas pointed out that the true documentary work in cinema had been going on in New American Cinema all along. For Mekas, Carolee Schneemann's investigation of her sexuality and her active handling of the film itself offered more real cinema than anything coded as "real," including cinema vérité documentary.[50] Parker Tyler argued that underground films were always "curiously 'documentary' " because they "document the traditional social activity of making life itself into a work of art."[51] According to David James's assessment, "By far the majority of underground films were essentially documentaries of these [homosexual, women's, Bohemian, drug, anti-war] subcultures . . . instances of minority social groups representing themselves." Moreover, "the radical innovation of the underground . . . invent[ed] film as practice rather than as manufacture."[52] Art of life, practice of art, life as art—"the movie equivalent of off Broadway, fresh and experimental and personal" was how Clarke described it. This was *avant la lettre*, the aesthetic flowering of Firestone's dream of "anti-culture," the cinematic dispersion of Hanisch's "personal is political."

"IF YOU'RE GOING TO CHANGE THINGS, YOU'RE GOING TO MAKE A MESS—EVERY HOUSEWIFE KNOWS THAT!" (CAROLEE SCHNEEMANN)

Cheap, lightweight equipment and the "cinema of an effortless (as much as it can be) self-expression, which culminated in *Blonde Cobra* and *Flaming Creatures* and 8mm" had made possible a new wave of "women . . . coming to cinema," commented Jonas Mekas in 1963 after viewing new work by Naomi Levine, Storm De Hirsch, and Barbara Rubin. "Now," he declares, "Marie Mencken is no longer alone."[53] In 1966, Marie Mencken, heiress to Maya Deren as mother of the avant-garde, appears as Gerard Malanga's mother in *The Chelsea Girls*. Mencken's career as a filmmaker, like that of her many avant-garde sisters began in collaboration with her husband, Willard Maas.[54] The "istory" of women in art features a litany of wives, lovers, and models tagged on as afterthoughts. For instance, Sheldon Renan concludes his profile of Robert Nelson in the "Gallery of Film-Makers" with the following sentence: "His wife Guvnor [sic] has, with Bill Wiley's wife, Dorothy, made a film called *Schmeerguntz* (1965), which satirizes the modern woman."[55] Both Gunvor and Dorothy, who rarely appear in accounts of underground film history can claim a decent pedigree—the history of modernist women artists is an "istory" of wives and lovers serving as footnotes to greater male visionaries.[56] Jane Brakhage—her body a central image and her camera work a central element of "Brakhage" films—is incorporated within the final title of the films shot in Colorado: "By Brakhage" flickers at the end of *Thigh Line Lyre Triangular* and *Dog Star Man*. These homemade movies of birth and wood chopping are family productions, but celebrating whose personal "metaphors on vision"?

In a 1971 interview with Brenda Richardson, entitled "Women, Wives, Film-Makers," which mocks, but cannot fully escape, the legacy of belittling artists' wives as second-class artists, Nelson and Wiley described the beginning of their collaboration: "Dorothy and I made two little 8mm movies, and Bob went with Bill Wiley, Bob Hudson, and Ron Davis and made *Plastic Haircut*, and that was more like a professional thing—Dorothy and I just fiddled around with little stuff."[57] Four years before, in a conversation recorded in 1967 and transcribed in *Film Culture*, Shirley Clarke and Storm De Hirsch had pointed out that despite being acclaimed filmmakers, "we are both little women" patronized constantly as women artists. Clarke begins their conversation with the tongue-in-cheek question: "Do you think that lady film-makers are mechanically equipped to handle their field?" She compares their status to female trolley drivers in the Soviet Union as the two proceed to circle the woman question in the history of independent cinema.[58] Both of these conversations shy away from declaring women's experimental filmmaking as a form of "women's liberation." Yet each emphasizes the different treatments male and female artists receive from journalists, other artists, and friends. Nelson and Wiley remember bitterly how, after

Schmeerguntz received first prize at the 1966 Ann Arbor Film Festival, male artist friends started speaking to them; Clarke notes that journalists always comment first on her demure appearance.[59]

In this curious diminution of themselves and their work, no matter how resentful, each of these filmmakers calls attention to her difference from her male colleagues, lovers, and husbands. Much as Mexican painter and wife Frida Kahlo had continually referred to herself as "little" compared to her muralist husband Diego Rivera's "giant" presence and art, these women stress the miniature; in so doing, however, they invert its value. Like Esther Bubley, who at 5' 4" started body building after an assignment at a Brooklyn boxing gym because she was so small that she tired from carrying her equipment, they muscled their way into a male domain, then relied on their petite size to get their cinematic results. Standing behind a 35mm camera, as Clarke had, but even holding a smaller 16mm one, offers a way to strap on the phallus and then utterly undo its power by filming the insignificant. In their quests for a tactile, hand-held medium, by the 1970s, Wiley worked exclusively in 8mm and Clarke had turned to video. Were they accepting that they "just fiddled around with little stuff"? Or were they anticipating the image revolution provided by digital cameras?

These pre-Women's Liberation Movement underground cinematic revisions of home movies paved the way for a new radical feminist cinema, but even more daringly, for radical feminism itself. When it screened in 1968, Carolee Schneemann's film *Fuses* got a rave from Mekas as heir(ess) apparent to his pantheon. In production for three years, *Fuses* features long sequences of Schneemann and her lover, James Tenney, having sex as viewed from the point of view of her cat, Kitch. She then scratched the film, baked it in the oven, left it out in the rain, until bodies and film fused. Like Clarke's early film, it too was the object of a censorship battle, which, unlike the cases over films by Anger and Jack Smith (both of which were highly public and theatrical) was unsuccessful in part because of its intensely private disclosure.[60] Private life, in all its trashiness, was what public culture deemed obscene. "With *Schmeerguntz*," notes Nelson, "we wanted to make a 16mm movie, I think. But we had no subject. And one day I was looking at all the gunk in the sink and thought of the contrast between what we do, and what we see that we 'should' be—in ads and things—and that was the idea right from

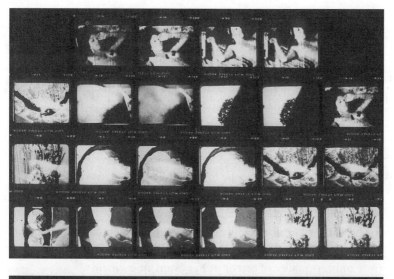

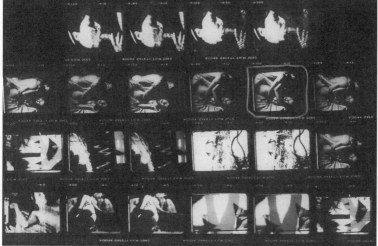

FIGURES 45 and 46. Carolee Schneemann, *Fuses* (1965). Self-shot color silent 20 minutes. Pacific Film Archive.

there, from the sink."[61] Joyce Weiland's *Rat Life and Diet in North America*—premiering in 1968 at the Jewish Museum—uses close ups of gerbils and cats scurrying amid food left out on her kitchen table to allegorize Canadian and feminist resistance to imperialism, war, and the violence of daily life. Since Maya Deren's *Meshes of the After-noon* investigated the multiplying uncanniness found within a southern California bungalow, its objects—phonograph, telephone, bread knife, windows, and mirrors—demonically animated as the body of a woman replicates again and again, women's experimental cinema has been imbricated in noir. Like Esther Bubley, Maya Deren was documenting the effects of war. Even domestic spaces are dangerous when the world's skies are filled with bombers; the home no refuge for her or for her refugee husband. She too invented the iconography and thematics of film noir *avant la lettre* as the living room took on a sinister quality of terror in her avant-noir cinema.[62]

Domesticity continued to be the focus of Dorothy Wiley's later 8mm works, such as *Cabbage* (1972), about which she says: "[W]hile watching film, I can abandon myself to the event. I don't find that so easy to do in the kitchen in the morning. I still don't understand that part."[63] Unsettling domestic settings, by turns inviting and erotic and violent and repulsive—domesticity with a vengeance, something Arbus accomplished in her 1963 portraits of New Jersey nudists, making the home into an uncanny place—is part of the complicated interrelationship of photography and image under capitalism, as much an aspect of the publicity of the private as of a "personal politics," which women's film work and feminist politics highlighted.[64] "*Schmeerguntz* is one long raucous belch in the face of the American Home. A society which hides its animal functions beneath a shiny public surface deserves to have such films as *Schmeerguntz* shown everywhere—in every PTA, every Rotary Club, every club in the land. For it is brash enough, brazen enough and funny enough to purge the soul of every harried American married woman," declared Ernest Callenbach in its sole review.[65] Following the leads of Deren and Mencken, Wiley, Nelson, Schneemann, and Weiland domesticated the wars at home and abroad. Personal cinema—home movies of sex and ordinary objects—flowers in women's filmmaking during the 1970s; but it, like *Meshes*, brings the war home. For instance, Chick Strand's 1979 *Soft Fiction* used her girlfriends' weird stories—concluding with a terrifying tale about how, as a young girl, one woman flirted with a Gestapo enabling her family to escape the Nazis—to parody the sincere talking heads of much earnest feminist documentary as it tracked a vaguely noir narrative of a woman escaping her bungalow by train. Homey images eventually became a way to entice women into filmmaking, as Liane Burton explained: "If you can thread a sewing machine, you can thread a projector, and if you can follow a recipe, you can do still photography developing."[66] Yet women reshot underground home movies and documented women's struggles for private audiences—the cognoscenti of the New American Cinema and the committed of the New Left.

"FREE IN THE DUSTY BEAM OF THE PROJECTOR"
(ADRIENNE RICH)

Looking back through Women's Liberation's *Notes* from the First, Second, and Third Years, it becomes clear that if the 1960s marked the emergence of late capitalism, in Ernst Mandel's term, then the long 1968 of feminism and film hints at a brief triumph of the Cultural Revolution. The woman question had been lurking behind Marxism for more than a hundred years, popping its head out at various times only to be pushed back from view. But the late 1960s reorganization of capital and desire opened the floodgates as public space became the site of private conscience, freeing the imagination in Paris and Prague, declaring "Sisterhood is Powerful" in the United States and around the world. "The superstructural movement and play enabled by the transition from one infrastructural or systemic stage of capitalism to another" mitigated, for a time, class-based analyses of social and political change by unleashing "social energies" in the form of new cultural movements, including feminism.[67]

Viewed from today's perspective, in which the distinction between culture, consciousness, and commodity is increasingly elided, the struggles of feminists to "name the system" that oppressed women, as Paul Potter had exhorted the New Left at the 1965 antiwar March on Washington, was exceedingly prescient; Potter later recounted that he had purposely evaded naming the system, capitalism, "because capitalism was for me and my generation an inadequate description of the evils of America—a hollow, dead word tied to the thirties."[68] In part, this explains why guerilla theater actions inspired by film and television became a key form of feminist political organizing. It appeared certain that women's liberation, understood by radical feminists as freedom from men's control, individual men as well as systems of male chauvinism, would never be achieved solely by structural changes in the economic relationships between classes, even sex classes; only a fundamental change in consciousness and in its public expression would accomplish a feminist revolution. After all, like Maya Deren in *Meshes*, Barbara Stanwyck ended up dead, even after admitting she really loved the guy, at the end of both *Double Indemnity* and *The File on Thelma Jordan*. Simply unleashing women's fury at domesticity was not enough.

With its dual struggle against censorship (to gain visibility) and for revolution (to change the world), the work of the underground, both cultural and political, was lodged, in part, within film. Censorship crucially acts as an official refusal to circulate knowledge publicly, by, on the one hand, insisting that the private remain hidden (inhibiting sex), and, on the other, hiding state secrets (waging war), in effect privatizing public information. Politics and culture in the 1960s unraveled and tangled these threads—underground films and Happenings, often public displays of private love and friendship, were raided by the police while the nightly news brought the brutality of state-sponsored death in Vietnam into American living rooms. Thus it makes wacky sense that *Medium Cool* would be given an X-rating by the MPAA; it was deemed pornographic for pointing out how obscene war is. Battling censorship meant forcing a public acknowledgment of this hypocrisy.

If censorship relies on keeping knowledge private, revolution demands the public demonstration of a refusal, bringing the masses into the streets because their solely private existence as individual subjects becomes untenable and they seek power collectively. Women's work in film during the long 1968 united, as radical feminism did, the struggles to fight censorship and make revolution. It located the woman's body—its private spaces and its public consumption—as the uncanny site of a new kind of politics—a politics of the image and of the personal. Fighting censorship meant bringing into view the noirish elements of middle-class women's lives— the vomiting pregnant woman, the sink full of dirty dishes, the shitty diapers, and the images of Miss America—as much as it meant a self-revelation of women's erotic desires. Making revolution meant refuting the culture of images that depended upon the female body and documenting the long history of women's presence yet invisibility in politics by the very mechanisms that had both objectified and ignored women's bodies; it meant celebrating "our bodies ourselves." Exposure, expression, exploitation, excess: the cinema as metaphor for daily life (a theme prevalent in much twentieth-century literature and criticism) became cinema as a design for living—its creation charted in a clunky, curious documentary. Cinema not only documented 1960s movements, however; it actively structured both their politics and poetics. Adrienne Rich's 1970 poem, "Images for Godard" concludes:

> the mind of the poet is the only poem
> the poet is at the movies
>
> dreaming the film-maker's dream but differently
> free in the dark as if asleep
>
> free in the dusty beam of the projector
> the mind of the poet is changing
>
> the moment of change is the only poem[69]

The long 1968 offers a prehistory to feminist film work. First generation feminist films may not have made the revolution; but, through a medium uncool, they did project the moment of change.

Fifth Reel:
"Women's Cinema as Counter Cinema" (Claire Johnston, 1973)
Legend of Maya Deren Project (begun in 1973, first edition appeared in 1988)
Popcorn Venus (Marjorie Rosen, 1973)
Women in Film and Video Conference (Buffalo, New York, 1974)
From Reverence to Rape (Molly Haskell, 1974)
"Visual Pleasure and Narrative Cinema" (Laura Mulvey, 1975)
Women and Film (1975)

Jeanne Dielmann, 23 Quai du Commerce, 1080 Bruxelles (Chantal Akermann, 1975)

Camera Obscura (1977)

Telluride Film Festival—includes Agnes Varda's *L'Opera Mouffe*, Marie Menken's *Orgia*, Nelson and Wiley's *Schmeerguntz*, Anne Severson's *Near the Big Chakra*, and *Fuses* and *Plumb Line* by Schneemann in a program entitled: The Erotic Woman (1977)

Women's Pictures: Feminism and Cinema (Annette Kuhn, 1982)

Women and Film: Both Sides of the Camera (E. Ann Kaplan, 1983)

Thelma and Louise (1991)

1997 Shirley Clarke dies.

CHAPTER 9

MAPPING NOIR

DEAD RECKONING

The Hutchinson River Parkway winds north from the Bronx. Cutting a path through granite hillocks, shadowed by oak and maple and pine, it is a dark somewhat haunted roadway. It is the only federal highway in the United States named for a woman, commemorating the site where Anne Hutchinson, her family, and followers were massacred after they had been banished first from the Massachusetts Bay Colony and then from more religiously tolerant, yet still repressive, Rhode Island. Hutchinson should be considered the first "dark lady" of American political pulp history: a woman who defied her elders—men, both ministers and governors—because she dared to speak openly about her ideas and beliefs. A midwife who herself had sixteen children, Hutchinson began informally recounting Sunday sermons to the women lying in before and after childbirth. Her biblical readings and interpretations drew more and more women, who eventually brought along their husbands as well as their children, until she was running a counter church, preaching her own, not merely recounting others', sermons, declaring her belief in radical predestination. Imprisoned for months while pregnant, she delivered a "monstrous birth" whose death sealed the verdict John Cotton, a supporter of hers, was forced to draw about her—that she was a danger to the community, a heretic to be cast out from the "city on the hill" into the wilderness. Hutchinson's story haunted Nathaniel Hawthorne, whose ancestor Hathorne (Nathaniel adding the letter W as a vague disguise) sat in judgment at the Salem witch trials; she (and her latter-day reincarnation, Margaret Fuller) is the model for defiant Hester Prynne.

The Scarlet Letter, beginning with its long scene in the Custom-House, establishes the basic formula for film noir. Just as almost all of the classic noirs rely on a voice-over narration told from the grave—Mildred Pierce, Al Roberts in *Detour*, Walter Neff in *Double Indemnity*, and, quite literally, Joe Gillis in *Sunset Boulevard*, to name just a few—Hawthorne's tale begins by divulging the story of how the buried story surfaces. The cache of letters and the bizarrely ornamented piece of cloth the narrator finds among the items stored in the attic of the Custom-House where he works a dull office job, the nineteenth-century version of Neff's Pacific All-Risk Insurance Company office. Its secretary pool and its Dictaphones and telephones are merely technological updates of the paper, wood, and charcoal used to record the comings and goings of freight. Paralyzing boredom and routine work mark the daily existence of the men working in offices whether in a Salem Custom-House, a Los Angeles insurance agency, or, like Joe Gillis, a rewrite desk in a Hollywood studio. Each man finds release from his dead-end job in the allure of a diabolical woman.

Barbara Stanwyck may seem a far cry from Hester Prynne, but Billy Wilder (in *Double Indemnity*) and Robert Siodmak (in *The File on Thelma Jordan*) stage her entrance into the plot in practically the same manner that Hester emerges into view in Hawthorne's romance. Framed by the prison door, as her story is framed by that of the Custom-House, Hester appears out of the dark, her mark of disgrace, the scarlet *A*, gleaming in the late-afternoon New England sunshine. Her momentary pause at the door, on view by the spectators mobbing the entrance, offers them a full glimpse of her body and of the small baby she cradles. Reversing the direction Jane Greer comes from when she materializes out of the bright daylight in the doorway of the gloomy Mexican cantina in *Out of the Past*, radiating a pervasive glow into the dark café, Hester leaves behind the dank prison for the light of day; yet those watching her, shrouded in black

FIGURE 47. Sunglasses as Armor. Barbara Stanwyck and Fred McMurray in Jerry's Market in *Double Indemnity* (d. Billy Wilder, 1944).

clothing, present a dark vision. She, like Phyllis Dietrichson or Lizabeth Scott as Coral Chandler in *Dead Reckoning*, an apparition of white light—her blond helmeted hair glowing, her white skin wrapped in a white towel—draws the eye. Walter Neff stares up at Stanwyck as she looks down from the second-floor balcony at him, and we in the audience are pulled into her orbit as well. The camera, like Hawthorne's narrator, forces us to look.

This cinematic spectacle beginning Hester's story is repeated at various moments in the tale—at the marketplace, at the scaffold, at the pulpit, at the minister's window—when visual display and its necessary other, concealment, which is the curse of Arthur Dimmesdale and his townspeople, structure the narrative. Italian critic Sandro Portelli calls *The Scarlet Letter* a grammar of America; American critic Patricia Crain finds it to be America's primer.[1] I prefer the metaphor of the road map. The threads embroidered across Hester's chest provide the contours for what would eventually unfold so daringly in film noir—a framed landscape viewed through headlights and windshield wipers in which women's desires are always open to inspection, suspect precisely because they refuse to be concealed, yet endlessly appearing as an enigma, a problem to be solved, a crime needing punishment. What Hawthorne's map acknowledged was precisely that a representation is all that is necessary because there is no truth to be found either out there or in here. The visually cryptic red markers tell all, if one cares to follow their directions. Secrets are always laid bare, like highway markers announcing each town—Emblem, Wyoming, population 11—along its route. Thus in mapping the paths of America's darkness, Hawthorne outlines how romance—the framed stagy form he insisted best described his work—is essential for uncovering the nation's past politics.

Hawthorne may have borrowed his form and content from the publication of Frederick Douglass's narrative registered in the Clerk's Office of the District Court of Massachusetts in 1845. Douglass too frames his life's story—this time in the form of two testimonials by white men assuring readers of Douglass's legitimacy because the racist ideologies of antebellum America could not accomodate an articulate black writer. William Lloyd Garrison and Wendell Phillips have heard Douglass speak and can verify his words; their reports authenticate his. Douglass begins his tale with an account of witnessing his Aunt Hester's beating by his cruel master, Captain Anthony. Douglass discerns the central facts of his condition as "a witness and a participant" while hiding "terrified and horror-stricken . . . in a closet": "It was the blood-stained gate, the entrance to the hell of slavery, through which I was about to pass. . . . It was a most terrible spectacle." Understanding his impotent complicity in the sexualized racial violence of slavery, and in the peculiar role he now occupies as its witness and narrator, Douglass connects himself and his readers to the visual spectacle of blood and bondage, as well as the erotics of pain and degradation that Hawthorne's Hester also sets into motion. As a young boy, he is dimly aware that his master is overreacting to finding Aunt Hester had disobeyed his orders not to leave his property when she was discovered with (her lover) another slave, Ned Roberts. Douglass notes that Aunt Hester was "a woman of noble form, and graceful proportions, having very few equals, and fewer superiors, in personal appearance, among the colored or white women in our neighborhood." Aunt Hester is a beauty. Frederick, often "awakened at the dawn of day by the most heart-rending shrieks of an own aunt of mine," senses that Captain Anthony seems to take particular relish in torturing her: "[H]e used to tie [her] up to a joist, and whip upon her naked back till she was literally covered with blood." The day Douglass moves from auditor to voyeur, however, that is, the day he stands at the doorway of slavery—its witness and participant—the beating is especially brutal: "Before he commenced whipping Aunt Hester, he took her into the kitchen, and stripped her from neck to waist, leaving her neck, shoulders, and back, entirely naked. He then told her to cross her hands, calling her at the same time a d--d b--h."[2] Tying her hands, he made her stand on a stool stretched out on display before the young boy hiding in the kitchen closet, who watches through the keyhole, waiting his turn. Douglass's Aunt Hester must be degraded by Captain Anthony because of her desirability; he punishes the body her finds so attractive, and does so publicly, as a spectacle performed on the threshold of America's hell. Her bloody back, striped in red—like the lines on a road map—by her master's whip, reappears on Hester Prynne's chest winding amid the red embroidery of her emblem of debasement.

Film noir did not appear—or at least was not named—until French critics got to see the storehouse of embargoed American films after the end of World War II. However, Hawthorne makes clear in Hester's resurrection of Anne Hutchinson—and the hanged Salem witches and perhaps his knowledge of Douglass's aunt as well—that a noir plot underlay the entire history of this continent.[3] The crime story in which a woman figures as bearer of chaos and the resulting trial to ascertain guilt and assess punishment is a narrative that did not begin with European settlers, of course. It goes way back to the Lady Eve (played, naturally, by Barbara Stanwyck). It's a typology in which political history can only be discerned through a framed fictional form. Film noir makes legible a long undercurrent within American political culture—its essential pulpiness, its scandalous dependence on revealing fallen women's crimes with and against their doomed, slightly dimwitted (or at least faint-hearted, remember Dimmesdale) men. Thus we need Barbara Stanwyck to help make sense of Hester Prynne as much as Hester and her riveting *A*, or Aunt Hester and her bloodied back, stand Phyllis in brilliant relief.

We only know Aunt Hester through Douglass's recollections, and Anne Hutchinson through her reported speech recorded at her two trials. Rita Copeland explains how our understanding, even our knowledge, of dissent—until quite recently—is always mediated through a legal and rhetorical system designed to suppress it.[4] While Puritans were a highly literate culture—directly reading the Bible's word was essential to the Reformation—Hutchinson never wrote her readings of text down. What we have is a transcript—a recording in the technology of the time, handwritten probably from notes after the events occured, like the Dictaphone cylinders that Walter Neff keeps filling with his memo to insurance investigator and friend Barton Keyes. Film noir obsessively dwells on devices that mechanically reproduce and transmit the voice—Mike Hammer's telephone answering machine in *Kiss Me Deadly*, Myra Hudson's tape recorder in *Sudden Fear*, the ubiquitous telephones so central to Leona Stevenson in *Sorry, Wrong Number*;[5] or on photography as a record of bodies of evidence—for instance, in *Call Northside 777*, *Pickup on South Street*, and *The File on Thelma Jordan*; or the binoculars attached to a camera, and the tape recorder bugging the telephone in *Pushover*.[6] Thelma Jordan's cinematic punch derives, in part, from identifying Barbara Stanwyck's character as a bleached-blonde prostitute who looks exactly like Phyllis Dietrichson through an old gangland photograph circulating between District Attorney Wendell Corey's office and one from Miami. The scenario mirrors the ship captain's use of an old mug shot to clue Henry Fonda that Stanwyck and her father are gambling hustlers in Preston Sturges's *The Lady Eve*.

The tools of reproduction, faulty as they are, nevertheless enable dissenting and resisting women's voices to be deciphered long after their deaths, but they also may reveal their hidden deceptive pasts. Buried within these forms is a repetitive tale of replication as Anne Hutchinson's monstrous birth grew into Hester Prynne baring her emblazoned breast, whose wild daughter, Pearl, is later revealed to be Daisy Miller glimpsed by Winterbourne kneeling in the enormous oval of the Coliseum before the gigolo Giovanelli, who, like Mrs. Ansley, the "quiet" woman knitting in view of the Coliseum in Edith Wharton's "Roman Fever," begets still another ravishing daughter, Barbara, this time as Phyllis Dietrichson (or Joan Crawford's Mildred Pierce, whose diabolical daughter, Vera, assumes her look and her man), who begets, in the most recent version of a dark lady and her machinery—telephones and (the appropriately named trip-up Linda Tripp's) tape recorders again—Monica Lewinsky.

President Clinton's affair in the lesser oval (office) of the White House played out against the backdrop of this perverse plot. His former lover, Gennifer Flowers mentioned in an interview with

FIGURE 48. The mechanics of noir—visual and audio surveillance. Phil Carey as voyeur and Fred McMurray as auditor in *Pushover* (d. Richard Quine, 1954).

Larry King that as soon as she saw the ubiquitous footage of black-bereted Monica hugging the president, she knew he was involved with the young intern. Monica Lewinsky, revealed Flowers, looked just like her when she, a young reporter at a Little Rock television station, first met Clinton. "Back then, I had dark hair, like his mother," she noted coolly. Thelma Jordan disguised herself by turning into, or returning to, a mousy brunette; the women surrounding Clinton's impeachment—Hillary Rodham Clinton, Paula Corbin Jones, Linda Tripp, Gennifer Flowers, Monica Lewinsky—underwent a series of makeovers, transforming themselves through changing make-up and hair color and styles, weight loss and plastic surgery, into an evolving catalogue of film noir's female types. Each of these women was demonized in highly predictable ways. For instance, in a fundraising letter sent during the 2000 Senate race in New York, the Republican Party described Hillary Clinton with great alliterative flair as "abrasive and annoying, brash and bitter, calculating and scheming, distant and deceitful, polarizing and power-hungry."[7] Without the armor of fiction, it would be practically impossible to make sense of Kenneth Starr's obsessive inquiry into Clinton's personal life, which itself repeats a familiar plot. Roger Chillingworth and Barton Keyes, men who doggedly search out the truth, resisting temptations usually found in the shape of a woman, cannot fathom the ones who cannot stay away—Walter Neff or Cleve Marshall (in *The File on Thelma Jordan*), Arthur Dimmesdale and Bill Clinton as well. Film noir provides the context for understanding the replication of America's dark ladies and the men who fall for them, as well as those who relentlessly seek their exposure. The deep shadows and the glaring light put the shades of gray into high relief.[8] Bill Clinton gleaned the political efficacy of "triangulation" when he stole Republican Party platforms on the sexually loaded and racially coded issues of crime and welfare and refashioned them into his own policy. Douglass viewed these interlocking triangles through a closet door; Hawthorne found them in the moldy papers stuffed in the Custom-House attic; my parents spent Saturday night watching them at the Rialto; I absorbed them on *Million Dollar Movie*; my sons peruse them on the World Wide Web.

DETOUR

I have been arguing for attention to narrative history—to the history of narratives as much as to the narratives of history—found in the trash of America's popular and political cultures. Only a pulp theory can make sense of the strange lineage connecting Monica Lewinsky to Anne Hutchinson; so to conclude, let me take you on a feminist excursion into narrative history, a detour on the road through noir. We begin driving north on the Hutchinson River Parkway heading toward Vermont where poet Anne Stevenson's "family history in letters" (as she subtitled her volume of poetry) was uncovered. *Correspondences*, whose title plays on the varied meanings of the word— epistles back and forth, the harmonious reverberations between one set of objects or representatives and others, sexual intercourse, religious communion—is a saga of two hundred years of New England women's crises over family, work, money, and thwarted dreams of creative expression and sexual desire derived from an actual archival source found in the barn of her family's Vermont farmhouse. Her poems rewrite the letters she found molding there to appear truly authentic by mimicking eighteenth- and nineteenth-century diction and including the archivist's footnotes (in the form of marginalia detailing damage by fire, water, or rodents). As the poems move into and through the twentieth century, various poetic styles are picked up and discarded as first one then another generation of women suffer humiliation at the hands of mothers and lovers, editors and husbands.

The long confessional poem, "From an Asylum: Kathy Chattle to her mother, Ruth Arbeiter," dated May 2, 1954—years before Betty Friedan named the "Feminine Mystique" as the problem that had no name, but only a few years after Olivia de Havilland survived *The Snake Pit*—written by one of the last heirs of the dynasty, is posted from The Good Samaritan Hospital, a mental institution. Once a worker (arbeiter is her maiden name), she is now, as a wife and mother, a slave (chattel), suffering perhaps from "involutional melancholia," like the women Esther Bubley photographed for the *Ladies Home Journal*. The letter offers a litany of middle-class domestic hells: a screaming, colicky baby and cheating, absentee husband leave her a raging new mother perpetually drunk. It concludes with a typical 1950s explanation mounted by the "whitecoats" for why Kathy abandoned her own daughter—"they think you're to blame."[9] Kathy's husband, feeling trapped in "the prison of a family / Baby / shaping him into the / middle class, money-earning / ulcered American Dad," declares her a "slut . . . / [s]lovenly, drunken bitch." Kathy takes off one day on "the first train" into "a wind full of / knife-edged, excitable sunlight. // Walking from Central Station / feeling slenderer, blonder . . ." Her trip to New York—fleeing suburbia for the city streets where she is "Too scared to go to bars. . ." like a femme fatale—sends her "wandering like a schoolgirl from / museum to museum . . ." until she collapses at the Cloisters and ends up "where they've taken my belt and my / wedding ring, where they / specialize in keeping me weeping." Unable to transform from the "nice girl" she was raised to be into a femme noire, Kathy ends up installed in psychological melodrama (65–70). However, Stevenson's family history concludes with a 1972 letter from this same woman, now renamed after her divorce and an expatriate writer, to her estranged father: "It is a poem I can't continue. / It is America I can't contain" (88). Moving away from the enclosure of domestic space, she discovers the nation itself is as constricting. These private episodes of loss cannot contain the nation; yet they are precisely the stuff of 1970s feminist revisions of American political discourse. During the Vietnam War, the noir vision of domestic hell lurking within the middle-class family extends to the political realm to include the gunk in the kitchen sink.

The tradition of Marxist-feminist criticism argues for the importance of analyzing both social and literary texts as complementary, interruptive, and, sometimes, competing narratives, suggesting that literary scholarship must never forget social relations.[10] How could it? Even the most personal confessions, those that "can't continue . . . can't contain," failing at Whitman's democratic "I am large. I contain multitudes" seek other voices, reveal whole nations, in caches of secret and hidden documents that are the heart of contemporary feminist historical inquiry. We write literary history not to escape or forget the troubling geography in which the clipping or the letter or the drawing now dwells, but precisely to detail this climate as well as its earlier one. Situating a book in history or fancying literature from history—doing both kinds of literary history—reveals the past and so enables a close reading of the pulpy present.

When Stevenson came upon the cache of family letters in the early 1970s, women's historians were busily reinventing the discipline of history to include and understand such private forms as the diary or letter as legitimate data—seen then as a window on that supposedly separate sphere of woman: private life. Recently, Felicity Nussbaum has argued that the construction of the private self in those diaries and letters is preeminently a public and political act enabling Enlightenment subjectivity, and so empire and capitalist accumulation—the big stuff of politics and economics. At a time when feminist historians find the public/private split useless, is it any wonder that feminist novelists, like Hawthorne a century and a half ago, pick up history—that no longer exclusive realm of public truth—for their fiction?; or more accurately, turn again to historical fiction to argue contemporary political issues?

BELOVED ARROGANCE AND VINDICATION

Three late twentieth-century novels by American women—Toni Morrison's *Beloved* (1987), Frances Sherwood's *Vindication* (1993), and Joanna Scott's *Arrogance* (1990)—take their subjects from historical figures and incidents in order to circulate feminist political theory within contemporary popular culture.[11] These books, as literary histories, allow us to think about why writing historical narratives or narrating writerly histories offers us a politics for and a history of the present. They put forth a pulp theory of this present trashy era. These works are all dilettante's histories—works by those "lovers of the fine arts," those "refusers of a profession," rank "amateurs," "parasites," to quote from some of the citations found in the *Oxford English Dictionary*. Novelists are really counterfeit dilettantes (the true ones being artists or musicians and their fans), which makes them even more likely to tell the truth than those in the profession of truth-telling: "I'm suspicious about the nature of history or biography, and what really happened and what didn't happen," says Frances Sherwood. "The biographers might rely on Mary's letters, but have you ever written a letter that was a lie? I have."[12] Critics severely chastised each author—even as they praised each for her poetic erudition—for wholesale "fiction-mongering," lying, tampering with the historical record, such as it is, then meddling in the politically correct.[13] The controversies surrounding these novels point to the uneasiness with which we approach those transgressors of boundaries—be they poets, dilettantes, femmes fatales, or feminists.

Toni Morrison took what had been a footnote in histories of the slave community—Margaret Garner's murder of her child (which she found in Angela Davis's citation of Herbert Aptheker's offhanded remark published in a Communist Party USA journal during the cold war years)—as the center of her massive novel about the secret heart of the nation—slavery and racism—and spun pages and pages of sensuous descriptions of clothing, food, work, tools, and instruments of torture.[14] Certain critics faulted her for not leaving these "unspeakable things unspoken."[15] When Morrison tapped the mind of the enslaved mother, she provided a counterhistory from Davis's footnote to the gap in Frederick Douglass's narrative (one of the sources for *Beloved*) about his mother's absence: "I do not recollect of ever seeing my mother by the light of day. She was with me in the night. She would lie down with me, and get me to sleep, but long before I waked she was gone. Very little communication ever took place between us. . . . Never having enjoyed, to any considerable extent, her soothing presence, her tender and watchful care, I received the tidings of her death with much the same emotions I should have probably felt at the death of a stranger."[16] Morrison lets us see a woman who worked from sun to sun then walked miles to sleep briefly with her son. She lets us know that a mother's love can go unrecognized. The tree on Sethe's back, scars left from the horrendous beating she endured as a slave, grow out of his Aunt Hester's whippings; they are her darker scarlet letter. Morrison was savaged, much as Zora Neale Hurston had been during the 1930s, for staging a minstrel show in prose, pandering to the sensational desires of a mass white public—in this case, a white feminist one.

Beloved focuses on "what a woman suffers as a slave," motherhood, and maternity, the emotions, but also the legalities, of blood bonds, ownership, and parental rights, and the racial history of reproduction and property rights, in short, the gothic residue of racialist sexuality.[17] The novel links the history of American racism and the legacy of slavery to contemporary debates on abortion, welfare, and teen pregnancy, which have galvanized the New Right in its backlash against the movements for liberation among African Americans and other racial minorities, and among women and gays of all races. Morrison's novel investigates questions about legitimate and illegitimate mothering, about the work of the reproductive body in the political economy of America, about the discomfort female sexuality elicits within patriarchal culture. Its presentism, its conscious "design to placate sentimental feminist ideology," and its (critical and theoretical) controversies left it open to political attack. Critic Stanley Crouch denounced its "melodrama" and its "biblical grandeur." Because its supernatural elements moved it out of the realm of history into that of fantasy, Crouch likened Morrison's politics and poetics to those of "P. T. Barnum."[18]

Lest it appear that only critics at *The New Republic* express outrage that a novelist tampers with history, Margaret Forster, the feminist biographer of Daphne Du Maurier, revealed a surprisingly similar panic a few years later about Frances Sherwood's *Vindication*. Frances Sherwood's stunning 1993 novel so provoked its *New York Times Book Review* critic that she felt compelled to warn readers that the story of Mary Wollstonecraft being told by Sherwood in this novel was not factually verifiable. But truth is not really what was at issue. In her biography *Love, Anarchy and Emma Goldman*, Candace Falk revealed that the 1970s feminist heroine had been the love slave of Ben Reitman. Doing the work that feminist historians do, Falk had discovered a cache of letters between the anarchist and the hobo in the archives of the Bancroft Library at UC Berkeley. These same sources from private life—diaries and letters—have been the means feminist historians use to place women as a subject in history. However, it seemed from the response to Falk's research that they only attain value if they reinforce positive images about women. With few exceptions, Falk's disclosure about Goldman's "sexual slavery" (the title of Kathy Barry's 1978 book), coming as it did at the height of the feminist sex wars, were met with outrage by feminists.

Unlike Falk, whose facts debunked a kind of feminist heroine worship seeking to align the personal with the political, Sherwood's crime was to embellish the scanty facts and question why we think personal life corresponds to political ideology and action at all. Damned if you do, damned if you don't. Forster's concerns revolve around three distressing scenes in Sherwood's novel: Wollstonecraft's slippage into madness after her break-up with Henry Fusili; her pleasure as a s/m bottom; and her abuse of her first-born daughter, Fanny. None of these incidents, asserts Forster, could possibly have occurred: "Mary Wollstonecraft? Whipped? It's just as likely that she would have snatched the whip and turned it on him," she declares in a huff.[19] That Sherwood's novel takes liberties, if you will, with Wollstonecraft's life and art (Mary Wollstonecraft was after all not only a historian, political theorist, and journalist but a novelist herself) in order to discuss what the reviewer for the *Library Journal* notes as "so many trendy topics—child abuse, mental illness, homosexuality, and drug addiction—without departing from the basic facts" is precisely what makes the novel convincing as a literary history.[20] And, if one takes seriously complaints about biographies and their failure to bring their subjects to life, it is clear that only novelists might be able to animate "the indirect author/hero of this mess."[21]

What else is historiography but a continual revision? Forster's sense that history is cheapened when called to serve the present as if it has sold itself like some bar maid is akin to Crouch's anger at Morrison's appeal to the "ideology . . . [of] the black woman as the most scorned and rebuked of victims." In her own justification of the liberties taken with literary decorum, however, Wollstonecraft argued "I have rather endeavoured to pourtray [sic] passions than manners. . . . I could have made the incidents more dramatic [but] would have sacrificed my main object, the desire of exhibiting the misery and oppression, peculiar to women, that arise out of the partial laws and customs of society. In the invention of the *story*, this view *restrained* my fancy; and the *history* ought to be considered, as of woman, than of an individual."[22] Wollstonecraft's last piece of writing fails as a novel, according to critic Moira Ferguson, because it returns to her treatise on education, coming full circle to reproduce the effect of a political exhortation; in other words, it is not about a character but about a class, womankind.[23] For Wollstonecraft, however, the novel served as a pedagogical tool, another vehicle by which she could traffic in the political arguments of her day. (This is precisely the strategy Caroline Slade employed a century and a half later; see chapter 6.) The reviewer for London's *New Statesman and Society* ultimately champions Wollstonecraft's didactic fiction over Sherwood's fabulation: "If we are Wollstonecraft, then she is us, and the conclusion is somehow much more presumptuous than the premise."[24] But why must this be so? Both authors narrate a feminism that complicates the picture of woman's story and history by depicting women as victims, or, more dangerously, exonerating them as victimizers, or, more damning still, suggesting that they may be both at the same time, constructing, as reviewer Fletcher calls it, "a feminist continuous present." By participating in contemporary political debates through literary history, Sherwood embraces Wollstonecraft's (and indeed feminism's) best history, but the slippage among genres so common in the eighteenth century is highly questionable these days.

Vindication airs many of the dark corners of this continuous contradiction, such as, the noncongruence between ideology and desire as played out in the feminist sex debates of the 1980s. Until the publication of books by Nadine Strossen, Sally Tisdale, and Katha Pollitt, Sherwood's novel was one of the few mainstream publications to push a so-called prosex line.[25] The feminist antiporn argument received wide attention in the mass-marketed form of Andrea Dworkin's tome, *Intercourse*; it was mainstreamed by feminist slicks like *Ms.* and rarefied by the academic legal credentials of Catherine MacKinnon.[26] However, the feminist anticensorship and prosex arguments circulated in work by Pat Califia, Alice Echols, Suzie Bright, and Carol Vance only within small presses and little magazines—Cleis Press, Monthly Review Press, *On Our Backs*.[27] *Vindication* is a history of the present dressed up, in perfect period costume, as a historical fiction from the eighteenth century. If *Vindication* is a history of the present, then of course Wollstonecraft is us. Yet foremothers' names are not to be sullied; women's history celebrates remarkable and exceptional women. To suggest that an Amazon such as Wollstonecraft may have harbored a less-than-PC set of desires is troubling within a backlash world. Sherwood's Wollstonecraft took her cues from the controversies about pornography, s/m, butch/femme, engaging, or rather rupturing, American academic feminism during the 1980s and from 1940s femme fatales.

Joanna Scott's 1990 novel pivots on Viennese artist Egon Schiele's twenty-four day prison sentence in 1912 for "disseminating indecent drawings and endangering public morality." These charges were the only ones to stick after he was accused of abducting a young peasant girl who had posed for his life drawings of nude girls masturbating and embracing.[28] Schiele's case, tried in the village of Neulengbach, was no cause célèbre in prewar Austria, but Scott effectively distills the events preceding and following his arrest to elaborate her rococo meditation on his obsessive artistic genius. The novel is narrated retrospectively by the young girl but relies often on the voice of Schiele's new model and lover. Taking these few weeks as the central instance in the artist's short life, Scott composes a novel that explores the political history of fin-de-siècle Vienna and, of course, anticipates American millennial concerns as well.

As in the other examples, Scott stretches a footnote into a full-length alternative history of the artist and his city.[29] Art historians usually hurry over the "tragic time" of Schiele's imprisonment, minimizing and even dismissing the grim and clearly political poetry screaming from his self-portraits made in his cell.[30] Intent on viewing Schiele as "one of the most normal" people whose life "was relatively eventless," critics declare in no way was he a "rebel"; rather he was only concerned with his art, which figurative and erotic, to be sure, is really just abstraction because the images are not fixed spatially. They float without orientation to ground.[31] However, as curator James Demetrios has implied, precisely because these works are aberrations in Schiele's career—they are dated, titled, and the figures do appear in spatial contexts—they should be seen as significant; they interrupt the more purely formalist considerations dominating art history, in general, and Schiele criticism in particular.[32] These twelve charcoal, pencil, and watercolor studies of the artist curled under thin blankets on his bare cot are captioned with such inflammatory titles as "To Confine the Artist Is A CRIME, It MEANS MURDERING UNBORN LIFE" or "For My Art I Will Gladly Endure to the END." Schiele's melodramatic *cri du coeur* anticipated a history of censorship within European nations, from Hitler's Germany to Stalin's Soviet Union, that destroyed works and lives. However, his more local, seemingly less political, trial and imprisonment has even more in common with recent events in the United States.

Again, Scott's exaggerated literary history provides a device for probing the present. Like Sherwood, she pushes fiction into an argument with biography. Scott, too, was chastised by critics, who could not fault the novel's "sensuous, provocative patterns" detailed through "rich experiences, intriguing perceptions." Yet she failed to "bring either Schiele or his art to life" being "more . . . a treatise than a novel, it's often bulky with exposition, and perilously short on active characters and dramatic scenes."[33] Of course, because Scott chooses to focus on the trial and imprisonment of the artist for pornography, one can hardly miss her very contemporary references to arts' funding and censorship controversies circulating around the Cincinnati Art Musuem's exhibit of Robert Mapplethorpe's photography, Andre Serranos's "Piss Christ," performance artists Karen Finley, Holly Hughes, and the rest of the NEA Four, and other cases that figured so prominently in the sexual hysteria of the Reagan/Bush years. Less well known perhaps was the case of Jacqueline Livingston, a photographer who was fired from her Cornell University job after complaints surfaced about a series of nude photographic portraits she took of her father-in-law, then husband, and son. What caused the ruckus was a sequence of images of her young son masturbating; these were interpreted to be child pornography. Other cases—such as the furor over Sally Mann's book of photographs about her children, or Jock Sturges's investigation by the FBI after lab technicians claimed his nude images of his and friends' children trafficked in child pornography—were less well publicized than the case of the NEA Four but are even more chilling in their implications. Feminist artists and curators, such as Connie Samaras, Carol Jacobson, and Carole Vance, have repeatedly demonstrated—in their work, their writings, and most particularly in their struggle to present others' work—that there are large and dangerous unintended consequences to feminist challenges to pornography.[34] Those most interested in policing degrading images enable the state to determine deviance, which includes even feminists. Art and female desire suffer in the name of protection. But anyone who had been watching film noirs already knew this.

CORRESPONDENCES

Even if critics have had a rough time recognizing the singular contributions of these women's literary histories, I hope I have made it clear that the novels borrow from a feminist literary tradition operative since Wollstonecraft. Like the femme fatale, feminist literary history emerges on the threshold between the enigma and the stereotype, the unwritten and the rewritten.[35] Like Walter Benjamin's "Angel of History," this angle on history ever looks over its shoulders even as it plants itself firmly in the present, only to be blown forward by the storms of complaint. Anne Stevenson's verse history reimagined America from the perspective of those just barely outside its center—middle-class WASP women—and returns the novel to its epistolary origins, even as she pushed poetic diction into everyday vernacular. The many women who write most of these letters are shown to be willful, contemptible, self-involved, racist, pathetic, anguished; they speak of money, violence, war, civil unrest, madness, sex, children, and poetry, tracing how families produce and reproduce themselves. In short, they survey all the debates raging among feminists during the late 1960s and 1970s.

For two hundred years, the work of feminism has been, in part, to peer into the recesses of private life, to locate it within public and political culture. Unraveling family and, by extension, social history through the discovered sack of letters hanging like the Moor's shriveled head at which the young Orlando jousts his make-believe lance in the chilly attic of his ancestral home formed Josephine Herbst's 1930s Trexler trilogy.[36] Herbst's one-hundred-year saga of her family's struggle to achieve and maintain middle-class stability developed from the stories Herbst heard her mother tell during long hours spent hiding in storm shelters against the tornadoes of western Iowa. Her mother's stories, retold by Anne Trexler, were kept alive through her words, but their veracity depended on the "bags of old letters hanging from the rafter like beheaded corpses as if the written works of the dead somehow pledged the family to immortality."[37] Letters in the attic, mildewed and moth-eaten, like the moldy packet found in Hawthorne's Custom-House, keep memory and history alive. They legitimate the secret history of any family lucky enough to possess a house, eventually becoming the sources for subsequent social histories once their location has been discovered and their secrets deposited in the archives for future generations of scholars to peruse. The novelist has privileged access to this source of family immortality, of history—her letters may even be among those saved. Herbst obliquely makes this point by including excerpts of her own reportage, often written in the form of letters to *The New Masses* from various sites of struggle: foreclosed farms and dairy cooperatives in the Midwest; sugarcane workers' soviets in Realengo, Cuba; the anti-Nazi underground in Berlin. These documentary narratives shore up the literary history of postbellum America encapsulated in the Trexler saga.

As Woolf and Herbst knew, stealing the words of one's forebears provides fodder for exactly the kind of story most fitting for pulp modernist narrative. Hart Crane reveals a secret affair in his poem, "My Grandmother's Love Letters," which were "pressed so long / Into a corner of the roof / That they are brown and soft, / And liable to melt as snow."[38] Discovered, we learn from his biographer, in the secret hideout Crane found for his boyhood masturbation, they let us in on the author's desires more than his grandmother's. Crane's discovery of his grandmother's secret literary history, "hung by an invisible white hair," then rummaged in the family archives of the attic, updates an American Gothic convention—revealing the secret of the purloined letter or the Custom-House.[39] Nathanael West's *Miss Lonelyhearts* trafficked in the sad, absurd letters sent to his desk by those lacking the stability of a house with an attic, those on the margins of a commodified world of canned emotion, in search of hope and advice from the all-knowing soothing voice of a dissipated, alienated journalist. Anne Stevenson, like Herbst and West, shifted the modernist focus from the secret reader of (scarlet) letters to the social saga they narrated, returning to Hawthorne's romance, turning private dispatch into political diatribe. The racial and sexual inversions connecting Anne Hutchinson to Aunt Hester in *The Scarlet Letter*, on the one hand, or Stevenson's Kathy Chattle to Morrison's Sethe, on the other, crisscross the map of noir. Esther Bubley's bus trip west through Ohio then south through Kentucky reversed the direction the pregnant Sethe took after she escaped bondage at Sweet Home. Perhaps Bubley's Greyhound passed the train hurtling Cross Damon east to Penn Station where he might have glimpsed Lutie Johnson waiting on the platform enroute to Chicago. The forces that banished the pious Anne Hutchinson from the city on the hill were different from those that sent Bubley, a Russian-Jewish girl from the heartland of Superior, Wisconsin, to New York and Washington, D.C., three hundred years later, but they were not that different: a restless, rebellious desire spurred by the darkness lurking within themselves and their landscapes. They followed the map of the hundreds of film noirs from the postwar years and the thousands of photographs from the Depression decade, as well as the many novels and poems that echo them, as they strayed off the highway and found the detour toward the political truth of pulp fiction, which charts, in black and white and noir, America's pulp modernism.

NOTES

INTRODUCTION: ON PULP MODERNISM

1. Simone de Beauvoir, *America Day by Day*, trans. Carol Cosman (Berkeley: University of California Press, 1999), 113.

2. Theodor Adorno, *Minima Moralia: Reflections from Damaged Life*, trans. E. F. N. Jephcott (1974; reprint, London: Verso, 1984), 48.

3. Mary McCarthy, "Mlle. Gulliver en Amerique," in *On the Contrary: Articles of Belief, 1946–1961* (New York: Farrar, Strauss, Cudahy, 1962), 24–31.

4. As this book was going to press, the Twin Towers of the World Trade Center were destroyed by two hijacked airplanes killing thousands and transforming the New York skyline. De Beauvoir's prescience about the aftermath of World War II was horribly fulfilled.

5. Nelson Algren, *Chicago: City on the Make* (Sausalito, Calif.: Contact Books, 1961), 105.

6. Richard Severo, "Jane Greer, 76, Film Noir Star Who Returned to Do a Remake," *New York Times*, August 28, 2001, A17. In her obituary, Jane Greer, co-star with Robert Mitchum in *Out of the Past*, is quoted as replying to her son, when he told her she was the "Queen of Film Noir," that she really didn't know what film noir was.

7. Quoted in C. L. R. James, *American Civilization*, ed. Anna Grimshaw and Keith Hart (Oxford: Basil Blackwell, 1993), 130.

8. See Nino Frank, "A New Kind of Police Drama: The Criminal Adventure" (1946) and "Americans Are Also Making *Noir* Films" (1946), in Alain Silver and James Ursini, eds., *Film Noir Reader 2*, 15–24 (New York: Limelight Editions, 1999).

9. Quoted in Jane Jacobs, *The Death and Life of Great American Cities* (New York: Vintage, 1961), 310.

10. Ann Douglas, *The Feminization of American Culture* (New York: Knopf, 1977), argues that with the rise of sentimental female fiction in the mid-nineteenth century, American intellectuals were forced to resort to a rhetoric of cheap emotions to effect political change. Andreas Huyssen, "Mass Culture

as Woman," *After the Great Divide: Modernism, Mass Culture, Postmodernism* (Bloomington: Indiana University Press, 1986), argues that a virile modernist poetics raged against the decadence of a feminized popular realm.

11. For a new assessment of the many vernancular modernisms found in mid-century America, see Jani Scandura and Michael Thurston, eds., *Modernism, Inc.: Body, Memory, Capital* (New York: New York University Press, 2001).

12. Michael Szalay, *New Deal Modernism: American Literature and The Invention of The Welfare State* (Durham: Duke University Press, 2000); Saverio Giovacchino, *Hollywood Modernism: Film and Politics in the Age of the New Deal* (Philadelphia: Temple University Press, 2001); Jani Scandura and Michael Thirston, eds. *Modernism, Inc.: Body, Memory Capital* (New York: New York University Press, 2001) refer to "vernacular modernism," as does Paul Buhle among others; Cary Nelson discusses the modernism "we have wanted to forget" in *Revolutionary Memory: Recovering the Poetry of the American Left* (New York: Routledge, 2001); Marshall Berman speaks of "low" and "street" modernism in *All That is Solid Melts into Air: The Experience of Modernity* (New York: Penguin, 1988). Houston A. Baker, Jr., *Modernsim and the Harlem Renaissance* (Chicago: University of Chicago Press, 1987) outlines an "Afro-American modernism." In his address to the 2001 Modernist Studies Association convention, Ramon Saldívar identified a "transnational modernism" in the poetry of Americo Paredes.

13. Kenneth Fearing, "C Stands for Civilization," *Collected Poems of Kenneth Fearing* (1940), New York: AMS Press, 1977, p. 101. All further references appear in the text.

14. For a discussion of Fearing's use of advertising slogans, see Rita Barnard, *The Great Depression and the Culture of Abdundance: Kenneth Fearing, Nathanael West, and Mass Culture in the 1930s* (Cambridge: Cambridge University Press, 1995), esp, chapter 5.

15. Klaus Theweleit, *Male Fantasies, vol. 1.: Women, Floods, Bodies, History* Trans. Stephen Conway (Minneapolis: University of Minnesota Press, 1987).

16. Gilles Deleuze, *Coldness and Cruelty*, in *Masochism* (New York: Zone Books, 1991), 72.

17. Adorno, *Minima Moralia* , 218.

18. See Laurence Miller, "Evidence for a British *Film Noir* Cycle," *Film Criticism* 16 no. 2 (1991): 42–51, which lists 331 films made between 1940 and 1959; Tony Williams, "British *Film Noir*," in Alain Silver and James Ursini, eds., *Film Noir Reader 2* (New York: Limelight Editions, 1999), 243–70, also lists hundreds of films and stresses the interplay between American directors, actors, and writers and their British counterparts to suggest that there is both a distinctive British version, and to argue that it had an impact on American film as much as it borrowed from it.

19. For an extended analysis of the markings of race and ethnicity in this film, see E. Ann Kaplan, " 'The Dark Continent of Film Noir': Race, Displacement and Metaphor in Tourneur's *Cat People* (1942) and Welles's *The Lady from Shanghai* (1948)," in E. Ann Kaplan, ed. *Women in Film Noir*, 2nd ed. (London: British Film Institute, 1998), 183–201.

20. Rosita Forbes, *Women Called Wild* (New York: E. P. Dutton, Inc., 1937). The final chapter of her book, which follows female slaves and prostitutes and communists and soldiers around the world, concludes with the stories of a fox woman from Central America and a hyena woman from Abyssinia. Bram Dijkstra, *Evil Sisters: The Threat of Female Sexuality and the Cult of Manhood* (New York: Alfred Knopf, 1996), details how the "endless procession of gigantic spiders, vampires, cats, tentacled monsters, snake-bedecked women, women with (or better yet, turning into) wolves, black panthers, gorillas, bats, cobras, and whatever other gaping-mouthed predators . . . were to become the most lasting cultural heritage of turn-of-the-century biological 'science' " (146). He uses the *Amazing Stories* cover from October 1949 to illuminate how "the biology of female reversion [was] revealed by pulp" (caption, 147).

21. Charlotte Nekola, "Ida Lupino," *Dream House: A Memoir* (New York: W. W. Norton, 1993), 89–92.

22. This catalog could go on and on, an ever-proliferating list of neo-retro-noir films, novels, photographs, fashion, neighborhoods, etc. See, among many such examples, William L. Hamilton, "Style Noir," *New York Times*, September 15, 1997, B1, 6; Peter Marks, "As It Turns Artistic, A Noirish Enclave Steps Into the Light," *New York Times*, October 10, 1997, B1, 26 [about Dumbo in Brooklyn]; Constance C. R. White, "Why Coy Can Sizzle Hotter Than Brazen," *New York Times*, November 5, 1997, A23, which describes designer John Bartlett's "noir-inspired tomato-red leather coat" for "vixens." The year 1997 marked the fiftieth anniversary of the Hollywood blacklist; a commemoration held at the Academy of Motion Picture Arts and Sciences was organized by the industry's unions. Shunned by studio executives, it ended in a noir fashion: "A sad footnote to the evening was the death of the 82-year-old screenwriter Paul Jarrico, another blacklist victim, whose car ran off the road when he was on his way home," reported Bernard Weinraub, " At the Movies," *New York Times*, October 31, 1997, 11. For the twentieth anniversary of Roman Polanski's "renovating" the genre in *Chinatown*, see Jim Shepard, "Jolting Noir With a Shot of Nihilism," *New York Times*, February 9, 1999, Arts and Leisure, 24. Spike Lee's noirish resurrection of the 1977 Son of Sam summer, *Summer of Sam*, used an advertisement splashing the tabloid headlines from the *Daily News* across a full page of the Arts and Leisure section of the *New York Times*, May 2, 1999, 31. A Turner Classic Movies channel film noir series featuring less–well known noir films provided the occasion for Bernard Weinraub to gather four surviving femme fatales showcased in this series to remi-

nisce about their screen personae. "They're Gorgeous, Mysterious and Ready to Make a Sap Out of You," *New York Times*, August 23, 1999, B1, 5. In 1999, the Oscars were disrupted by supporters of Abraham Polonsky and other black-listed directors protesting the unanimous decision of the Academy of Motion Picture Arts and Sciences presentation of an honorary Oscar to Elia Kazan, see Bernard Weinraub, "Early Oscars Go to Coburn, Dench, and 'Shakespeare'," *New York Times*, March 22, 1999, B1, 3.

23. Janet Maslin, "The Rewards of Obsessing About Film," *New York Times*, April 14, 2001, A20.

24. Michael Pye noted that the protagonist "is also, noticeably, a film creature. She's in dark glasses, with a classy car and perfect makeup, a mouth like a red gash—like every thieving, conniving woman in a film noir. Like, say Janet Leigh in the start of *Psycho*. Her wig comes off, to shocking effect, in sexual fights, just like Connie Towers (remember?) in *The Naked Kiss*. "Serial Mom," *New York Times Book Review*, April 10, 1999, 29. The month before, Ed McBain described the formula for the "2 or 3 cents a word" pri-vate eye story: "I always started a P.I. story with a blonde wearing a tight shiny dress. When she crossed her legs, you saw rib-topped silk stockings and garters taut against milky white flesh, boy." "She Was Blond. She Was in Trouble. And She Paid 3 Cents a Word.," *New York Times*, March 29, 1999, B1, 3. However, commenting on the "explosion in the ethnicity of the detectives," Martin Arnold notes "the ranks of the new-breed fictional detective include gay teachers, a lesbian restaurant owner, a document examiner, psychologists, a forensic anthropologist, a quadriplegic police criminologist, a sports agent, an Egyptologist. . . . In short, all have profes-sions. They don't have to depend on a sexy woman slipping them a pair of greasy Ben Franklins." "Making Books," *New York Times*, April 15, 1999, B3.

25. Nicholas Christopher, *Somewhere in the Night: Film Noir and the American City* (New York: Free Press, 1997), insists with the French critics that film noir is "*a way of seeing the world*" (63; emphasis in original). He dis-sects the interconnections among the cell-like rooms of each apartment building, every office building in the modern city, and the bridges, cars, trains traversing them and linking them that reveal the inner workings of an alienating yet all-pervasive postwar capitalism. Eddie Muller, *Dark City: The Lost World of Film Noir* (New York: St. Martins. 1998), places the films and their audiences within this wild imaginary landscape. He understands that all film noirs, no matter where they are set, are about this doomed place.

I. ALREADY FRAMED: ESTHER BUBLEY INVENTS NOIR

1. See Giuliana Bruno, *Streetwalking on a Ruined Map: Cultural Theory and the City Films of Elvira Notari* (Princeton: Princeton University Press,

1993), for a discussion of the role urban movies—both as sites and as sights, that is, both the theater spaces themselves and the images that were shown there—played in unleashing urban Italian women from the constraints of the home.

2. Esther Bubley, United States Office of War Information Negative #LC22132-D. All citations from the Esther Bubley Collection of the FSA/OWI photographs in the Library of Congress.

3. Andrea Fisher, *Let Us Now Praise Famous Women: Women Photographers for the U.S. Government, 1935 to 1944* (London: Pandora, 1987), 105.

4. Bubley, OWI Negative #LC21005-E.

5. Bubley, OWI Negative #LC21016-E

6. Bubley, OWI Negative #LC21021-E.

7. Cornell Woolrich [William Irish], *I Married a Dead Man* (1948) (New York: Penguin Books, 1982), 19. The novel was made into the 1950 noir melodrama starring Barbara Stanwyck, *No Man of Her Own*. (Like *Raw Deal*, it was one of the rare examples, *Mildred Pierce* being another maternal noir that also starts with a woman's [Joan Crawford] recollections, to feature a female voice-over narration).

8. OWI Negative #LC38314-E. Esther Bubley's caption.

9. Naremore deconstructs the famous sex scene in *Out of the Past*, which is encoded through actions that reposition a lamp and the door, suggesting that "the codes of erotic lighting have an affinity with the codes of mystery lighting." He goes on: "After drying Kathie's [Jane Greer] hair with a towel, Jeff [Robert Mitchum] passionately embraces her and tosses the towel across the lamp, which pitches over in a gust of wind from the open doorway." Then the camera shifts outside the cabin returning as Jeff's silhouette looms up from the dark to shut the door. James Naremore, *More Than Night: Film Noir in Its Contexts* (Berkeley: University of California Press, 1998), 182.

10. These are all images from OWI negative nos. 32333–32353, specifically, 32340-E, 32334-E, 32351-E, and 32342-E.

11. See Miles Barth, ed., *Weegee's World* (New York: International Century of Photography/ Boston: Bulfinch Press, 1997), for information on Weegee.

12. See, for instance, Eunice Fuller Barnard, "College Girl: 1932–33," *Scribner's Magazine* 94 (January 1933): 51. For more on the educated, professional woman's image during the 1930s, see Laura Hapke, *Daughters of the Great Depression: Women, Work, and Fiction in the American 1930s* (Athens: University of Georgia Press, 1995), ch. 6.

13. In "Kiss the City Goodbye," *Lusitania* 7 (Spring 1996): 56–66, and "City of Fear: Defensive Dispersal and the End of Film Noir," *Any* 18 (1997): 14–18, Edward Dimendberg argues that these two zones of film noir imagi-

nation are differentiated not only spatially but temporally as well when the road became significant with postwar suburbanization and highway subsidies; however, many early and classic film noirs—*Detour* and *Out of the Past*, among them—are located in the movement from one zone to the other, anticipating the zigzagging back and forth between the old neighborhood and the new by the embourgeoisment of the white ethnic working class throughout the 1950s and '60s.

14. Minneapolis College of Art and Design Calendar of Events, Special Commencement Edition, May 1998, n.p.

15. From a handwritten biographical résumé in her working notebook of 1965. Uncataloged papers, Esther Bubley estate. Jean Bubley, executor.

16. Rosita Forbes, *Women Called Wild* (New York: E. P. Dutton & Co., Inc., 1938). The volume is illustrated with incredible woodcuts by Isobel R. Beard.

17. Two novels from the late 1930s—Bessie Breuer's *The Daughter* (New York: Simon and Schuster, 1938) and Leane Zugsmith's *A Time to Remember* (New York: Random House, 1936)—consider the emerging conflicts building within young Jewish women who have been provided with an education and are trying to Americanize themselves. Zugsmith's novel, which addressed family conflicts arising when daughters, rather than fathers, found work, was based on the League of Women Shoppers' support for the newly organized shopgirls at Orbach's. Breuer's novel focused on an alienated teenager whose divorced mother is too preoccupied to notice that her daughter's growing suicidal depression stemmed only when the girl meets up with striking fisherman and farmworkers in Florida. Both link a crisis in lower-middle-class Jewish life to the economic crisis facing the nation during the Depression. Part of what unsettles these young women is the ways in which they must enter the workforce despite family conflicts about the resulting freedom. Zugsmith's Aline Weinstein and Breuer's daughter test out sexual and political autonomy opened up for middle-class Jewish girls by the Left; they meet Gentile men with whom they have relationships, and they join political groups antithetical to their parents' limited political involvements. Moreover, middle-class possibilities of shopping, white-collar work, and travel have dislodged them from ghetto or community ties, secured by religion, labor unions, and family. Only the Left offers a replacement for these. By the 1940s, Communist Party membership was almost 50 percent female, and with almost 50 percent of the Party being Jewish, this became a space of Jewish female circulation. Bubley's upper Midwestern Jewish background is reflected back at her in the mirrors of the girls in rooming houses, with one, Pearl Ginsburg, clearly a radical, who has refused to pay her rent increase. See Paula Rabinowitz, *Labor and Desire; Women's Revolutionary Fiction in Depression America* (Chapel Hill: University of

North Carolina Press, 1991), and "Not Sappho, Sacco: Women, Art and Movement in the 1930s," *Intellectual History Newsletter* 19 (1997): 15–18; Laura Hapke, *Daughters of the Great Depression: Women, Work, and Fiction in the American 1930s* (Athens: University of Georgia Press, 1995).

18. Simone de Beauvoir, *America Day by Day*, trans. Carol Cosman (Berkeley: University of California Press, 1999), 165.

19. Unpublished typescript excerpts of a transcription of an interview by Tony Van Witsen of NBC, November 4, 1984, p. 6. Esther Bubley estate.

20. "Life in a Waiting Room," Photograph from series with text about the "entire story of bus transportation . . . made for the Standard Oil Co. of New Jersey." Esther Bubley estate. The series won first prize in the Picture Sequence category of the annual competition sponsored by the Encyclopaedia Brittanica Book of the Year and the University of Missouri School of Journalism.

21. Katherine Dieckmann, "Photography: A Nation of Zombies," *Art in America* 77 (November 1989): 55–57.

22. Bubley, OWI Negative #LC37670-E (Chicago, Ill., Sept. 1943).

23. Bubley, OWI Negative #LC37932-E. Bubley's caption reads: "A girl getting off the Macon bound Greyhound bus in Georgia. Passengers can get off at any place they wish along the road." September, 1943.

24. Bubley, OWI Negative #LC37468-E "A gas station on the road between Columbus and Cincinnati, Ohio, which is now used as a home. It is only one of many which are so converted." September, 1943.

25. Bubley, OWI Negative #LC37684-E (Chicago, Ill., Sept. 1943).

26. In a 1956 diary entry logging a job for Pepsi International (between Managua and Mexico City), she lists the following images: "air travel, passengers, baggage, cargo, behind scenes, different kinds of country, drinking (Pepsi), eating, embarking, disembarking, meeting and greeting, leave taking, reservations." Esther Bubley estate.

27. Caption for OWI Negative #37430, Esther Bubley Bus Trip, September 1943. This list runs down two pages and includes various brand names as modifiers– "Barbasol shaving cream," "Lux soap," as well as explanations for "ammonia inhalant (in case you get sleepy at night)," and "witness pad (for accidents)." Typescript, 5-6; Esther Bubley collection. In the typescript entitled "Bus Driver and Family," Bubley narrates the stories of the drivers and of the passengers in greater detail. This packet of materials included bus schedules and advertisements, as well as a detailed twenty-page description of the driver and passengers, featuring the recount of "Us on a Bus."

28. See note 26.

29. Bubley, OWI Negative #LC36894-E

30. de Beauvoir, *America*, 165.

31. 1948 diary/workbook. Esther Bubley estate.

32. Joan Younger, "What *Is* Mental Illness?" *Ladies Home Journal* 64 (April 1949): 36–37, 234. Follow-up articles by Joan Younger urged consideration of "Public Enemy # One: Mental Illness" and called for solutions in "Psychiatry Needs You," showing the necessary work of psychiatric nurses.

33. There are two boxes of photographs from "Mental Hospitals" in the Esther Bubley estate.

34. This picture won a prize in an exhibit at the University of Missouri. It became a standard image in psychiatry textbooks.

35. The *DSM-I* (1950) called this depression "involutional psychotic reaction." The *DSM-II* (1968) defines involutional melancholia as a "disorder . . . characterized by worry, anxiety, agitation, and severe insomnia. Feelings of guilt and somatic preoccupations are frequently present and may be of delusional proportions." In 1969, Francis J. Braceland was reporting on "Changes in the Treatment of Involutional Melancholia," in *Hospital and Community Psychiatry* 20 (May 1969): 136–40, and touting the improvements found in patients undergoing the "safeguards" in electroshock that aided recovery, where previous uses of endocrine replacement therapy had been unsuccessful on the women diagnosed. He describes those he encountered in the 1930s as follows: "Their child-bearing period was over; their children were grown, their husbands busy; their early dreams and desires were not to be fulfilled; their sexual life, if it ever was interesting, was waning. The future held little for them but old age and loneliness. To those who had traded upon their physical attractiveness, it was an especially distressing time. It was an era when women hated and resented middle-age and the menopause, and their anxiety and hostility could be expressed only against themselves. It was a period, too, when women were not as emancipated as they are today. They seemed to age more quickly in the culture of the 1930s, and what the future held had little charm for them" (29). However, a decade later, when the next *DSM* was in preparation, Margaret Weissman was unmasking "The Myth of Involutional Melacholia" in the pages of *Journal of American Medicine* 242 (August 24–31, 1979): 742–44. Her research set off a slew of investigations questioning "Is There an Involutional Melancholia?," which noted that by the end of the Second World War, the "place of involutional melancholia seemed well assured." P. Pichot and C. Pull, in *Comprehensive Psychiatry* 22 (January/February 1981): 2–10; yet a decade after feminism, it had disappeared.

36. *The Story of Serpasil* (Summit, N.J.: Ciba Pharmaceutical Products, Inc., 1955). This promotional brochure is in the Esther Bubley estate and can be found in the University of Minnesota Biomedical Library.

37. Esther Bubley, "Research for November *Profile of Youth* for 1949 *Ladies Home Journal*, p. 3. Esther Bubley estate.

38. Title of the photo essay done for OWI. Esther Bubley Collection.

39. "Working School Girl," "Teen-Age Poison," "Teen-Age Cruelty," *Ladies Home Journal* (November 1949): 62–66.

40. Journal entry, Feb. 18 (n.d. [1950?]). Rome, Italy. Esther Bubley estate. In this entry, Bubley notes that she has discovered her "ancestors." "I have joined the human race. It is like finding ones [sic] family at last."

41. Telephone conversation with Sally Forbes, Bubley's assistant, September 29, 1999.

2. DOMESTIC LABOR: FILM NOIR, PROLETARIAN LITERATURE, AND BLACK WOMEN'S FICTION

1. James Naremore, *More Than Night: Film Noir in Its Contexts* (Berkeley: University of California Press, 1998), 240–41. Naremore connects this to Norman Mailer's "White Negro" and the emergence of a critique of racism within Hollywood cinema in the wake of the Second World War.

2. Walter Benjamin, "The Work of Art in the Age of Mechanical Reproduction," in Hannah Arendt, ed., *Illuminations*, trans. Harry Zohn (New York: Schocken Books, 1969), 220.

3. Benjamin, "The Work of Art," 223–34.

4. Speaking of the 1940s', " 'woman's film' (or more accurately, the 'white woman's film')," Mary Ann Doane's notes: "When black women are present [in the 'woman's film'], they are the ground rather than the figure; often they are made to merge with the diegesis. They inhabit the textual sidelines, primarily as servants." *Femmes Fatales: Feminism, Film Theory, Psychoanalysis* (New York: Routledge, 1991), 232–33.

5. Fanny Hurst's novel *Imitation of Life* (1933) was immediately turned into a film by John Stahl (1934), then revived in 1959 by Douglas Sirk. It has served as a nodal point for much feminist theorizing on race, identity, and sexuality. See Mary Ann Doane, "Dark Continents: Epistemologies of Racial and Sexual Difference in Psychoanalysis and Cinema, in *Femmes Fatales*, 209–48; Marian Heung, " 'What's the Matter with Sara Jane?': Daughters and Mothers in Douglas Sirk's *Imitation of Life*," *Cinema Journal* 26, no. 3 (Spring 1987): 21–43; Sandy Flitterman-Lewis, "*Imitation(s) of Life*: The Black Woman's Double Determination as Troubling 'Other'," *Literature and Psychology* 34, no. 4 (1988): 44–57; Lauren Berlant, "National Brands/National Body: *Imitation of Life*," in Hortense Spillers, ed., *Comparative American Identities: Race, Sex, and Nationality in the Modern Text* (New York: Routledge, 1991), 110–40.

6. The whole question of what the "Left" was during this period is up for grabs; however, James Smethurst describes the nexus of intellectuals, writers, and organizations in Chicago that nurtured Gwendolyn Brooks as the "CPUSA subculture" of Chicago; he notes that Ann Petry wrote for "the Left-influenced newspaper," *People's Voice*. He cites a 1950 *Phylon*,

review of "New Poets," where Margaret Walker called Brooks a "forties" writer. James Smethurst, *The New Red Negro: The Literary Left and American American Poetry, 1930–1946* (New York: Oxford University Press, 1999), 58, 41, 179. See also William J. Maxwell, *New Negro, Old Left: African-American Writing and Communism Between the Wars* (New York: Columbia University Press, 1999), 2.

7. For a materialist reading of American naturalism, see June Howard, *Form and History in American Naturalism* (Chapel Hill: University of North Carolina Press, 1985); for a reading of *Cat People* as a racial allegory, see E. Ann Kaplan, "The 'Dark Continent' of Film Noir: Race, Displacement and Metaphor in Tourneur's *Cat People* (1942) and Welles's *The Lady from Shanghai* (1948)." In E. Ann Kaplan, ed., *Women in Film Noir*, 2nd ed. (London: British Film Institute, 1998), 183–201.

8. Alan Wald, *Writing From the Left: New Essays on Radical Culture and Politics* (London: Verso, 1994), and Michael Denning, *The Cultural Front: The Laboring of American Culture* (London: Verso, 1996), have different perspectives on this subject; but both agree that limiting cultural radicalism to the novels written during the 1930s [as Barbara Foley, *Radical Representations: Politics and Form in U.S. Proletarian Fiction, 1929–1941* (Durham, N.C.: Duke University Press, 1993); Robert Shulman, *The Power of Political Art: The 1930s Literary Left Reconsidered* (Chapel Hill: University of North Carolina Press, 2000); and many others, myself included, have done], skews the cultural vision of American radicalism by connecting it firmly to an established genre and a conventional period. When I was thinking through the difference gender made on the proletarian novel in *Labor and Desire: Women's Revolutionary Fiction in Depression America* (Chapel Hill: University of North Carolina Press, 1991), I limited my investigations to the years between Agnes Smedley's *Daughter of Earth* (1929) and Mary McCarthy's *The Company She Keeps* (1941), including works by Tillie Olsen and Meridel Le Sueur that had been completed during the 1930s but never published until the 1970s; however, I excluded Margaret Walker's *Jubilee* because she spent more than twenty years writing it. By delimiting the subject as I had— trying to read the novels produced in direct response to the pronouncements of literary radicals, like Michael Gold and Philip Rahv—I had contributed to another form of what I criticized them and their subsequent literary historians and critics of doing. Just as they failed to see women's literary radicalism, because gender and sexuality reconfigured the form and content of proletarian culture, by limiting my study to a period and a genre, I failed to see how black nationalism and feminism further revised proletarian literature.

9. But, as I will show in chapter 3, Richard Wright's 1953 answer to *Invisible Man*, *The Outsider*, is a postwar work.

10. Grace Hutchins, *Women Who Work* (1934), summarized the double burden of the working-class woman as follows: "[O]n top of a long day's work in the home, the working mother goes out for another stretch of five or six hours' work, scrubbing and cleaning floors and stairs and toilets. . . . " in Charlotte Nekola and Paula Rabinowitz, eds., *Writing Red: An Anthology of American Women Writers, 1930–1940* (New York: The Feminist Press, 1987), 339.

11. Mel Watkins, "Gwendolyn Brooks, 83, Passionate Poet, Dies," *New York Times*, December 5, 2000, C22. " 'I wrote about what I saw and heard in the street,' Ms. Brooks once said. 'I lived in a small second-floor apartment at the corner, and I could look first on one side and then the other. There was my material.' " The Bronzeville poems were recommended to the editors of Harper & Row by Richard Wright, who admired her ability to capture "the pathos of petty destinies, the whimper of the wounded, the tiny incidents that plague the lives of the desperately poor, and the problems of common prejudice." Watkins notes that "Ms. Brooks wrote a novel, *Maud Martha*, which received scant consideration when it was published in 1953. [It] was overshadowed by her achievements as a poet and invidiously compared with Richard Wright's *Native Son* and Ralph Ellison's *Invisible Man*, epic novels with clear-cut socio-political themes."

12. Belle Traub, "Discovered: A Modern Slave Block!" *The Negro Liberator* (June 15, 1935), quoted in Mary Battenfeld, "The World Problem is a Personal Problem: Women Document the 1930s," which analyzes this article. (Paper delivered at American Studies Association, New Orleans 1988.)

13. Ella Baker and Marvel Cooke, "The Bronx Slave Market," *The Crisis* 42 (November 1935): 330–31, 340.

14. Louise Mitchell, "Slave Markets Typify Exploitation of Domestic," *The Daily Worker* (May 5, 1940). Reprinted in Gerda Lerner, ed., *Black Women in White America: A Documentary History* (New York: Vintage Books, 1973), 229–31.

15. Barker and Cooke, "Bronx Slave Market," 331. Two years later, Marvel Cooke described the efforts of domestics to organize the Domestic Workers' Union and win uniform contracts. Marvel Cooke, "Modern Slaves," *The Amsterdam News* (October 16, 1937), in Lerner, *Black Women in White America*, 232–34.

16. Marita Bonner Occomy, "One True Love," in Joyce Flynn and Joyce Occomy Stricklin, *Frye Street and Environs: The Collected Works of Marita Bonner* (1941; reprint, Boston: Beacon Press, 1987), 219–27. Originally published in *Opportunity*, this story of the futility of black female struggles for education may have been an impetus for Brooks's character, Hattie's, bitter assessment of night school.

17. Gwendolyn Brooks, *Blacks* (Chicago: Third World Press, 1994), 52.

All further citations to Brooks's works come from this collection and appear in the body of the text.

18. Jacqueline Jones, *Labor of Love, Labor of Sorrow: Black Women, Work and the Family from Slavery to the Present* (New York: Vintage Books, 1985), 220.

19. "Harlem Crime," *The Crisis* 46 (December 1939): 366, 377–78.

20. Ann Petry, *The Street* (Boston: Houghton Mifflin, 1946), 41, 45. All further references from this edition appear in the body of the text.

21. Chester Himes, *The Quality of Hurt* (New York: Paragon House, 1972), 28.

22. Ibid., 18–19. Frederick Douglass, *Narrative of the Life of Frederick Douglass, An American Slave, Written by Himself* (1845; reprint, Garden City, N.Y.: Dolphin Books, 1963), 3.

23. Doc and Lou reported in the *Daily Worker* that it was "Not Sunny for Girl Slaves in 'Sunny' Florida," who worked fifteen-hour days as waitresses for $5 and picked up "a little extra on the side" from a "man friend" (January 4, 1929): 4. Waiting tables, as a public form of domestic service, thus is directly linked to prostitution; it is through the restaurant that the woman finds her clients. Another issue of the *Daily Worker* features two articles headlined: "Scrub Women Slave While World Sleeps; Wages Miserable" and "In Chicago, Waitresses Slave 70 Hour Week as Union Officials Fail Them" (March 13, 1929): 4. Again these women are defined as slaves because they serve and scrub, like domestics, in public places.

24. *Daily Worker* (September 23, 1929): 3.

25. Bessie Smith, "Washerwoman's Blues," 1928. *Empty Bed Blues* (Columbia G30450).

26. Phyllis Palmer, *Domesticity and Dirt: Housewives and Domestic Servants in the United States, 1920–1945* (Philadelphia: Temple University Press, 1989), 6.

27. In her discussion of the NBC/PBS series *I'll Fly Away*, Cheryl Johnson makes clear the necessary distinction between the iconography and history of the black mammy and that of the black maid. She shows how actress Regina Taylor resists the ideological pull of the racist image of the mammy by appearing as a "beautiful woman" who has her own family, narrates her own story, and participates as an activist in the civil rights movement of the 1950s. Cheryl Johnson, "A Restless Domesticity: Feminizing the Black Domestic in *I'll Fly Away*," After the American Century Conference, Oregon State University, April 19–21, 2001, forthcoming in *Wide Angle*.

28. David R. Roediger, *The Wages of Whiteness: Race and the Making of the American Working Class* (London: Verso, 1991), p. 85.

29. See Paula Rabinowitz, *Labor and Desire*, esp. 34–58; Elizabeth Faue, *Community of Suffering and Struggle: Women, Men and the Labor Move-*

ment in Minneapolis, 1915–1945 (Chapel Hill: University of North Carolina Press, 1991), esp. 69–99; Barbara Melosh, *Engendering Culture: Manhood and Womanhood in New Deal Public Art and Theater* (Washington, D.C.: Smithsonian Institute Press, 1991), esp. 15–32. On the connections between masculinity and interracial solidarity, see William J. Maxwell, *New Negro, Old Left*, esp. ch. 4.

30. Fannie Austin, "The Negro Working Women," *The Daily Worker* 2 (May 1930): 4 (emphases added).

31. Roediger explains that in Republican rhetoric this term allied artisans, small manufacturers, craftsmen, as well as mechanics, workingmen, and tradesmen against "the parasitic designs of bankers, undeserving paupers, monopolists, aristocrats and corporations," as well as slaves. See *The Wages of Whiteness*, 50–55.

32. Katherine Q. Seelye, " 'Working Families' Becomes a Theme Meant to Attract Female Voters," *New York Times*, August 22, 2000, A18. The phrase was meant to appeal to the "waitress mom," but it seemed to resonate well with more professional women—teachers and day care licensers are the two interviewed in the article—who also called themselves "working class."

33. The lyrics to Florence Reece's "Which Side Are You On?"can be found in Charlotte Nekola and Paula Rabinowitz, eds., *Writing Red*, 182–83.

34. "Domestic Workers Too Must Organize and Fight," by a Worker Correspondent to the "Working Woman Special" *The Daily Worker*, March 2, 1931, Sec. 2, p. 8, exhorts houseworkers, maids, chambermaids, day workers and live-ins to "build a union of domestic workers to defend our interests." By the time the United States entered the Second World War and better-paying jobs opened up in various industries for black women, notes Jacqueline Jones, Baltimore newspapers were trumpeting that "The Whip Changes Hands," as black domestics organized to raise wages and improve working conditions. In the South, "mysterious 'Eleanor Clubs' (named for the notorious busybody of a First Lady)—groups of black women who colluded to withhold their labor from the job market"—demanded concessions from white employers (*Labor of Love, Labor of Sorrow*, 237).

35. Trudier Harris, *From Mammies to Militants: Domestics in Black American Literature* (Philadelphia: Temple University Press, 1982), 14.

36. See Nancy Armstrong, *Desire and Domestic Fiction: A Political History of the Novel* (New York: Oxford University Press, 1987); Terry Eagleton, *The Rape of Clarissa: Writing, Sexuality and Class Struggle in Samuel Richardson* (Minneapolis: University of Minnesota Press, 1982), among other critical histories of the novel.

37. For some examples of interracial women's alliances during the 1930s, see Mollie V. Lewis, "Negro Women in Steel"; Mary Heaton Vorse, "Hard-

Boiled;" Myra Page, "Leave Them Meters Be!" and "Water!," in Nekola and Rabinowitz, eds., *Writing Red*, 276–78, 291–98; Lauren Gilfillan, *I Went to Pit College* (New York: Viking, 1934); *Union Maids* (d. Julia Reichert, Miles Mogeluscu, and James Klein, 1976).

38. See Doane's analysis of the complicated "act" that Sarah Jane performs, in "Dark Continents" in *Femmes Fatales*, 237–38.

39. In its first issue, *Ebony* interviewed black stars about these roles; Butterfly McQueen complained about being still being relegated to the maid, Lottie, in *Mildred Pierce*. "*Mildred Pierce*" *Ebony* 1 (January 1946): 30.

40. James M. Cain, *Mildred Pierce* (1941; reprint, New York: Penguin Books, 1946), 50.

41. Doane argues that "pretense, ontology, and the visible real" are "the core of its [the maternal melodrama] discourse." Moreover, "blacks are insistently *there*, never central, but an important component of the discourse, of its reality-effect" ("Dark Continents" in *Femmes Fatales*, 235, 239).

42. Langston Hughes, "Madam's Past History," in Arnold Rampersad and David Roessel, eds., *The Collected Poems of Langston Hughes* (New York: Alfred Knopf, 1995), 301. In *The New Red Negro*, 106, 172–75, Smethurst argues that the Madam series may have been written in response to Brooks's "Hattie Scott" poems, which he claims were a response to Richard Wright's *Native Son*, 247, n. 8. See also Bill Mullen, *Popular Fronts: Chicago and African-American Cultural Politics, 1935–1946* (Urbana: University of Illinois Press, 1999), 167–76.

43. [Dorothy] Myra Page, *Gathering Storm: A Novel of the Black Belt* (London: Martin Lawrence, 1932), 122. For a discussion of the interracial dynamics between women in this and other white women's proletarian novels from the early 1930s, see Susan Sowinska, "Writing Across the Color Line: White Women Writers and the 'Negro Question' in the Gastonia Novels," in Bill Mullen and Sherry Linkon, eds., *Radical Revisions: Rereading 1930s Culture* (Urbana: University of Illinois Press, 1996), 120–43.

44. In "Madam's Calling Cards," instead Alberta K. Johnson "had some cards printed." (Rampersad and Roessel, eds., *The Collected Poems of Langston Hughes*, 301).

45. Fannie Hurst, *Imitation of Life* (1933; reprint, New York: Permabooks, 1959), 77.

46. See any number of feminist readings of film noir, but especially relevant is Mary Ann Doane, "*Gilda*: Epistemology as Striptease," in *Femmes Fatales*, 92–118.

47. Gwendolyn Brooks, *Maud Martha* (1953), reprinted in *Blacks*, 141–321.

48. Smethurst notes in particular "at the hairdresser's," the section of the multipart poem about domestic worker "Hattie Scott," who "Got Madam

C. J. Walker's first. /Got Poro Grower next. / Ain't none of 'em worked with me, Min" (Brooks, *A Street in Bronzeville*, in *Blacks*, 53).

49. Ramona Lowe, "The Woman in the Window," in Nekola and Rabinowitz, eds., *Writing Red*, 79–83, (emphasis in original). Langston Hughes's "Madam and Her Madam" deatils the tense "love and theft," as Eric Lott called minstrelsy, in the exchange characterizing white women's misguided relationship to black women. It, like Ramona Lowe's story, takes a damning and ironic view of Fannie Hurst's fantasy (Rampersad, 285).

50. Roediger, *Wages of Whiteness*. Lauren Berlant, "Race, Gender, and Nation in *The Color Purple*," *Critical Inquiry* 14 (Summer 1988): 831–59, notes that Sofia's refusal to accept the mayor's wife's offer to her that she work as her maid, with her vocal "Hell no!" represents the first time Celie imagines rebellion to the rule of racial oppression. That ultimately Sofia lands in prison for this refusal, and is then further punished by being paroled into service as the mayor's maid suggests just how imbricated the state is with the private family (843).

51. Michael Denning, *The Cultural Front*, 60–62.

52. For a contemporary history of black migration, which means black men and their labor power, see Arna Bontemps and Jack Conroy, *They Seek a City* (Garden City, N.Y.: Doubleday, Doran and Co., Inc, 1945).

53. Doane, "Dark Continents" in *Femmes Fatales*, 241.

3. DOUBLE CROSS: WRI(GH)TING AS *The Outsider*

1. See Alain Bergala, "Weegee and Film Noir," trans. Alexandra Bonfante-Warren, in Miles Barth, ed., *Weegee's World*, (New York: International Center of Photography/Boston: Bullfinch Press, 1997), 69–77.

2. David Madden, *Proletarian Writers of the Thirties* and *Tough Guy Writers of the Thirties* (Carbondale: Southern Illinois University Press, 1968). By the 1950s, during the height of McCarthyism, many literary radicals had turned exclusively to popular genres. For instance, Ed Lacy's *Lead with Your Left* (New York: Harper and Bros., 1957), a crime novel set in New York, refers not too subtly to the author's political leanings. See Alan Wald, *Exiles from a Future Time* (Chapel Hill: University of North Carolina Press, 2002), for a detailed account of the mass cultural turn made by many writers affiliated with the Popular Front.

3. Georgia O'Keeffe, *Georgia O'Keeffe* (New York: Viking Press, 1976), n.p. Commentary to plate #58.

4. For only one example: In the scene in *The Outsider*, where Cross Damon kills both Gil Blount, the communist, and "Herr Herndon," the fascist landlord, Wright employs cinematic conventions from many film noirs—the darkened angled stairway (from *The Big Clock*), the fight in a

cramped apartment lit only by the flickering flames of a smoldering fire (from *Out of the Past*), the sounds of blows landing mixed with the tinkling of broken glass (from *The Lady from Shanghai*), a phone left dangling off the hook (from *Detour*), the bloody corpses left on the rug (from *Mildred Pierce*), the bloody weapons wiped with a handkerchief (from *Lady in the Lake*). Richard Wirght, *The Outsider* (1953; reprint New York: Perennial Library, 1965), pp. 223–28. All further references to this edition appear in the text.

5. See Dick Hebdige, *Subculture: The Meaning of Style* (London: Methuen, 1979); and Angela McRobbie, "Gender and Subculture," in Stuart Hall and Tony Jefferson, eds., *Resistance Through Rituals: Youth Subcultures in Postwar Britain* (Birmingham: Center for Cultural Studies, 1975).

6. All this seems far removed from race relations, but seeing enough of the films, it jumps out at you, so that the glaring lack of scholarship on it is bizarre. Manthia Diawara, "*Noir* by *Noirs*: Toward a New Realism in Black Cinema," in Joan Copjec, ed., *Shades of Noir* (London: Verso, 1993), 261–78, looks at movies made from Chester Himes' *Rage in Harlem* and focuses on the black revisions of the genre. A few critics have looked at the new black gangsta films as a third flowering of the style, but only a few critics have explored noir's racial codings. See also Mary Ann Doane, *Femmes Fatales: Feminism, Film, Theory, Psychoanalysis* (New York: Routledge, 1991); Eric Lott, "The Whiteness of Film Noir," *American Literary History* 9 (1997): 542–66; E. Ann Kaplan, ed., *Women in Film Noir*, new edition (London: British Film Institute, 1998); James Naremore, *More Than Night: Film Noir in Its Contexts* (Berkeley: University of California Press, 1998); Jonathan Munby, *Public Enemies, Public Heroes: Screening the Gangster from Little Caesar to Touch of Evil* (Chicago: University of Chicago Press, 1999).

7. "Roots and Branches," unpublished typescript (foreword to *Eight Men*), 5. Quoted in Michel Fabre, *The World of Richard Wright* (Jackson: University Press of Mississippi, 1985), 71.

8. Fabre, "From Tabloid to Myth" and "The Man who Killed a Shadow," in *The World of Richard Wirght*, 93–121.

9. For information on Wright's direct quotations from the *Tribune*, see Fabre, *World*, 65; and on the tradition of Chicago crime fiction derived from newspaper accounts, see Nelson Algren, *Chicago: City on the Make* (Sausalito, Calif.: Contact Press, 1961), 21–22. Margaret Walker, *How I Wrote Jubilee and Other Essays on Life and Literature* (New York: The Feminist Press, 1990), 33–49, tells of her aiding Wright's *Native Son*.

10. Yale Collection of American Literature (YCAL), Beinecke Manuscript and Rare Book Library, Richard Wright Papers, Box 95, Folder 1255, Horace Cayton, letter to Richard Wright, around August 29 or 30 [1945?]. Hereafter refered to as "Wright Papers."

11. See Richard Wright's "A Blueprint for Negro Writing," *New Challenge* 2 (Fall 1937): 58–65, on the importance of inventing an African-American realism. Wright's criticism of Zora Neale Hurston's 1934 novel, *Their Eyes Were Watching God*, turned on its use of folksy dialect, which, he felt pandered to white audiences used to viewing black culture through the distorted lens of the "minstrel show." Richard Wright, "Between Laughter and Tears," *New Masses* (October 5, 1937): 22, 25.

12. Michel Fabre, *The Unfinished Quest of Richard Wright* (New York: William Morrow and Co., 1973), 316

13. See Wright Papers, Box 53, Folder 639: Milton Rugof, *Herald Tribune*, Sunday, March 22, 1953, 4, calls it "sheer melodrama, a compost of sex and crime—lurid." An unidentified March 22, 1953, review by Carter Brooke Jones in the "Richard Wright Scrapbook" declares: "*The Outsider* is a melodrama. . . . It's almost as if Henry James took over a plot devised by Mickey Spillane." Lewis Vogler of the *San Francisco Chronicle*, April 5, 1953, called it "a full-scale ideological melodrama." The *New Yorker*, March 28, 1953, coins a neologism, "melodramative," to describe the novel. Granville Hicks's front-page Sunday *New York Times Book Review*, March 22, 1953, notes "*The Outsider* is both a melodrama and novel of ideas." Rey L. Gillespie of the *Cleveland Plain Dealer*, April 19, 1953, states simply: "[T]he climax is melodrama involving the Communists." Even the Clarksdale, Mississippi, *Press-Register* weighed in commenting on the book's noir-like jacket: "*The Outsider* is a gripping, melodramatic story of violence and psychology that has the shocking effect of shattered glass—which is, incidentally, symbolized by a solarized cover design." Arna Bontemps sums it all up in the *Saturday Review*, March 28, 1953, when he asserts that "Richard Wright's mind has always run to melodrama."

14. Wright Papers, "Richard Wright Scrapbook," Box 50, Folder 653. Jones, unidentified review in note 13. Melvin Altshuler in the *Washington Post*, March 22, 1953, declares: "If Mickey Spillane were to rewrite *The Outsider*, even he—with his formula that nothing succeeds so well as excess—would not tax credulity as much as Wright has." James N. Rhea writing in the Providence, Rhode Island, *Journal* condemns "*The Outsider* [a]s the worst novel I have ever read. . . . Without the intellectual and symbolic trappings, it might have been a corking good Mickely Spillane sort of thriller."

15. Wright Papers, Box 53, Folder 639. Rhea review in note 14. Herman Kogan called it a "cops-and-robbers story," in *Chicago Sun and Times*, March 22, 1953; while *Jet*, March 26, 1953, decried it as a "whodunit."

16. James Naremore, *More Than Night: Film Noir in Its Contexts* (Berkeley: University of California Press, 1998), 45

17. Wright Papers, Box 53, Folder 639. *Jet*, March 26, 1953.

18. Wright Papers, Box 97, File 1314. Ralph Ellison, letter to Ellen Wright, March 26, 1952.

19. John F. Callahan notes Ellison's debt to Wright for sparking his literary career after Wright, coeditor of *New Challenge*, asked the younger man to review a novel for the Fall 1937 issue. " 'On the basis of this review,' Ellison recalled, 'Wright suggested that I try a short story, which I did.' " Wright accepted the story about riding the rails, it was set into galley proofs, but bumped for space. *New Challenge* then failed. John F. Callahan, introduction to Ralph Ellison, *Flying Home and Other Stories* (New York: Random House, 1996), x.

20. Wright Papers, Box 97, File 1314. Ralph Elison, letter to Richard Wirght, January 21, 1953. He even includes a sales figure around 15,000.

21. Wright Papers, Box 97, File 1314 [p.41]. Ralph Ellison, letter to Richard Wright, February 1, 1948.

22. Ibid.

23. Ralph Ellison, "The Seer and the Seen," in *Shadow & Act* (New York: Signet, 1966), 112.

24. See Ellison letter dated February 1, 1948, in note 21.

25. Ellison letter dated January 21, 1953, in note 20.

26. Wright Papers, Box 53, Folder 639. March 30, 1953, and placed in the Richard Wright Scrapbook unsourced.

27. Wright Papers, Box 52, Folder 637. "Biographical Remarks."

28. Wright Papers, Box 52, Folder 636, "Introductory Section," n.d. In a typescript of this statement, Wright details how after 1946, when he and his family traveled to France, "a lull set in," during which he was sorting out his personal philosophy after leaving both the country and communism. He explains, "Elementary honesty prompts me to testify that the basic reality of our world—its meaninglessness, its poverty, its wars, its oppressions!—that once compelled me to be a Communist has not altered; indeed, the sickness of our time has not waned but waxed." Wright Papers, Box 52, Folder 637, Typescript 1,1952–53.

29. Wright Papers, Box 52, Folder 631. Early draft, n.d. In notes to himself about the court martial incident, Wright outlines the plot of *Cornering a Man*, which begins with "Negro in Army," tracks his increasing isolation from "order," and concludes with his "Disappearance." Other titles that Wright considered early on included "Cross: a novel," and "Man Upside Down: a novel." As late as August 7, 1952, Wright's editor at Harper's, Jack Fischer, offered these alternative titles: "A man Called Damon"; "The man with Two Names"; "The Victim"; "Man of Violence"; "Second Chance"; "A Name from a Grave"; "Man in Trouble."

30. Wright Papers, Box 105, Folder 1589. Letter to Richard Wright, March 19, 1948.

31. Dashiell Hammett, *The Maltese Falcon* (1929; reprint New York: Pocket Books, Inc., 1945), 200.

32. Richard Wright, *The Outsider* (1953; reprint, New York: Perennial, 1965), 130.

33. Ibid. See Joan Copjec, "The Phenomenal Nonphenomenal: Private Space in *Film Noir*," in Joan Copjec, ed., *Shades of Noir* (London: Verso, 1993), 167–97, for a discussion of "the detective function" played by Barton Keyes in *Double Indemnity* and his use of statistics and numbers to confound bureaucracies even as he feeds their murderous enterprise (171). Ely Houston clearly owes much to Edward G. Robinson's savory performance of this role.

34. For a discussion of knowledge and how "it changes the *impossible* into the *prohibited*" in film noir, see Slavoj Žižek, " 'The Thing That Thinks': The Kantian Background of the *Noir* Subject," in Joan Copjec, ed., *Shades of Noir*, 199–226.

35. W. E. B. Du Bois, *The Souls of Black Folk* (1903; reprint, New York: Vintage Books, 1990) 42.

36. The book-jacket cover illustration implies the connections between the novel and film noir; it looks just like a movie title: A black solarized photograph of a shattered pane of glass (a bullet-smashed windshield?) on the front; Wright's somber face matching it against the black background on the back. See Figure 28.

37. Wright Papers, Box 93, Folder 1167. Nelson Algren, letter to Richard Wirght, March 12, 1940, pp. 1–3.

38. Wright Papers, Box 98, Folder 1354. Richard Wright, typescript draft of letter to Mike Gold [1940?], pp. 5–6, 7.

39. Ibid., p. 10.

40. The same year, Vera Caspary, whose novel about a working-class girl who "passes" herself off as high class, *Laura*, would become one of the important film noirs of the 1940s, published *The White Girl* (New York: Grosset and Dunlap, 1929), a novel about light-skinned Solaria Cox, who "passes" for white in Chicago. Caspary, like Larsen, is concerned with the ways passing and criminality (or at least guilt) intertwine with desire. After being revealed as having "got nigger blood in your veins," she begins to unravel psychologically (161). "She thought of a spot on the hem of her white moiré dress and of a colored man in Chicago, and of a little boy with coppery brown curls, then she opened her eyes and she saw a rectangle of pale yellow light shining on the floor, and she heard the horns of lonely taxicabs querulously wailing" (171). A few years later, another Jewish woman writer of melodrama, Fannie Hurst, patron of Zora Neale Hurston, published her passing novel, *Imitation of Life*. Clearly, for these Jewish left-wing (or at least left-leaning) women, the story of African-American women pass-

ing offered a cogent metaphor for their own struggles to assimilate. Like many left-wing Jewish writers, actors, and composers—Guy Endore (*Babouk*), Elie Seigmeister, Al Jolson—racial cross-dressing served as a way to assert one's Americanness without assuming the mantle of racist "whiteness" and to challenge Hitler's anti-Semitism without calling attention to one's Jewishness. See Alan Wald's discussions of this in *Writing From the Left: New Essays on Radical Culture and Politics* (London: Verso, 1994); Susan Gubar, *Racechanges: White Skin, Black Face in America* (New York: Oxford University Press, 1997); Michael Rogin, *Blackface, White Noise: Jewish Immigrants in the Hollywood Melting Pot* (Berkeley: University of California Press, 1996). That this is a theme with enduring power is clear from Philip Roth's 2000 PEN/Faulkner Award-winning novel, *The Human Stain*, in which its protagonist is a light-skinned black classics professor who passes as a Jew.

41. Perhaps one of the most damning jibes at *The Outsider* occurred because of this repeated phrase. A September 26, 1953, *New Yorker* "No comment" passage features quotations mentioning "woman as body of woman," from pages 22, 26, 27, 39, 47, 85, 128, 217, concluding: "about time, too." Wright Papers, Box 53, Folder 639.

42. *The Outsider* plays with the lists of alliterative words Wright was constantly scribbling as he worked through the novel. One dated June 12–22, 1947, for a draft entitled "Cross Damon: The Age of Man," reads as follows: "Dread, Despair, Delirium, Deliverance, Destiny, Damnation, Dream, Decision, Death, Defeat, Damnation, Doubt." Wright Papers, Box 48, Folder 606.

43. See Caren Irr, *The Suburb of Dissent* (Durham: Duke University Press, 1998), ch. 5, and Barbara Foley, *Radical Representations* (Durham: Duke University Press, 1994), ch. 5, for excellent analyses of the ways in which Wright inverts and twists the proletarian novel plot to deal with racial conflicts.

44. Wright Papers, Box 48, Folder 601, ms. p. 158 [?]. This synopsis offers the story of both Cora in James M. Cain's *The Postman Always Rings Twice* and Gloria in Horace McCoy's *They Shoot Horses, Don't They?*

45. See Harold T. McCarthy, *The Expatriate Experience: American Novelists and the Idea of America* (Rutherford, N.J.: Fairleigh Dickinson University Press, 1974), 185, on Wright's reliance on newspaper clippings to write *The Outsider*.

46. Nicholas Christopher, *Somewhere in the Night: Film Noir and the American City* (New York: Free Press, 1997), 163–65, highlights the "wholesale political corruption, graft, and racketeering—with cities so sick as to be on the verge of moral implosion," notable in *The Racket* (1951) and *The Street with No Name* (1948), as a "hyperbolic" Baudelairean "hyperreality."

47. Many noir screenwriters were active in the CPUSA and the Screen

Writers Guild—Daniel Mainwaring, Clifford Odets, Dashiell Hammett, Ben Maddow, among them. See Otto Friedrich, *City of Nets: A Portrait of Hollywood in the 1940's* (New York: Harper and Row, 1986), 72–82, who links the Screen Writer's Guild to film noir through Hammett's Sam Spade. Many left-wing writers turned to writing detective and other genre fiction under pseudonyms in 1940s and '50s after McCarthyite blacklists were instituted. See Alan Wald, *Writing from the Left* (London: Verso, 1994), for an account of the process by which writers in the CPUSA moved into genre fiction after the 1930s. David Madden notes in his introduction to *Proletarian Writers of the Thirties* (Carbondale: Southern Illinois University Press, 1968) that he got the idea for the anthology after putting together a collection on *Tough Guy Writers of the Thirties* because of the similarities in names and styles among the authors.

48. Nelson Algren, *Chicago: City on the Make*, 22.

49. Mark Naison, *Communists in Harlem During the Depression* (New York: Grove Press, 1983), 300.

50. Wright Papers, Box 98, Folder 1354. Richard Wright, typescript draft of letter to Mike Gold [1940?], p. 9.

4. BLANC NOIR: RURAL PULP AND DOCUMENTARY MODERNISM

1. The 2000 census shows a marked reverse for many cities as their populations grew dramatically in the wake of the massive immigration during the 1990s. New York's population, for instance, tops eight million again; however, in most large cities now, whites constitute a minority, with Hispanics and Asian immigrants representing the largest percentage of growth, thus sealing the image of the urban center as a foreign zone. Lenny Bruce's routines about how everyone in New York was Jewish but no one in Minneapolis could be, even if her name were Rabinowitz, and Woody Allen's 1977 film, *Annie Hall*, clearly satirize but also perpetuate this urban/rural, ethnic/white bread cultural divide.

2. As I completed the final copyediting on this book, nineteen men hijacked four commercial jets, which were used to damage the Pentagon and destroy the Twin Towers of New York's World Trade Center, killing thousands. It now becomes clear that the international face of the United States is, as it has always been, New York City and Washington, D.C. The meaning of the Oklahoma City bombing, as an act of *domestic* terrorism, becomes even clearer. In fact, the slow response of President George W. Bush to New York's plight suggests just how difficult it is for post-1960s political leaders to acknowledge the totality of America. The outpouring of support from the nation to New Yorkers will perhaps revise the paradigm I am outlining in this chapter.

3. Sarah Boxer, "How the Other Half Defies Its Image," *New York Times,* News of the Week in Review, April 30, 1995, 6.

4. In his June 4, 1995, column for the *New York Times Sunday Magazine,* "Who's John Doe," William Safire provides an etymology of the word, "heartland," that makes clear its connection to both militaristic and folk discourses.

5. Russell Baker, "Not Quite Paradise," *New York Times,* May 2, 1995, A17, reminds his readers that this was the same place that was home to the rural gangsters of 1930s fame—John Dillinger, Bonnie and Clyde, Pretty Boy Floyd, and before them the site of Andrew Jackson's deadly Indian wars. In his remarks, Baker echoes Nelson Algren's assessment of Bonnie and Clyde: "They were outcasts of the cotton frontier. They were children of the wilderness whose wilderness had been razed; who came to maturity in the hardest of times. Clyde might have survived to a sad old age by chopping cotton. Bonnie might have knocked about as a sharecropper's wife or a prostitute until worn out by hard use. The two chose, instead, to give everyone a run for their lives. And, having once committed themselves, made a run which verged upon the uncanny." Nelson Algren, introduction to *The True Story of Bonnie and Clyde,* ed. Jan I. Fortune (New York: New American Library, 1968), 16–17. Since the bombing, revisited six years later through the closed-circuit televised coverage of Timothy McVeigh's execution in another heartland locale, Terre Haute, Indiana, the nation has witnessed a series of brutal school shootings by teenagers. In each case—Colombine High School in suburban Denver, Santana High School in suburban San Diego, an elementary school in Paducah, Kentucky, and so on—the refrain echoes that already heard: "This sort of thing doesn't happen here." The meaning is clear: we're white, middle-class, church-goers, who moved out of the city to protect our children from the dangers of the inner city—guns, drugs, gangs—the violent milieu of a minority underclass.

6. Jonathan Munby argues for continuity among 1930s gangster films and the German expressionist cinema of the preceding decades (made by many of the same directors) and film noirs of the 1940s and 1950s (many of whose directors were also German refugees). He points to the sounds of urban culture as distinctly ethnic and anticorporate as the reasons for instituting the censorship of the Hays Production Code and shows how this earlier code paved the way for the HUAC hearings' blacklist in the postwar era. Munby finds many links between the earlier and later period, effectively countering traditional film histories that speak of noir style as aberrant. Moreover, he argues, classic Hollywood genre films, far from being rigidly determined to solidify an oppressive corporate regime, remain far more open to subversive play than formalist film critics would usually allow.

Jonathan Munby, *Public Enemies, Public Heroes: Screening the Gangster from Little Caesar to Touch of Evil* (Chicago: University of Chicago Press, 1999).

7. See Abigail Solomon-Godeau, *Photography on the Dock*, (Minneapolis: University of Minnesota Press, 1992), on the various editions of Engels's book and the changing uses of visuals within each text. According to Solomon-Godeau, within a few decades visual aids were essential to the construction of knowledge about urban industrial plight. Nancy Armstrong details the cultural work of city photography in Britain, *Fiction in the Age of Photography: The Legacy of British Realism* (Cambridge, Mass.: Harvard University Press, 1999).

8. See Alan Wald, *Writing from the Left* (London: Verso, 1994), on the continuities between 1930s literary radicalism and later popular genre fiction and film. For the interconnections between proletarian and tough-guy writing in the 1930s, see David Madden, ed., *Proletarian Writers of the Thirties* and *Tough Guy Writers of the Thirties* (Carbondale, Ill.: Southern Illinois University Press, 1968; 1967). For technological connections between 1930s genre films and later film noir, see the Public Broadcasting Service series, *American Cinema*, especially the segment on film noir.

9. Patricia Zimmermann links images of Albanian refugees from the Kosovo War to Lange's portrait in "Matrices of War: Digitality and Destruction," paper presented at "After the American Century" Conference, Oregon State University, April 19, 2001.

10. However, virtually all recent advertising and prime-time TV, from *Cops* to *Hill St. Blues* to *Homicide* to Nike and EPT (Early Pregnancy Testing) ads to MTV music videos, rely on documentary techniques, especially those established by cinema vérité; infomercials which seamlessly blend the rhetoric of testimonial common to both documentary and advertisement rely on the talking head. So-called reality television depends on product placement and the ubiquity of surveillance cameras to secure its verisimilitude. Raymond Williams, *Television: Technology and Cultural Form* (New York: Methuen, 1975), has pointed out that television's "flow" blurs any differences between one image and another—scan lines resembling a mantra (as Nam June Paik has shown in such works as *TV Buddha*), indiscriminately filled with one thing or another, blend into a seamless whole.

11. See Margaret Walker's reminiscences of Richard Wright in *How I Wrote Jubilee and Other Essays on Life and Literature* (New York: Feminist Press, 1990), 33–49.

12. Noted in Hope Hale Davis's memoir, *Great Day Coming: A Memoir of the 1930s* (South Royalton, Vt.: Steerforth Press, 1994), 326–27. Nelson Algren wonders whether Bonnie Parker's devotion to Clyde Barrow occured because she was "acting out a *True Confessions* epic that could end

no other way than in death beside her dying lover." In Jan Fortune, *True Story of Bonnie and Clyde*, 14.

13. See Paula Rabinowitz, *Labor and Desire: Women's Revolutionary Fiction in Depression America* (Chapel Hill: University of North Carolina Press, 1991), 194, note 52, which quotes from a letter to the editors of *New Masses*. Minnesota Historical Society, Meridel Le Sueur papers, Miscellaneous Correspondences, 1940–1961. Folder 6. Henry Cheney, letter to Meridel le Sueur. Thanks to Julia Mickenberg for bringing this to my attention.

14. Kenneth Burke explains how this rhetorical move instills a sense of identification between the powerful and their followers in *A Rhetoric of Motives* (New York: Prentice Hall, 1950). See also James Agee and Walker Evans, *Let Us Now Praise Famous Men* (1941; reprint, Boston: Houghton Mifflin, 1980), 115, where Agee with biting irony uses FDR's words as the epigraph for the section entitled "Money."

15. See Raymond Williams, *The Country and the City* (London: Paladin, 1975), 23. I am indebted to Susan Kollin for pointing out how the interconnections between modernism's dependence on the distinctions between pulp and documentary are related to the older divisions of rural from urban.

16. Quoted in Milton Meltzer, *Dorothea Lange: A Photographer's Life* (New York: Farrar, Strauss and Giroux, 1978), 161–62.

17. For a detailed analysis of the form and content of this genre, see John Roger Puckett, *Five Photo-Textual Documentaries for the Great Depression* (Ann Arbor, University of Michigan Press, 1984).

18. For an anatomy of this dualism, see chapter 1, "Sunshine or *Noir*," Mike Davis, *City of Quartz: Excavating the Future in Los Angeles* (1990; reprint, New York: Random House, 1992), 15–98.

19. Quoted in Jack Hurley, *Portrait of a Decade: Roy Stryker and the Development of Documentary Photography in the Thirties* (Baton Rouge, La.: Louisiana State University Press, 1972), 70. For a discussion of the change in Stryker's mandate to the FSA photographers as a triumph of the corporate state, see Terry Smith, *Making the Modern: Industry, Art and Design in America*, (Chicago: University of Chicago Press, 1993), especially chapter 7.

20. These documentary images followed such negative literary portrayals of the hypocrisy of rural America, as Sinclair Lewis's *Babbitt* and *Main Street* or Willa Cather's disturbingly erotic visions of prairie life. But by the 1930s, modernist sensibility had turned middlebrow and was redeeming the very places skewered a decade before. Of course, a facet of American identity since the Puritans, who were performing an "errand into the wilderness," has been precisely the intense ambivalence elicited by the new world's vast open space, appearing uninhabited and untamed.

5. MELODRAMA/MALE DRAMA: THE SENTIMENTAL CONTRACT OF
AMERICAN LABOR FILMS

1. Tillie Lerner, "The Strike," *Partisan Review* 1 (November 1936). Reprinted in Charlotte Nekola and Paula Rabinowitz, eds., *Writing Red: An Anthology of American Women Writers, 1930–1940* (New York: The Feminist Press, 1987), 245.

2. Florence Reece, "Which Side Are You On?," in Nekola and Rabinowitz, *Writing Red*, 182.

3. See Ruth McKenney, *Industrial Valley* (1939; reprint, Ithaca: Cornell University Press, 1992; Martha Gellhorn, *The Trouble I've Seen* (New York: William Morrow, 1936); Lallah Davidson, *South of Joplin* (New York: W. W. Norton, 1939); and selections in *Writing Red*.

4. Lauren Gilfillan, *I Went to Pit College* (New York: Literary Guild, 1934). For a detailed discussion of this book, see Paula Rabinowitz, *Labor and Desire: Women's Revolutionary Fiction in Depresion America* (Chapel Hill: University of North Carolina Press, 1991), chapter 4.

5. Georg Lukács, "Reportage or Portrayal?" [1932] in Rodney Livingstone, ed., *Essays on Realism*, trans. David Fernbach (Cambridge, Mass.: MIT Press, 1981), 49.

6. Claudia L. Johnson, *Equivocal Beings: Politics, Gender and Sentimentality in the 1790s: Wollstonecraft, Radcliffe, Burney, Austen* (Chicago: University of Chicago Press, 1995), 2.

7. See Raymond Williams, *Culture and Society: 1780–1950* (1953; reprint, New York: Columbia University Press, 1983), 3–12.

8. Lukács, "Reportage or Portrayal?," 50.

9. On the complicated refusal of femininity in the rejection by modernism of sentimentality, see Rey Chow, *Women and Chinese Modernity: The Politics of Reading Between East and West* (Minneapolis: University of Minnesota Press, 1991), and Suzanne Clark, *Sentimental Modernism: Women Writers and the Revolution of the Word* (Bloomington: Indiana University Press, 1991). On the gendered iconography of the Left, see Rebecca Zurier, *Art for the Masses: A Radical Magazine and its Graphics, 1911–1917* (Philadelphia: Temple University Press, 1988); Barbara Melosh, *Engendering Culture: Manhood and Womanhood in New Deal Theater and Art* (Washington, D.C.: Smithsonian Institute Press, 1991); Elizabeth Faue, *Community of Suffering and Struggle: Men, Women and Labor in Minneapolis, 1915–1945* (Chapel Hill: University of North Carolina Press, 1991).

10. For critical analyses of melodrama as a debased form that allowed marginalized peoples, especially women and the working class, a popular platform for resistance within generic and social containment, see Martha

Vicinus, "Helpless and Unfriended: Nineteenth-Century Domestic Melodrama," *New Literary History* 13 (Autumn 1981); Jackie Byars, *All That Hollywood Allows: Re-Reading Gender in 1950s Melodrama* (Chapel Hill: University of North Carolina Press, 1991); Christine Gledhill, "The Melodramatic Field: An Investigation," in *Home Is Where the Heart Is: Studies in Melodrama and the Woman's Film* (London: British Film Institute, 1987); Lynn Hunt, *The Family Romance of the French Revolution* (Berkeley: University of California Press, 1992); Ien Ang, *Watching Dallas: Soap Opera and the Melodramatic Imagination* (London: Routledge, 1989); Michael Denning *Mechanic Accents: Dime Novels and Working-Class Culture in America* (London: Verso, 1987). The standard theoretical work on the mechanics of melodrama is Peter Brooks, *The Melodramatic Imagination: Balzac, Henry James, Melodrama and the Mode of Excess* (New Haven, Conn.: Yale University Press, 1976).

11. Lewis W. Hine, *Men At Work: Photographic Studies of Modern Men and Machines* (1932) (New York: Dover Publications, Inc., 1977).

12. Terry Smith, *Making the Modern: Industry, Art and Design in America* (Chicago: University of Chicago Press, 1993), analyzes the way in which 1930s celebrations of machines enabled the rise of a corporate state. See also Michael Szalay, *New Deal Modernism: American Literature and the Invention of the Welfare State* (Durham, N.C.: Duke University Press, 2000). Left-wing filmmakers, such as Leo Hurwitz, however, celebrated the "machine itself, as an instrument for the transformation of labor and material into what people need." Michael and Jill Klein, "Native Land: An Interview with Leo Hurwitz," *Cineaste* 6 (1974): 7. The aesthetics of streamlining, Raymond Loewy, one of its most creative designers, told *Life*, meant "that society could be industrialized without becoming ugly." Quoted in Jane N. Law, "Designing the Dream," in Fania Weingartner, ed., *Streamlining America*, (Dearborn, Mich.: Henry Ford Museum and Greenfield Village, 1986), 21.

13. See Joan W. Scott's critique of Gareth Stedman Jones's reading of the Chartist's political claims in *The Language of Class* in *Gender and the Politics of History* (New York: Columbia University Press, 1988); Elizabeth Faue, *Community of Suffering and Struggle* on women's organizing during the 1930s Minneapolis Truckers' Strike, and Rabinowitz, *Labor and Desire* on the gendered iconography of class in proletarian novels of the 1930s.

14. Hugo Gellert, *Karl Marx's "Capital" in Lithographs* (New York: Ray Long and Richard Smith, 1934).

15. But there is some truth to it. In an interview with Carol Brightman, "Mary, Still Contrary," *The Nation* (May 19, 1984): 611–20, Mary McCarthy describes the faces of the men in the Gdansk shipyard as familiar, like those of the workers in this country she watched picket the great industries during her youth in the 1930s; their supple muscles and slender figures assuming the

heroic poses Hine pictured. "Those young workers [in Solidarity]," she says, "I've never seen such handsome men. . . . You know, we haven't had a worker in this country that looked like that in fifty years." The bodies of 1930s American workers photographed by Hine have Renaissance proportions in stark contrast to the physiques of late twentieth-century workers pictured by Milton Rogovin, in Rogovin and Michael Frisch, *Portraits in Steel* (Ithaca, N.Y.: Cornell University Press, 1993). However, "brawny, heroic, manly men . . . are back," as heroes since September 11, 2001, according to Patricia Leigh Brown, "Heavy Lifting Required: The Return of Manly Men," *New York Times*, News of the Week in Review (October 28, 2001), 5. Brown quotes "conservative social critic" Camille Paglia's echo of Mary McCarthy: "I can't help noticing how robustly, dreamily masculine the faces of the firefighters are. These are working-class men, stoical, patriotic."

16. See Harriet Arnow, *The Dollmaker* (1954; reprint, New York: Avon Books, 1972). This story had been a staple of 1930s proletarian fiction. The many novels about the Gastonia, North Carolina, strike centered on the transition from folk culture to a culture of capitalist exploitation and the especially difficult time women, as repositories of family lore and tradition, had adjusting to the changes. See Joseph Urgo, "Proletarian Literature and Feminism: The Gastonia Novels and Feminist Protest," *Minnesota Review* 24 (Spring 1985): 64–84.

17. While the Corporation for Public Broadcasting has been a primary funder for many documentaries, including those investigating class relations in America, its audience is decidedly middle class. In *Pets or Meat*, Moore may have been working out a certain ambivalence toward PBS, which funded his films but which does not "bring the working class of this country into its network. . . . [T]hey don't ever seem to speak to people like us." Jay Bobbin, "Moore Moves 'Nation' to Fox," Glens Falls *Post-Star*, July 20, 1995, D8.

18. Speaking of *TV Nation*, Moore comments, "[I]t's very bizarre and rare that a group of people such as me and my friends would be able to come from Flint, Mich., and have a network TV show." Bobbin, D8.

19. Paul Arthur, "Jargons of Authenticity (Three American Moments)," in Michael Renov, ed., *Theorizing Documentary* (New York: Routledge, 1993), 104.

20. This is Douglas Wixson's name for those Midwestern proletariat authors, such as Jack Conroy, who came out of the working class, see *The Worker-Writer in the Midwest* (Urbana: University of Illinois Press, 1993). In the late 1920s, Mike Gold's editorials in the *New Masses* often called for a new movement of worker-correspondents to "Tell us your story . . . in the form of a letter. . . . Write as you talk. Write." Michael Gold, "A Letter to Workers' Art Groups," *New Masses* 5 (September 1929): 16.

21. In *Industrial Valley*, her reportage novel about the United Rubberworkers Union strike in Akron, Ohio, McKenney remarks on the geography of the company town in which the heights are reserved for the ruling families, with managers situated midway between them and the vast working-class neighborhoods spread around the plants in the valley.

22. Walter R. Baranger, "On Line, Management Also on Picket Line," *New York Times*, July 24, 1995, D6. This tactic has been employed as well by cyberspace corporations: "a section on Amazon[.com]'s internal Web site gives supervisors antiunion material to pass on to employees" and alerts managers of tell-tale warning signs that a union is trying to organize. Be wary of " 'hushed conversations when you approach which have not occurred before' and 'small group huddles breaking up in silence on the approach of the supervisor.' " Steven Greenhouse, "Amazon.com Is Using the Web to Block Union's Effort to Organize," *New York Times*, November 29, 2000, C1–2. At the same time, however, organizing efforts have been carried out in cyberspace. In 1996, the University Faculty Alliance and the AAUP at the University of Minnesota successfully fought a Board of Regents' effort to revise the tenure code by effectively using e-mail to communicate with the more than three thousand faculty members.

23. See Ben Hamper, *Rivethead: Tales from the Assembly Line* (New York: Warner Books, 1992), for a full accounting of Hamper's fascinating gendering of mental illnesses. Thanks to Carol Mason for bringing this to my attention. The effects of unemployment are among the most devastating chronicles of work life in late twentieth-century America. The stories of displaced workers are full of alcoholism, depression, suicide, abuse, and so forth. The alienation of labor Marx detailed seems even more exacerbated by the loss of self accompanying loss of work. See the interviews in *Portraits of Steel* conducted by oral historian Michael Frisch for moving accounts of the psychic wreckage caused by plant closures.

24. Jay Bobbin, columnist for the Tribune Media Services, quotes Moore's remarks on "one of a series of really wonderful ironies" that his television show, *TV Nation*, which often scrutinized corporate America, aired in 1994 on NBC, moved in 1995 to Fox, owned by international media tycoon, Rupert Murdoch, CEO of the News Corporation, which owns Fox among many other tabloids. Glens Falls *Post-Star* July 20, 1995, D8.

25. "Warner Acquires 'Roger' Docu for World Distribution," *Variety* 337 (November 1, 1989): 12.

26. See Chester Burger, "What Michael Didn't Say About Roger," *Public Relations Journal* 46 (April 1990): 40–42; Susan Duffy, "The Real Villain in *Roger & Me*? Big Business," *Business Week* (January 8, 1990): 42–45; David C. Smith, "Michael & Roger: GM Critic's Film Makes No Pretense at Fairness," *Ward's Auto World* 25 (November 1989): 5.

27. See Carl Plantinga, "Roger and History and Irony and Me," *Michigan Academician* 24 (Spring 1992): 511–20; and Carley Cohan and Gary Crowdus, "Reflections on *Roger & Me*, Michael Moore and His Critics," *Cineaste* 17: 4 (1990): 25–30.

28. This controversy was played out in the pages of the *New York Times* among other widely read national media venues and took on new life after it was learned that the film was not nominated for an academy award: on January 19, 1990, D. P. Levin reported that "Maker of Documentary That Attacks GM Alienates His Allies," C12; then on February 1, 1990, Richard Bernstein asked "*Roger & Me*: Documentary? Satire? Or Both?," C20; on March 2, 1990, D. Bensman contributed an op-ed piece stating: "*Roger & Me*: Narrow, Simplistic, Wrong," A33; on March 26, 1990, V. J. Dimidjian responded in a letter to the editor, "*Roger & Me*," A16. In the midst of this, *Newsweek* asked "Will GM Retaliate?" (February 26, 1990): 4.

29. Bobbin, "Moore Moves 'Nation' to Fox," D8.

30. In *The Family Romance of the French Revolution* (Berkeley: University of California Press, 1993), historian Lynn Hunt argues that melodrama was a key factor in the decision to behead royalty because this popular theatrical form securely differentiated between the righteous and evil ones, and applauded ridding the stage of evil power. Moore is hardly advocating Roger's death; but his ability to collapse the situation into a struggle between himself and his adversary—richer, more powerful, more deceitful—recalls this plot.

31. Of course, the title *American Dream* refers to the post–World War II promise, which film noir undercuts and exposes, made to the white working class of a home, a car, a stable job, and so forth earned at the expense of militant unions and through the build-up of a militarized federal budget. But I also think that because of the way the film portrays family conflicts, it is not entirely wrong to sit Freud before this dream and put his analytic powers to work.

32. Earl Browder, *The People's Front* (New York: International Publishers, 1938), 56, 235.

33. For a devastating critique of the vestiges of Popular Front culture lurking within left-wing expressions of solidarity with the working class, see Jesse Lemisch, "I Dreamed I Saw MTV Last Night," *The Nation* (October 18, 1986): cover, 374–76.

34. Anthony McCall and Andrew Tyndal, "Sixteen Working Statements," *Millennium Film Journal* 1 (Spring/Summer 1978), 36. See also Noel King, "Recent 'Political' Documentary: Notes on *Union Maids* and *Harlan County, USA*," *Screen* 22, no. 2 (1981): 7–18.

35. Peter Rachleff, review of *American Dream*, *The Oral History Review* 20 (Spring/Fall 1992): 94–96.

36. Peter Rachleff, *Hardpressed in the Heartland* (Boston: South End Press, 1993), details the history of the UFCW in Austin, as well as offers a completely different picture of the effects of the P-9 strike for the U.S. labor movement. A labor historian at Macalester College in St. Paul, Minnesota, Rachleff was instrumental in establishing the Twin Cities Support for P-9. Rachleff alerted me to the footage stored in Wisconsin's archives. (Personal communication, April 21, 1996). Tim Leland, business agent for the building trades union in Minnesota, voiced a great deal of criticism of the P-9ers, echoing Andersen that the strike was hopelessly doomed and thus resulted in hundreds of Hormel workers in Austin and Owatonna, Minn., losing their jobs. (Personal interview, November 10, 1994)

37. Rachleff's book is one of the two; the other is Hardy Green, *On Strike at Hormel: The Struggle for a Democratic Labor Movement* (Philadelphia: Temple University Press, 1990).

38. See Wini Breines, *Community and Organization in the New Left, 1962–1968: The Great Refusal* (New York: Praeger; South Hadley, Mass.: J. F. Bergin, 1982), on the 1960s movements' adoption of this model for organizing. I will take this up at length in chapter 8.

39. Robert Markley, "Sentimentality as Performance: Shaftesbury, Sterne and the Theatrics of Virtue," in Felicity Nussbaum and Laura Brown , eds., *The New Eighteenth Century* (New York: Methuen, 1987), 211–12.

40. James Agee and Walker Evans, *Let Us Now Praise Famous Men* (Boston: Houghton-Mifflin, 1941).

6. NOT "JUST THE FACTS, MA'AM": SOCIAL WORKERS AS PRIVATE EYES

1. Horace McCoy, *They Shoot Horses, Don't They?* (New York: Simon and Schuster, 1935), 126, 128. All further citations appear in the text. McCoy's novel, a tour-de-force of noir images about Hollywood's lowlife, precursor by four years to both Nathanael West's *The Day of the Locusts* and Raymond Chandler's *The Big Sleep*, is framed by the blaring sentence of the court, broken into thirteen chapters, concluding with the exhortation that the narrator will be "executed and put to death." As in many noir narratives, a retrospective voice from the grave recounts the crime that inexorably followed the regular guy's descent into the underworld because of his fatal encounter with a woman.

2. Kevin Brownlow, *The Parade's Gone By* (New York: Ballantine, 1968), includes a long interview with Joseph Henabery, assistant director of *Intolerance*, in which he describes how, *The Mother and the Law*, this "little, cheap, quickie picture," evolved from a "potboiler"and "tearjerker" into the monumental saga *Intolerance* (55–56).

3. In her 1932 reportage, "Women on the Breadlines," Meridel Le Sueur comments that there really isn't a name, a category, much less an agency that can address the plight of single impoverished women. *New Masses* 7 (January 1932): 5–6; reprinted in Elaine Hedges, ed., *Ripening* (Old Westbury, N.Y.: Feminist Press, 1982), 137–43. See also, Ruth E. Bowles, "A Social Worker Looks at Black Bottom," *Crisis* (July 1930): 211–13, about black women waiting on Cincinnati street corners for day work as maids, and night work as prostitutes, after their men have left them.

4. See Burton Bledstein, *The Culture of Professionalism* (New York: W. W. Norton, 1976); Julia Swindells, *Victorian Writing and Working Women* (Minneapolis: University of Minnesota Press, 1985); Linda Gordon, *Heroes of Their Own Lives* (New York: Viking, 1988); Denise Riley, *Am I That Name?: Feminism and the Category of "Women" in History* (Minneapolis: University of Minnesota Press, 1988); Carolyn Steedman, *Childhood, Culture and Class in Britain* (New Brunswick, N.J.: Rutgers University Press, 1990); Carolyn Steedman, *Past Tenses: Essays on Writing, Autobiography and History* (London: Rivers Oram Press, 1992), on the interlocking relationship between the professionalization of middle-class women and the pathologizing of poor women in the United States and Britain, especially during the late nineteenth and early twentieth centuries.

5. Muriel Rukeyser, "Book of the Dead," *U.S. 1* (New York: Covici Friede, 1938), 15. All further citations appear in the text. For an analysis of this "modernist poem as a radical document," see Robert Shulman, *The Power of Political Art: The 1930s Literary Left Reconsidered* (Chapel Hill: University of North Carolina Press, 2000), chapter 6.

6. Clinch Calkins, *Some Folks Won't Work* (New York: Harcourt, Brace and Co., 1930), for what may be the first book-length example of popularizing American social workers' case studies through fiction. Of course, true crime sensations had been staples of dime novels. Steedman's essays on working-class girls' narratives in *Past Tenses* links them to the rise of public investigations of poverty.

7. Caroline Slade, *Sterile Sun* (New York: Vanguard Pres, 1936). All references appear in the text.

8. I am using Swindells's discussion of professionalism, which relies on Geoff Esland, "Professions and Professionalism," in Geoff Esland and Graeme Salaman, eds., *The Politics of Work and Occupations* (Milton Keyes: Open University Press, 1980), 216, an analysis of how the professional classes emerged in the nineteenth century as " 'reality definers' and organizers of dominant thought from their position in the division of labor" (Swindell, 4).

9. Linda Gordon, *Heroes*, 245–47. Further references appear in the text.

10. Carolyn Steedman, *Landscape for a Good Woman: A Story of Two Lives* (New Brunswick, N.J.: Rutgers University Press, 1987), 6, describes how

personal narratives (especially by those outside of the mainstream) construct "resolutely social" political theory.

11. Gordon, *Heroes*, 215–18, discusses how child protection services defined young poor girls' "sexual deliquency." Susan Rubin Suleiman, *Authoritarian Fictions: The Ideological Novel as a Literary Genre* (New York: Columbia University Press, 1983), claims the hallmark of "authoritarian fiction," such as Slade's, is its redundant didacticism.

12. In "Narrate or Describe?" Georg Lukács outlines the differences between realism (which allows the representation of totality through social narratives [good]) and naturalism (which sinks to pornographic descriptions of psychological states [bad]). Arthur D. Kahn, ed. and trans., *Writer and Critic and Other Essays* (New York: Grosset and Dunlap, 1970). Unfortunately, at least to my mind, Slade seems to have moved from description to narration in her 1940s novels. Caroline Slade, *Margaret* (New York: Vanguard Press, 1946), published after the War, participates in the democratization of social problems, making it a novel of significance for all mothers, whereas Slade's first novel was directed to an audience of professionals. For a comprehensive analysis of the expansion of progressive parenting during this period, see Julia Mickenberg, "Educating Dissent: Children's Literature and the Left," Ph.D. diss., University of Minnesota, 2000.

13. Caroline Slade, *The Triumph of Willie Pond* (New York: Vanguard Press, 1940), 25.

14. Martha Gellhorn, "Ruby," from *The Trouble I've Seen*, in *The Collected Novellas of Martha Gellhorn* (1936; reprint, New York: Knopf, 1993).

15. Rachel Swarns, "Welfare as We Know It Goes Incognito," *New York Times*, News of the Week in Review (July 5, 1998), 1, rehearses the history of welfare "reform." In Slade's second novel, *The Triumph of Willie Pond*, Willie Pond, the laid-off tubercular WPA ditch digger, eventually commits suicide in order to "provide" for his family, which can only receive ADC (the predecessor to AFDC) in his absence, once he is deemed an able-bodied (though still unemployed) worker after recovering from TB in a state-run sanatorium. In short, Slade foresaw the contradictory history of welfare by noting its corrosive effect on the family, its band-aid solutions to structural unemployment, and its nightmarish bureaucracy.

16. Slade's novels were part of a subgenre of 1930s radical novels featuring social workers; I discuss these in the context of "women's revolutionary fiction," in Paula Rabinowitz, *Labor and Desire: Women's Revolutionary Fiction in Depression America* (Chapel Hill: University of North Carolina Press, 1991), 92. Records show Slade, second cousin to Walker Evans, to have been a member of the League of American Writers in 1936. (Thanks to Alan Wald and Theodore Crane for these bits of biographical information.)

17. See jacket blurb on the back cover of Caroline Slade, *Margaret* (New York: Vanguard, 1946).

18. Luella R. North, review of *Sterile Sun, The Survey* (November 1936): 352. Gellhorn's novel was written while she was a guest of Eleanor Roosevelt at the White House.

19. William Dane, review of *Miss Bailey Says, Social Work Today* (June 1934): 21.

20. Gertrude Springer, review of *The Triumph of Willie Pond, Survey Midmonthly* (June 1940): 212.

21. Gertrude Springer, review of *Lilly Crackell, Survey Midmonthly* (August 1943): 223.

22. Frank C. Bancroft, review of *The Triumph of Willie Pond, Social Work Today* (November 1940): 29.

23. Jacket blurb, back cover, *Margaret.*

24. For a comparison of Chandler's narratives to *Ulysses*, see Fredric Jameson, "The Synoptic Chandler," in Joan Copjec, ed., *Shades of Noir* (London: Verso, 1993), 33–34. *Ulysses* was listed first of the top one hundred twentieth-century novels in English by the Modern Library.

25. Josephine Herbst, "Ignorance Among the Living Dead," *New Masses* (January 1929): 4. A similar point is made by Herbst in her short memoir, "Yesterday's Road," *New American Review* 3 (1968): 84–104.

26. Josephine Herbst tells the story in "A Year of Disgrace," *Noble Savage* 3 (1961); reprinted in Josephine Herbst, *The Starched Blue Sky of Spain and Other Memoirs* (Boston: Northeastern University Press, 1991), 53–98. My copy of Slade's novel, a signed first edition owned by Martha H. Gro, her back-slanting signature barely edging the cover, was found in an upstate New York used bookstore; I had read reviews of the novel years ago but was never able to track it down from libraries. See Cathy N. Davidson, *Revolution and the Word: The Rise of the Novel in America* (New York: Oxford University Press, 1985), 5–10, for an ethnography of the book and the importance of scrutinizing the object itself.

27. Gertrude Springer, *Ask Miss Bailey, The Midmonthly Survey Pamphlets*, Series II, 1933, 25. Miss Bailey's solution, empathizing with Carrie, was to send a younger woman social worker with a pair of donated silk stockings to the home.

28. Raymond Chandler, *The Big Sleep* (1939), in *The Raymond Chandler Omnibus* (New York: Knopf, 1964).

29. Gertrude Springer, *Ask Miss Bailey, The Midmonthly Survey Pamphlet*, Series I, 1933, 6–7. Gordon, *Heroes*, explains how providing food, clothing, and shelter had both positive and negative impact on child neglect cases.

30. Ann Petry, *The Street* (Boston: Houghton Mifflin, 1946), 389. Further references appear in the text.

31. Unfortunately, this story is still on-going. Pam Belluck reports that Catherine Ferguson, public defender for the seven-year-old Chicago boy falsely accused of murdering Ryan Harris with an eight-year-old accomplice, noted that parents in the black community were resigned to having the police and other authorities remove their children: "In a white middle-class community, parents would have broken down the door and said, 'Let me in there!' " "Murder Chrages Dropped Against 2 Boys in Chicago," *New York Times*, September 5, 1998, A1, 10.

32. Marita Bonner, "The Whipping" (1935), in Charlotte Nekola and Paula Rabinowitz, eds., *Writing Red: An Anthology of Women Writers, 1930–1940* (New York: Feminist Press, 1987), 75. Further references in text.

33. Gertrude Springer, *Ask Miss Bailey*, Series II, 1933, 29.

34. During the summer of 1998, another scandal about the welfare system in New York City exploded as, first, three children were discovered to have been sexually abused by their parents and relatives in Brooklyn after they were returned from foster care to their home, and then, a two-year-old boy was found starving and locked away in a dark room left on a urine-stained mattress while in foster care. In both cases, it appears that caseworkers neglected to inspect the homes and actually see the children for themselves. Visual inspection is essential to child protection.

35. For an explanation of how Oscar Lewis's thesis about the culture of poverty contributed to the Johnson administration's Great Society, see Diana Pearce, "Welfare Is Not *for* Women: Why the War on Poverty Cannot Conquer the Feminization of Poverty," in Linda Gordon, ed., *Women, the State and Welfare* (Madison: University of Wisconsin Press, 1990), 265–79.

36. Louis L. Bennett, "Problems of Homecoming," *Survey Midmonthy* (September 1944): 246–48. Some "problems" noted by the director of Veterans' Service Center in New York included "family difficulties," "education and jobs," "housing," and "emotional disturbance and instability."

37. Raymond Chandler's original screenplay revealed Buzz as the amnesiac murderer, but the U.S. Navy objected to this depiction of a veteran and insisted on a rewrite. See Alain Silver and Elizabeth Ward, *Film Noir: An Encyclopedic Reference to the American Style*, 3rd ed. (Woodstock, N.Y.: Overlook Press, 1992), 36–37; and James Naremore, *More Than Night: Film Noir in Its Contexts* (Berkeley: University of California Press, 1998), 107–14.

38. In fact, the trumpeting of this problem itself became a problem, forcing Sallie Bright, executive secretary for the National Publicity Council for Health and Welfare Services, to exhort everyone, especially social workers and journalists, to "Stop Calling Them Problems," *Survey Midmonthly* (May 1945): 139–40

39. *Social Work Today* (January 1938): 26.

40. Editorial, *Social Work Today* (June–July 1940): 5–6.

41. *Social Work Today* (October 1940): 11–12.

42. *Social Work Today* (February 1942): 30.

43. *Social Work Today* (January 1941): 12.

44. Caroline Slade, *Lilly Crackell* (New York: Vanguard, 1943), 602.

45. This is Fritz Redl's term in "Zoot Suits: An Interpretation," *Survey Midmonthly* (October 1943): 259.

46. Slade, *Lilly Crackell*, 602.

47. Eliot Ness, "Sex Delinquency as a Social Hazard," *Proceedings of 1944 National Conference of Social Workers*, 279.

48. Slade, *Lilly Crackell*, 602.

49. Ethel L. Ginsburg, "The Case Worker in a Veterans' Service Center," *Survey Midmonthly* (May 1945): 126.

50. "Study Says Welfare Changes Made the Poorest Worse Off," *New York Times*, August 23, 1999: A13.

51. For more on this history, see Theda Skocpol, *Protecting Soldiers and Mothers: The Political Origins of Social Policy in the United States* (Cambridge, Mass.: The Belknap Press, 1992), especially chapters 8 and 9; Barbara J. Nelson, "The Origins of the Two-Channel Welfare State," in Linda Gordon, ed., *Women, the State, and Welfare*, 123–51.

52. Johnnie Tillmon, "Welfare Is a Women's Issue," in Rosalyn Baxandall, Linda Gordon, and Susan Reverby, eds., *America's Working Women: A Documentary History—1600 to the Present* (New York: Vintage, 1976), 355–58.

53. Lest one forget the currency of this connection, see Dan Barry, "Police Used Brothel So Often, Madam Got Worried," *New York Times*, July 18, 1998, A1, 10.

54. Karen Tice, *Tales of Wayward Girls and Immoral Women: Case Records and the Professionalization of Social Work* (Urbana: University of Illinois Press, 1998); and Beverly Stadum, *Poor Women and Their Families: Hardworking Charity Cases, 1900–1930* (Albany: State University of New York Press, 1992), present feminist readings of early twentieth-century case histories about poor girls and women. The pages of *The Survey* and *Social Worker Today* turn from a concern with male unemployment and female prostitution during the Depression to the plight of those facing war mobilization (and later, demobilization) during the 1940s.

55. I have not read Caroline Slade's *Job's House* but have located a copy in the New York State Library in Albany.

56. Carolyn Steedman, *Landscape for a Good Woman: A Story of Two Lives* (New Brunswick, N.J.: Rutgers University Press), 2.

7. BARBARA STANWYCK'S ANKLET

1. Jacques Derrida, *The Truth in Painting*, trans. Geoff Bennington and Ian McLeod (Chicago: University of Chicago Press, 1987), 381.

2. "A pair of shoes is more easily treated as a *utility* than a single shoe or two shoes which aren't a pair. The pair inhibits at least, if it does not prevent, the 'fetishizing' movement; it rivets things to use, to 'normal' use; it shoes better and makes things walk according to the law." He goes on to question what either Heidegger or Schapiro would have done with "a painting with only one shoe, especially a single high heel as in Magritte's *La Lune* or Lindner's *The Shoe*. Would they have been able to produce . . .?" Derrida, *Truth in Painting*, 332–33.

3. "Shoes. Dream shoes. Shoes to power the imagination. We sat spellbound before *Mildred Pierce*. Our eyes followed her feet . . . her shoes. . . . Inevitably black, they featured three-inch talons, a slightly raised platform, and a delicate strap encircling the ankle. Her shoes were a sign—but of what?" ask Shari Benstock and Suzanne Ferriss in the introduction to their collection, *On Fashion* (New Brunswick, N.J.: Rutgers University Press, 1994), 1.

4. Thanks to Cora Leland for bringing this term to my attention, which comes from the interdiction against sandals outlined in the dress code governing employees at Arthur Andersen and other accounting firms in the United States. See Colin McDowell, *Manolo Blahnik* (New York: Harper-Collins, 2000), who quotes Blahnik as confirming that "the first two cracks" of toe cleavage is a "very important part of the sexuality of the shoe." Quoted in Penelope Green, "Fall Reading, From Head to Toe," *New York Times*, September 4, 2000, B10.

5. Derrida, *Truth in Painting*, 269. Sigmund Freud, "On Dreams," trans. James Strachey, *Standard Edition of the Complete Psychological Works of Sigmund Freud*, vol. 5: 633–86. Hereafter noted as *SE*.

6. Wendy Lesser, "Stanwyck," in *His Other Half: Men Looking at Women through Art* (Cambridge, Mass.: Harvard University Press, 1991), 225–61.

7. Farah Jasmine Griffin, "Style Heritage," *Harpers Bazaar* (October 2001): 176–78.

8. Sigmund Freud, "Fetishism," *SE*, vol. 21, 152–53.

9. Freud, "Fetishism," *SE*, vol. 21, 156.

10. Freud, "Three Essays on Sexuality," *SE*, vol. 7, 154, fn 2 [added 1920].

11. Freud, "Three Essays," *SE*, vol. 7, 153.

12. Freud, "Three Essays," *SE*, vol. 7, 155, (emphasis in original).

13. Gilles Deleuze, *Coldness and Cruelty*, in *Masochism* (New York: Zone Books, 1991), 31.

14. Victor Turner, *The Forest of Symbols: Aspects of Ndembu Ritual* (Ithaca, N.Y.: Cornell University Press, 1967), 28, 29, 30.

15. Samuel Beckett, *Waiting for Godot* (New York: Grove Press, 1954), 44.

16. The picture appears in Astrid Proll, ed., *Baader-Meinhof: Pictures on the Run, '67–'77* (Zurich and New York: Scalo, 1998), 35. Thanks to Christina White for bringing it to my attention. Its caption reads in English: "Rudi Dutschke's shoe in Kurfurstendam shortly after shots had been fired by a right-wing assailant, 11th April 1968."

17. On the "ideological" and historical differences between these two men, see Derrida, *Truth in Painting*, 281. Martin Heidegger, "The Origin of the Work of Art," in *Poetry, Language, Thought*, trans. Albert Hofstadter (New York: Harper and Row, 1971), 15–87. Meyer Schapiro, "The Still Life as a Personal Object—A Note on Heidegger and Van Gogh," in Marianne L. Simmel, ed., *The Reach of Mind: Essays in Memory of Kurt Goldstein* (New York: Springer Publishing, Colo., 1968), 203–09. Derrida's long essay on this "debate" appears in "Restitutions," in *The Truth in Painting*. It became the jumping off point for Fredric Jameson's *Postmodernism: Or, The Cultural Logic of Late Capitalism* (Durham, N.C.: Duke University Press, 1991), 6–11, as well as other less widely read texts; see below.

18. Karl Marx, *Capital: A Critique of Political Economy*, vol. 1, trans. Samuel Moore and Edward Aveling, (1887; reprint New York: International Publishers, 1967), 72, 74.

19. Marx, *Capital*, vol. 1, 76, 72 (emphasis added).

20. Walter Benjamin, *The Arcades Project*, trans. Howard Eiland and Kevin McLauglin (Cambridge, Mass.: Belknap Press of Harvard University Press, 1999), 662.

21. Emile Durkheim, *The Elementary Forms of the Religious Life*, trans., Joseph Ward Swain (1915; reprint, New York: The Free Press, 1969), 203.

22. For critiques of these sentiments, see a cryptic set of questions by Derrida: "What if Heidegger were already questioning beyond this already coded thematics? What if he were also wary of the concept of fetishism according to Marx or according to Freud? And what if he wanted to take the whole of this problem up again, and the whole question of the thing in truth which exercises the notion of fetishism?" (334). See also, the analysis of "the rhetoric of iconoclasm," in W. J. T Mitchell, *Iconology: Image, Text, Ideology* (Chicago: University of Chicago Press, 1986), 151–208.

23. Benjamin, *Arcades*, 669.

24. Walter Benjamin, "Unpacking My Library," in Hannah Arendt, ed., *Illuminations*, trans. Harry Zohn (New York: Schocken, 1968), 59–67.

25. Susan Stewart, *On Longing: Narratives of the Minature, the Gigantic, the Souvenir, the Collection* (Durham, N.C.: Duke University Press, 1993), 151.

26. Douglas Mao, *Solid Objects: Modernism and the Test of Production* (Princeton: Princeton University Press, 1998), 4.

27. Virginia Woolf, *Orlando: A Biography* (1928; reprint, Hammondsworth: Penguin Books, 1942), 212.

28. Walter Benjamin, *Arcades*, 594.

29. Roland Barthes, *Mythologies*, trans. Annette Lavers (New York: Hill and Wang, 1972), 39.

30. James Agee and Walker Evans, *Let Us Now Praise Famous Men* (Boston: Houghton Mifflin, 1941), 262–63.

31. Gertrude Jobes, *Dictionary of Mythology, Folklore and Symbols*, vol. 2 (New York: Scarecrow Press, 1961–1962), 1440.

32. Quoted in Jean Chevalier and Alain Gheerbrat, *A Dictionary of Symbols*, trans. John Bruckman-Brown. (Oxford: Blackwell, 1994), 876.

33. Joseph J. Kockelman, *Heidegger on Art and Art Works* (Dordrecht: Martinus Nijhoff Publishers, 1985), 127.

34. Schapiro, "Still Life," in Simmel, *The Reach of Mind*, 206.

35. See Otto Poggeler, "Heidegger on Art," in Karsten Harries and Christoph Jamme, eds., *Martin Heidegger: Politics, Art, and Technology* (New York: Holmes and Meier, 1994), 106–24.

36. Art Spiegelman, *Maus II: A Survivor's Tale: And Here My Troubles Began* (New York: Pantheon, 1991), 60–63.

37. Marjorie Garber, *Vested Interests: Cross-Dressing and Cultural Anxiety* (New York: HarperCollins, 1993), 44–45, cites *Information for the Female-to-Male Crossdresser and Transsexual*, which relies on John T. Molloy's note that "for the small man . . . the best shoes are traditional wingtip" and on Nancy Friday's *My Secret Garden* mention of female transvestites' interest in "wingtip shoes," to suggest that wingtips were part of the "imitation man look."

38. Agee and Evans, *Let Us Now Praise Famous Men*, 258.

39. Elin Schoen Brockman, "A Woman's Power Tool: High Heels," *New York Times*, March 5, 2000. In response, Deborah L. Rhode commented on the bizarre spectacle of powerful women lawyers mincing around in their "thigh-high stiletto-heeled boots" and other "footwear that maims" in an op-ed piece, "Step, Wince, Step, Wince," *New York Times*, October 18, 2000, A31.

40. Advertisement for pierresilber.com in *New York Times*.

41. Michael Wilson, *Salt of the Earth*, screenplay 1953, (Old Westbury, N.Y.: The Feminist Press, 1978), 61.

42. Erwin Panowsky defines iconography as the study of "the subject matter or meaning of works of art," *Studies in Iconology: Humanistic Themes in the Art of the Renaissance* (New York: Harper and Row, 1962), 3. In his rumination on the "theory of imagery," W. J. T. Mitchell notes: "We can

never understand a picture unless we grasp the ways in which it shows what cannot be seen." *Iconology: Image, Text, Ideology* (Chicago: University of Chicago Press, 1986), 39.

43. See "The Family of Little Feet," "Chanclas," and "A House of My Own," in Sandra Cisneros, *The House on Mango Street* (1984; reprint, New York: Vintage, 1991) 39–42, 46–48, 108.

44. The discovery of the bloody size-12 Bruno Magli shoeprints left on Nicole Simpson's walkway became only the most recent spectacular example of this. The search to identify the tread was undertaken by a Japanese firm specializing in shoe print recognition at crime scenes. The fact that only a few hundred pairs of this size existed worldwide and O. J. Simpson owned one of them, however, was not sufficient evidence to convict.

45. Leslie Kaufman, "A Walk on the Wild Side Stirs the Shoe Industry," *New York Times*, July 9, 2000, 3:1,8, notes that in the United States, women's shoe sales have been remarkably consistent since the end of World War II. During the 1990s, despite the consumer boom, women's shoe sales have grown steadily at only 1.8 percent per year, consistent with figures from the 1940s, excluding a spike during the 1980s when athletic footwear became popular.

46. See Carolyn Steedman, "Landscape for a Good Woman," in *Past Tenses: Essays on Writing, Autobiography and History* (London: Rivers Oram Press, 1992), 21–40. See also her book of the same title.

47. Charlotte Nekola, "Good Mothers, Bad Daughters," in *Dream House: A Memoir* (New York: W. W. Norton, 1993), 42–56.

48. C. L. R. James, *American Civilization*, ed. Anna Grimshaw and Keith Hart (New York: Blackwell, 1993), 131.

8. MEDIUM UNCOOL: AVANT-GARDE FILM AND UNCANNY FEMINISM

1. Sigmund Freud, "The 'Uncanny'" (1919), *On Creativity and the Unconscious* (New York: Harper Torchbook, 1958), 122–61.

2. "For structures of feeling can be defined as social experiences *in solution* . . ." Raymond Williams, *Marxism and Literature* (Oxford: Oxford University Press, 1977), 133 (emphasis in original).

3. Fredric Jameson, "Periodizing the '60s," in Sohnya Sayers et al. eds., *The Sixties Without Apology* (Minneapolis: University of Minnesota Press, 1984), 208.

4. For an excellent detailed account of France and film and 1968, but one that says nothing about women, much less feminism, see Sylvia Harvey, *May '68 and Film Culture* (London: British Film Institute, 1978).

5. Jay Boyer, "You Will Never Read the Novel You Might Like To," Sohnya Sayres et al., eds., *The Sixties Without Apology*, 309–10. Even when a

work of fiction appears about the New Left, such as Alix Kates Shulman's *Burning Questions*, it does so in the form of a nonfictional memoir, complete with a treatise on the history of radical women's autobiographies. Novels about Vietnam—such as Philip Caputo's *Rumor of War* or Tim O'Brien's *The Things They Carried*—are read as nonfiction memoir. In many ways, the legacy of Vietnam narratives is the memoir. For a discussion of how trauma informs genre, see Julia Bleakney, "Reproducing the Vietnam War: Bodies, Places, Memories," Ph.D. preliminary examination, English Department, University of Minnesota, November 2000.

6. Todd Gitlin, *The Sixties: Years of Hope, Days of Rage* (New York: Bantam, 1987), 242–43.

7. Gitlin, *The Sixties*, 243.

8. Henry Abelove, "Some Speculations on the History of Sexual Intercourse During the Long Eighteenth Century in England," *Genders* 6 (November 1989): 125–30.

9. Raymond Williams, *The Country and the City* (London: Paladin Press, 1975), describes this problem.

10. Roland Barthes, *Camera Lucida: Reflections on Photography*, trans. Richard Howard (New York: Hill and Wang, 1981), 98

11. Patricia Zimmermann, *Reel Families: A Social History of Amateur Film* (Bloomington: Indiana University Press, 1995). Freud notes that, "Many people experience the feeling [of the uncanny] in the highest degree in relation to death and dead bodies, to the return of the dead, and to spirits and ghosts." ("The 'Uncanny'," 149).

12. "The First Statement of the New American Cinema Group," *Film Culture* 22–23 (Summer 1961): 130–31.

13. Quoted in Lawrence Van Gelder, "Shirley Clarke Is Dead at 77; Maker of Oscar-Winning Film," *New York Times*, September 26, 1997, C19.

14. Stan Brakhage, letter to Dolores Daniels, *Film Culture* 40 (Spring 1966): 73–75.

15. Stan Brakhage, "Defense of the 'Amateur' Filmmaker," *Filmmakers Newsletter* (Summer 1971): 20

16. "An Interview with Kenneth Anger, Conducted by *Spider Magazine*," *Film Culture* 40 (Spring 1966): 68.

17. Carolee Schneemann, *More Than Meat Joy: Complete Performance Works and Selected Writings*, ed. Bruce McPherson (New York: Documentext, 1979), 122–27.

18. "Vietnam a Vegetable Culture Which Leaves No Garbage," notes about "Snows" in Schneemann, *More Than Meat*, 120.

19. Schneemann, "Naked Action Lecture," in *More Than Meat*, 180. The performance happened on June 27, 1968.

20. Schneemann, "Istory of a Girl Pornographer," in *More Than Meat*, 192.

21. Quoted in Van Gelder, "Shirley Clarke Is Dead at 77."

22. Don Langer, "Tips on Photography," *New York Herald Tribune*, September 29, 1957, 4:7.

23. Both Arbus quotations are from an interview with Ann Ray in *Newsweek*; quoted in Patricia Bosworth, *Diane Arbus: A Biography* (New York: Knopf, 1984), 248.

24. John Wakeman, *World Film Directors, Vol. 2, 1945–1985*, "Shirley Clarke," (New York: H. W. Wilson Company, 1988), 222.

25. See Patricia Bosworth, *Diane Arbus*, for more juicy details, 261–64, 295–98.

26. Ti-Grace Atkinson, "On Violence in the Women's Movement," *Amazon Odyssey* (New York: Links Books, 1974), 198.

27. Susan Sontag, *On Photography* (New York: Farrar, Strauss and Giroux, 1977), 178 (emphasis added).

28. Carol Hanisch, "Critique of the Miss America Protest," in *Notes From the Second Year: Women's Liberation* (New York: New York Radical Women, 1970), 86–87.

29. Quoted in Alice Echols, *Daring to Be Bad: Radical Feminism in America, 1967–1975* (Minneapolis: University of Minnesota Press, 1989), 86–7.

30. Echols, *Daring to Be Bad*, 86.

31. Ethan Morder, *Medium Cool: The Movies of the 1960s* (New York: Knopf, 1990), 287, delves into a history of 1960s Hollywood's "own apocalypse."

32. Robin Morgan, ed., *Sisterhood Is Powerful: An Anthology of Writings from the Women's Liberation Movement* (New York: Vintage, 1970), 496. Reprinted from *Women: A Journal of Liberation* (1970).

33. Gloria Steinem and George Barris, *Marilyn* (New York: New American Library, 1986).

34. Crowther's review appeared in *New York Times*, August 14, 1967; Schickel's in *Life*, October 13, 1967. All reprinted in John Cawelti, ed., *Focus on Bonnie and Clyde* (Englewood Cliffs, N.J.: Prentice Hall, 1973), 22–25.

35. Violence, and its almost slapstick visualization, propelled the renaissance of the genre film: *Bonnie & Clyde* updated the late 1930s rural gangster film; *Butch Cassidy & the Sundance Kid* cashed in on the western Sergio Leone had already restored; and with *Rosemary's Baby*, Roman Polanski resurrected an eerily contemporary monster movie. But the genres had been feminized; Faye Dunaway, Claudia Cardinale, and Mia Farrow figure centrally in these films.

36. Peter Biskind, *Easy Riders, Raging Bulls: How the Sex, Drugs and*

Rock 'n' Roll Generation Saved Hollywood (New York: Simon and Schuster, 1998), 46.

37. Shulamith Firestone, *The Dialectic of Sex: The Case for Feminist Revolution* (New York: Bantam, 1970), 188.

38. This 1967 film, *Shulie*, by Jerry Blumenthal, Sheppard Ferguson, James Leahy, and Allan Rettig was "adapted" as a "shot-by-shot, line-by-line recreation" in 1997 by Elisabeth Subrin. Director's notes. Program notes for "Fakes/Remakes: Stretching the Truth," Walker Art Center, Minneapolis, Minnesota, March 20, 1999.

39. "First Statement," *Film Culture* 22–23, 133.

40. Sherry Sonnett Trumbo, "A Woman's Place Is in the Oven," in *Notes from the Third Year: Women's Liberation* (New York: New York Radical Women, 1971), 91. Reprinted from the *New York Times*.

41. Muriel Rukeyser, *Theory of Flight* (New Haven, Conn.: Yale University Press, 1935), 87. See Rebecca Hill, "Fosterites and Feminists, Or 1950s Ultra-Leftists and the Invention of AmeriKKKa," *New Left Review* (1998), argues that these critiques of Hollywood are central to left-wing feminism in the postwar years and so offer a continuity between the two periods.

42. Barbara Burris, "Fourth World Manifesto," *Notes from the Third Year*, 109.

43. Francee Covington, "Are the Revolutionary Techniques Employed in *The Battle of Algiers* Applicable to Harlem?" in Toni Cade, ed., *The Black Woman: An Anthology* (New York: Signet, 1970), 244–54.

44. Susan Sontag, "The Third World of Women," *Partisan Review* 60 (1973): 180–206.

45. Newsreel Manifesto was reprinted by Mekas in his January 25, 1968, *Village Voice* column. Reprinted in Mekas, *Movie Journal: The Rise of a New American Cinema, 1959–1971* (New York: Collier Books, 1972), 305–6.

46. Charlotte Bunch, *Passionate Politics: Feminist Theory in Action, Essays 1968–1986* (New York: St. Martin's Press, 1987), 5-6; Echols, *Daring to Be Bad*, 54–59, describes these actions.

47. David James, *Allegories of Cinema: American Film in the Sixties* (Princeton: Princeton University Press, 1991), 217.

48. David Talbot and Barbara Zheutlin, *Creative Differences: Profiles of Hollywood Dissidents* (Boston: South End Press, 1978), 362. Ironically, both Kramer and Phillips, who also parted ways, became interested in narrative forms: Kramer, who died in 1998, made a number of feature-length narrative films with European financing, among them *Milestones*, which traced the demise of the 1960s New Left; Phillips moved into soap opera, seeing it as a popular female form whose never-ending story-line appeared to undo classic Hollywood cinema and mobilize a female mass audience. She and friends produced an alternative radio soap opera, "Winds of Change," in St.

Louis; eventually, she became a scriptwriter for the satirical television soap, *Mary Hartman, Mary Hartman.*

49. Quoted in Van Gelder, "Shirley Clarke Is Dead at 77."

50. Nancy Ellen Dowd, "Popular Conventions," provides a devastating critique of *Battle of Algiers*'s "cloying" fakery in *Film Quarterly* 22, no. 3 (Spring 1969). David James forcefully makes this point in his *Allegories of Cinema*, especially in the chapter on Brakhage.

51. Parker Tyler, *Underground Film: A Critical History* (New York: Grove Press, 1969), 69.

52. James, *Allegories*, 119–120.

53. Mekas, *Movie Journal*, 89–90.

54. Maya Deren made her first film with her husband, director and cinematographer Alexander Hammid; Chick Strand started Canyon Cinema with her filmmaker husband, Bruce Baillie; filmmaker Freude Bartlett was married to videographer Scott Bartlett; Emily Breer and Robert Breer both made films, and so forth.

55. Sheldon Renan, *An Introduction to the American Underground Film* (New York: E. P. Dutton, 1967), 174.

56. With the exception of the *Film Quarterly* review and interview and Renan's off-hand remark, I can find no mention of this germinal film in any accounts of underground, experimental, expanded, or avant-garde cinema, until a brief quotation of the Callenbach review in Wheeler Winston Dixon, *The Exploding Eye: A Re-Visionary History of 1960s American Experimental Cinema* (Albany: State University of New York Press, 1997). Even Patricia Mellencamp's *Indiscretions*, whose subtitle is: "Avant-garde Film, Video and Feminism" (Bloomington: Indiana University Press, 1990), fails to mention this momentous event. Of the mini-industry of memoirs and histories about the 1960s, only Alice Echols's careful recreation of those "Daring to Be Bad" mentions this film.

57. Brenda Richardson, "Women, Wives, Film-Makers: An Interview with Gunvor Nelson and Dorothy Wiley," *Film Quarterly* 25, no. 1 (Fall 1971): 34–41.

58. Shirley Clarke and Storm De Hirsch, "A Conversation," *Film Culture* 46 (Autumn 1967), 44–54 (published October 1968).

59. Richardson, "Women, Wives, Film-Makers," 36; Clarke and De Hirsch, "A Conversation," 50.

60. Kate Haug, "Femme Experimentale: Interviews with Carolee Schneemann, Barbara Hammer, and Chick Strand," *Wide Angle* 20 (January 1998): 1–19, reprints a letter from Adrienne Mancia on Museum of Modern Art stationery, dated August 1968, in which she "regret[s] that Carolee Schneemann's film, FUSES, is confronted with problems of censorship" (18).

61. Richardson, "Women, Wives, Film-Makers," 35.

62. In 1978, J. Hoberman noted that "*Meshes* seems less related to European surrealism than to the Freudian flashbacks and sinister living-rooms that typify Hollywood's wartime 'noir' films. Located in some hilly L.A. suburb, the house where Deren's erotic, violent fantasy was filmed might be around the corner from Barbara Stanwyck's place in *Double Indemnity*." J. Hoberman, "The Maya Mystique," *The Village Voice* 23, no. 20 (May 15, 1978): 54. However, Deren's 1943 film, like Esther Bubley's photographs, predates almost all film noirs. Repeating Hoberman, critic Lauren Rabinovitz notes that "*Meshes of the Afternoon* adopts the dominant visual vocabulary associated with the emerging *film noir*—high contrast lighting, extreme camera angles, character point-of-view shots—but displaces it onto a narrative of a woman subject contending with her own fragmentation and disequilibrium." Lauren Rabinovitz, *Plots of Resistance: Women, Power and Politics in the New York Avant-garde Cinema, 1943–71* (Urbana: University of Illinois Press, 1991), p. 56.

63. *Canyon Cinema Catalogue* #6 (1988), 247.

64. The phrase is taken from Sara Evans' book of the same name.

65. Ernest Callenbach, review of *Schmeerguntz*, *Film Quarterly* 19, no. 4 (Summer 1966): 67.

66. "Filmmaking," *The Second Wave* 2, no. 3 (1973): 32, transcript of a 1972 interview with Maureen McCue on Boston's public radio station, WBUR.

67. Fredric Jameson, "Periodizing the '60s," in *The Sixties Without Apology*, 208.

68. Paul Potter, *A Name for Ourselves*, quoted in Gitlin, *The Sixties*, 185. However, as David Bernstein, who was also present at the speech, suggests, underlying this sensibility were two others directly related to the productivity of censorship for revolution: McCarthyism had successfully indoctrinated even those radicals most critical of it into suspicion of anything that smacked of communism, on the one hand; and "the system" was at the same time tacitly understood by everyone who heard this phrase to be capitalism. Thus self-censorship served, paradoxically, to open up new metaphors and movements (personal communication).

69. Adrienne Rich, *Poems: Selected and New, 1950–1974* (New York: W. W. Norton, 1975), 169–172. Reprinted from *The Will to Change* (New York: W. W. Norton, 1971).

9. MAPPING NOIR

1. Personal communication with Sandro Portelli; Patricia Crain, *The Story of A: The Alphabetization of America from the New England Primer to The Scarlet Letter* (Stanford: Stanford University Press, 2000).

2. Frederick Douglass, *The Narrative of the Life of Frederick Douglass, An American Slave, Written by Himself* (1845; reprint, Garden City, N.Y.: Dolphin Books, 1963), 7–9.

3. We might ask, with Shelley Fisher Fishkin, "Was Hester Black?" It is quite possible, given her somewhat abolitionist sentiments, that Nathaniel's wife, Sophia, had read Douglass's narrative. See Fishkin, *Was Huck Black?: Mark Twain and African-American Voices* (New York: Oxford University Press, 1994) and arguments by critic Viola Sachs that Herman Melville's Ishmael is based on a black sailor as well. Lecture delivered at Terza Università degli Studi di Roma (Spring 2000).

4. See "Introduction," Rita Copeland, ed., *Criticism and Dissent in the Middle Ages* (Cambridge: Cambridge University Press, 1996).

5. J. P. Telotte notes that the "tangled networks" of the telephone are suggestive of the "anxious atmosphere that seems to surround every effort at speaking in the noir world." *Voices in the Dark: The Narrative Patterns of Film Noir* (Urbana: University of Illinois Press, 1989), 74.

6. For new research into film noir, the law, and the state, see the work-in-progress of Nancy West, Zoë Druick, and Helen Lennon.

7. Quoted in John M. Broder, "The Devil and Political Fund-raising," *New York Times*, News of the Week in Review, December 10, 2000, 4.

8. In a series of brilliant op-ed pieces, which netted her the Pulitzer Prize, Maureen Dowd understood this better than anybody else during the long impeachment saga: See, for example, "The 16th Minute," *New York Times*, September 1, 1999, A23, which details the afterlife of Monica Lewinsky's fortunes selling purses "with names resplendent of Hester Prynne," like "Garden Patch" on the World Wide Web; and "Pulp Nonfiction," *New York Times*, News of the Week in Review, September 13, 1998, 21, which reads Kenneth Starr's report as a "445-page Harold Robbins novel," and likens Monica Lewinsky's role in the narrative to "a stereotype, Monica became the raging, vengeful Glenn Close character in *Fatal Attraction*." In a post-Clinton recycling of the noir imaginary, Dowd revealed that she had learned that President George W. Bush's nickname for her is "The Cobra." "I Have a Nickname!!!" *New York Times*, April 29, 2001, 4:11.

9. Anne Stevenson, *Correspondences* (Middletown, Conn.: Wesleyan University Press, 1974), 70. Further citations appear in the text.

10. See June Howard, "Towards a Marxist-Feminist Cultural Analysis," *Minnesota Review* 20 (Spring 1983): 77–92, and Deborah Rosenfelt and Judith Lowder Newton, "Introduction: Toward a Materialist-Feminist Criticism," in Rosenfelt and Newton, eds., *Feminist Criticism and Social Change: Sex, Class, and Race in Literature and Culture* (New York: Metheun, 1985), for two examples from the mid-1980s.

11. I do not want to imply that only women novelists are engaged in dil-

letante historiography. Clearly, so are E. L. Doctorow (*Ragtime* and *The Book of Daniel*), Gore Vidal (*Hollywood, Burr* and the America cycle), Don DeLillo (*Libra, Underworld*), Robert Coover (*The Public Burning*), to name just a few. "The force of history," as DeLillo puts it, is the province of fiction. However, the works I consider seem to be doing more than the already mammoth task of setting the writer's "pleasure, his eros, his creative delight in language and his sense of self-preservation against the vast and uniform Death that history tends to fashion as its most enduring work" (Don DeLillo, "The Power of History," *The New York Times Magazine* [September 7, 1997]: 60–63). They are allowing the psychological expansiveness of fiction not only to reanimate the past but to intervene in the present.

12. Diane Prenatt, "Interview with Frances Sherwood," *Belles Lettres: A Review of Books by Women* 10 (Spring 1995): 22–26.

13. According to Marc Penka, Emerson condemned Hawthorne's "fiction-mongering" as unworthy of the philosophical questions with which he was concerned. " 'The Deep Taint of His Nature': Uncanny Allegory and Mr. Hawthorne's Gothic," Ph.D. diss., University of Minnesota, 2001.

14. Davis quotes Herbert Aptheker's passing comment that "[O]ne may better understand now a Margaret Garner, fugitive slave, who, when trapped near Cincinnati, killed her own daughter and tried to kill herself. She rejoiced that the girl was dead—'now she would never know what a woman suffers as a slave'—and pleaded to be tried for murder. I will go singing to the gallows rather than be returned to slavery.' " Angela Davis, *Women, Race and Class* (New York: Random House, 1981), 21; Herbert Aptheker, "The Negro Woman," in *Masses and Mainstream* 11 (February 1948): 12.

15. Toni Morrison, "Unspeakable Things Unspoken: The Afro-American Presence in American Literature," *Michigan Quarterly Review* 28 (Winter 1989): 1–34.

16. Frederick Douglass, *Narrative*, 2.

17. The vexed and strange interrelationship of fiction and history within slave women's literary cultures includes as well the research by Jean Fagin Yellin into Harriet Jacobs's *Incidents in the Life of a Slave Girl, Written by Herself*, which authorized it as a genuine slave narrative, not merely the sentimental fiction of Lydia Child as it had been presumed to be by literary historians. Because the conventions of the sentimental novel were more clearly recognizable within Jacobs's narrative than within that of Douglass (though his tale relies on virtually every coding of the sentimental, also), her story was viewed with suspicion by generations of scholars. Hers is surely a bizarre, even gothic, story; but the tale seemed fantastic in part because it conformed so accurately to popular narrative forms.

18. Stanley Crouch "Aunt Medea," review of *Beloved*, *The New Republic* 19 (October 1987): 38–48. See also Marilyn Judith Atlas, "Toni Morrison's *Beloved* and the Reviewers," for a comprehensive reading of the various responses to the novel. *Midwestern Miscellany* 18 (1990): 45–57.

19. Margaret Forster, "This Is Sort of Your Life, Mary Wollstonecraft," *New York Times Book Review* (July 11, 1993): 21.

20. Edward B. St. John, review of *Vindication*, *Library Journal* 118 (March 15, 1993): 109.

21. Stendhal writing of the scandal surrounding the Baron de Pontalba's attempted murder of his daughter-in-law and his subsequent suicide, quoted in Angeline Goreau, "A Spectacular Mess of a Marriage," (review of *Intimate Enemies: The Two Worlds of the Baroness de Pontalba* by Christina Vella) *New York Times Book Review* (August 31, 1997): 6–7. Goreau concludes her favorable review of the biography by longing "for a novelist who could explore the intricate workings of motivation, who could trace the seesawings of power and control, who could ask the tricky question of who the 'author' of this family's story finally was" (7).

22. Mary Wollstonecraft, *Maria, or The Wrongs of Women*, "Author's Preface," (1798; reprint, New York: W. W. Norton, 1975), 7 (emphasis added).

23. See Moira Ferguson's introduction to Wollstonecraft, *Maria*, especially p. 20.

24. Loraine Fletcher, review of *Vindication*, *New Statesman and Society* 6 (June 4, 1993): 40.

25. Katha Pollitt, *Reasonable Creatures: Essays on Women and Feminism* (New York: Knopf, 1994); Sallie Tisdale, *Talk Dirty to Me: An Intimate Philosophy of Sex* (New York: Doubleday, 1994); Nadine Strossen, *Defending Pornography: Free Speech, Sex and the Fight for Women's Rights* (New York: Scribners, 1995). All reviewed in *The Nation* (February 20, 1996).

26. Andrea Dworkin, *Pornography: Men Possessing Women* (New York: Putnam, 1981), and *Intercourse* (New York: Free Press, 1987); "Is One Woman's Sexuality Another Woman's Pornography?" *Ms.* [Special Issue] (April 1985).

27. The 1980s sex debates were often far more vicious than the relatively balanced term, "debate," would suggest. Some of the decade's key texts promoting the "prosex line" include: Angela Carter, *The Sadeian Woman and the Ideology of Pornography*, (New York: Pantheon, 1978); *Heresies* #12 "Sex Issue"(1981); *Diary of a Conference on Sexuality*, "The Scholar and the Feminist," Barnard Women's Center, 1982; Sue Cartledge and Joanna Ryan, *Sex & Love: New Thoughts on Old Contradictions* (London: The Women's Press, 1983); Ann Snitow, Christine Stansell, and Sharon Thompson, eds., *Powers of Desire: The Politics of Sexuality* (New York: Monthly Review Press, 1983); Car-

ole Vance, ed., *Pleasure and Danger: Exploring Female Sexuality* (Boston and London: Routledge and Kegan Paul, 1984); Jane Root, *Pictures of Women: Sexuality* (London: Pandora Press, 1984); Varda Burstyn, ed., *Women Against Censorship* (Vancouver and Toronto: Douglas & McIntyre, 1985); Joan Nestle, *A Restricted Country* (Ithaca, N.Y.: Firebrand Books, 1987). See Paula Rabinowitz, "Ethnographies of Women: *Soft Fiction* and Feminist Theory," in *They Must Be Represented: The Politics of Documentary* (London: Verso, 1994), 157–75, for an account of the ways in which the sex debates played out in women's experimental films. More mainstream conservative/libertarian 1990s reinventions include Camille Paglia, *Sex, Art and American Culture: Essays* (New York: Vintage, 1992) and *Vamps and Tramps: New Essays* (New York: Vintage, 1994); Katie Roiphe, *The Morning After: Sex, Fear, and Feminism* (Boston: Back Bay Books, 1993).

28. Erwin Mitsch, *The Art of Egon Schiele*, trans. W. Keith Haughan (London: Phaidon Press, 1975), 34–35.

29. Michiko Kakutani's predictably less-than-enthusiastic review was entitled "Portrait of a Tortured Artist in a Tortured City," *New York Times*, July 27, 1990, C25.

30. A rare critical essay on his prison work is Alessandra Comini, "Egon Schiele in Prison," *Albertina-Studien* 4 (1974): 123–37. All of the images are reproduced in Erwin Mitsch, *Egon Schiele in der Albertina* (Graphische Sammlung Albertina, 1990).

31. Serge Sabarsky, *Egon Schiele* (New York: Rizzoli, 1985), 8–9.

32. James T. Demetrios, *Egon Schiele and the Human Form: Drawings and Watercolors* (Des Moines, Iowa: Des Moines Art Center, 1971). After describing Schiele's coded inscriptions, however, Demetrios makes a point of not including any of the prison images in the show. It is not clear why, but the show's title stresses "form."

33. *Times* reviewers on both sides of the Atlantic concurred in their estimations of the novel. Scott Bradfield, "Onan and Egon," *New York Times Book Review* (August 19, 1990): 14, said the first and third things quoted in this sentence. Neil Taylor, review of *Arrogance*, *Times Literary Supplement* (July 26, 1991): 20, said the second.

34. Constance Samaras and Carol Jacobson detail these and other cases, such as Jacobson's first-amendment fight with the University of Michigan Law School over its censorship of an exhibition, "Porn'Im'Agery," she curated, and explore their effects in a special issue of *The New York University Law School Law Review* 38, nos. 1 and 2 [on "The Sex Panic: Women, Censorship, and Pornography"] (1995).

35. During the late 1980s, feminists retreated from earlier assumptions "distinguishing" public from private. Nancy Armstrong and Joan Scott jointly swept away any logical reasons for retaining them. Each laid bare the

underlying assumptions shoring up women's literature, one the one hand, women's history, on the other. With feminist literary critics such as Felicity Nussbaum arguing that the private expressions of self by eighteenth-century bourgeois women through diaries and autobiographies helped codify middle-class subjectivity, and feminist social historians such as Linda Gordon claiming the working-class home as a central site of state formation through the organization of social welfare programs, it is difficult to see just where the private ends and the public begins, or vice versa. Nussbaum, *The Autobiographical Subject: Gender and Ideology in Eighteenth-Century England* (Baltimore: Johns Hopkins Unviersity Press, 1989); Gordon, *Heroes of Their Own Lives: The Politics and History of Family Violence* (New York: Viking, 1998).

36. Woolf's 1928 novel, *Orlando: A Biography*, takes as its subject the slippage between fiction and biography as it traces the 300-odd-year life span of its eponymous wealthy boy-man-woman writer-hero. With its central concerns of tracing the political effects of gender, race, and class on the bodies of individuals, *Orlando* was the gold standard for materialist-feminist British literary history.

37. *Pity Is Not Enough, The Executioner Waits*, and *Rope of Gold* are the titles of the three Josephine Herbst novels that never actually appeared as a trilogy until Warner Books reissued them together in 1985. Herbst, *Rope of Gold*, (1939; reprint, New York: The Feminist Press, 1984), 169.

38. The poem appeared in Crane's 1926 volume, *White Buildings*. Hart Crane, "My Grandmother's Love Letters," in *The Collected Poems of Hart Crane* (New York: Liveright, 1933), 65. The poem goes on to ask "Are your fingers long enough to play / Old keys that are but echoes?" John Eugene Unterecker, *Voyager: A Life of Hart Crane* (New York: Farrar Strauss and Giroux, 1969), reads this poem in light of Crane's boyhood sexuality.

39. As noted above, "discovered" documents offer a source for American revisionist historiography in *The Scarlet Letter*. Hawthorne rethinks, in light of Republican failures, his family's and his nation's sordid past through Hester Prynne's tale. This tradition is particularly important to African-American women's literary tradition: from Harriet Jacobs waging guerrilla warfare against her master from her attic enclosure by writing a series of letters posted secretly from afar to Rita Dove narrating her grandparents' lives through lyrics culled from family letters, diaries and mementos in *Thomas and Beulah* (Pittsburgh: Carnegie-Mellon University Press, 1987).

INDEX

Adams, Ansel, 116
Adorno, Theodor, 1, 10–11, 178, 201
AFL-CIO, 133
African-American authors, 20
African Americans, 5, 61
Agee, James, 119, 141, 204; and mixed genres, 83; on objects, 48; on rural poverty, 109; on shoes, 181–82, 184, 186–87
Aid to Dependent Children (ADC), 146, 161, 163
Aid to Families with Dependent Children (AFDC), 163–64
Akermann, Chantal, 196
Aldrich, Robert, 12, 186
Algren, Nelson, 1, 3, 5, 91–92
Amazing Stories, 12
America Day by Day (de Beauvoir), 2
American Dream (Kopple), 20, 126, 131–41
American landscape, 228; Adorno on 1; de Beauvoir on, 43; in film noir, 14, 16, 243. *See also* City; Heartland; Rural
Andersen, Hans Christian, 189
Andersen, Lewie, 133, 136, 138
Anderson, Benedict, 16–17
Anger, Kenneth, 200–201, 218
Annals of the American Association

of Political and Social Sciences, 160
Ann Arbor Film Festival, 218
Aptheker, Herbert, 235
Arbus, Diane, 82, 202–205, 220
Arcades Project, The (Benjamin), 180
Archer, Bill, 164
Arden, Eve, 73
Armstrong, Nancy, 123
Arnow, Harriet, 129
Arrogance (Scott), 234, 239–40
Arzner, Dorothy, 119, 197
Astor, Mary, 19
Atkinson, Ti-Grace, 204–205
Avant-garde film, 22, 193. *See also* Experimental film; New American Cinema

Baker, Ella, 65, 70, 75, 78
Bakhtin, Mikhail, 17
Ball, Lucille, 119
Barclay, Gwen, 160
Barnard, Rita, 7
Barry, Kathy, 237
Barthes, Roland, 176, 181, 198
Barton Fink (Coen), 32
Basic Instinct (Verhoeven), 111
Battle of Algiers, The (Pontecorvo), 208, 212, 216